SONG OF HEYOEHKAH

Song of Heyoehkah

Hyemeyohsts Storm

Art designed by Hyemeyohsts Storm
Painted by Tom Kirby

BALLANTINE BOOKS · NEW YORK

Published in the United States by Ballantine Books, a division of Random House, Inc., New York, and simultaneously in Canada by Random House of Canada Limited, Toronto.

Library of Congress Catalog Card Number: 82-90829

ISBN 0-345-30731-3

This edition published by arrangement with Harper & Row, Publishers, Inc.

Designed by Paul Quin

Manufactured in the United States of America

First Ballantine Books Edition: February 1983

10 9 8 7 6 5 4 3

This book is lovingly dedicated
to my greatest teacher:
my mother,

CONTENTS

Each Thought that is Written
Has as its Reflection
A Trail
Within the Heart
Of the Forest.

Sandie Storm

SONG OF HEYOEHKAH

THE RED LODGE

There are many quiets, but the one that awakens
remembrance is by far the greatest. And so it is with this
memory.

"Fire dances among the rocks like magical rain," the
Shamaness sang, "And the rain sings the shy messages
hummed by willow reeds every spring. Colors held in the
hands of chieftains, holding silver flower rings . . ."

THE WIND moved around my head like angry bees that night. Tired, I
lay down in a small ravine and fell asleep. That happened a long time
ago. I wish to tell you about the man who shook me awake the next
morning, because he was to become my teacher.

I remember that meeting so clearly it still startles me to think of it. I was
wet and shivering from the night dampness, half awake and half asleep,
when the old man began shaking me. I believe I was more surprised by
his sudden presence than I was by his clothing. He was wearing a Sun
Dance robe, and his thick white hair gave him the appearance of a
magician. Of course in those days I had neither heard of a magician nor

a Sun Dance Chief, and to a sleepy child in the middle of a prairie, no surprise seems out of the ordinary. Surprises are just surprises.

I should have jumped up, ready to run, but I didn't. Instead, I took his outstretched hand and followed him. He led me to his lodge, not far from where I had been sleeping. Together we shared a wonderful breaking of the fast. When I had eaten and been sufficiently warmed from the sun to feel like moving, I suddenly noticed for the first time the strange animals that were grazing close to the old man's lodge.

"What are those?" I asked.

"Those are sheep," he answered.

"Sheep?" I echoed. "Why do they not run?"

"Because they know only of one place at a time," he answered.

Two days can be a week to a child, and a month a year, so after a few days I felt as if I belonged with the old man. He hadn't said much, except for asking about my health. I tended the flock with him for a few days, mostly lounging around while he herded them. It wasn't long before I was going out by myself to watch after them.

Because I had little else to do, I began to watch the habits of the old man. One of them in particular puzzled me for days before I found enough courage to ask him about it. Every morning he would spend a portion of his time looking at one of his possessions.

"What is that you look at?" I finally asked.

"It is a mirror," he answered. "Do you have a name?"

"Name?" I frowned.

"Something people say when they mean you," he said in a kind voice.

I answered with a shake of my head.

"I have a name," he said. "Would you like to hear it?"

"Will it do something to me if I hear it?" I asked.

"It is a way of you touching me," he answered, smiling. "It is a way in which you may become part of me."

I shook my head yes.

"My name is Twin Chiefs," he said and smiled.

"Twin Chiefs," I repeated, frowning. "Twin Chiefs."

"And I will give you the name of Estchimah—Sleep," he said, getting to his feet. "Come. We will tell your name to the trees."

He walked slowly, with me following excitedly beside him, to the edge of the small valley.

"Estchimah!" he called out to the trees, cupping his hands to his mouth.

"Estchimah . . . Estchimah . . . Estchimah . . . Estchimah . . ." the trees echoed.

"Estchimah!" I yelled. "Estchimah! Estchimah! Estchimah!"

Then I remembered to cup my hands and yelled again, "Estchimah! Estchimah! Estchimah! Estchimah!"

And we heard the echoes repeating the beautiful sound over and over again.

As we walked quietly back to the lodge my heart seemed to be completely filled with the joy of having a name. I repeated it over many times that day, and once more before I fell asleep that night.

When the old man began to look at the mirror the next morning, I remembered what he had told me the day before.

"You look at mirror," I said proudly, pointing at it.

"Do you remember my name?" he winked.

I thought and thought but ended up only staring at my hands. I couldn't remember.

"It is Twin Chiefs," he said softly.

I felt like crying because I had forgotten.

"You would have remembered," he said, smiling at me, "but I wanted to be able to say it to you again."

"Yes!" I said, brightening up. "Yes! I would have!"

"Today," Twin Chiefs smiled, "we are going to look into the mirror."

> *A million painted leaves sleep under the white robe of winter. They sleep in remembrance, mirroring all that was seen when they danced in the trees. Each reflection holds within it the summer place and touches rainbow medicines as the leaves come to the earth for rest. The moccasins of the People move through these singing leaves, even while winter protects them, changing what was into spring again.*
>
> *And so it was.*

ESTCHIMAH'S MEDICINE WALK began within the great hall of the sacred mountain. The hallway was totally dark. There was no light except for the strange light encircling her. There was no sound. Quiet surrounded Estchimah. It was part of the light, part of the seeker. Then there was a tiny sound, one tiny sound. It was breathing. Then there was a second sound that did not go beyond the light. It was the sound of bare feet upon the warm glasslike floor.

The darkness closed in about the light. It seemed to be alive, to want to imprison. The darkness appeared as an enemy.

The terror of the unknown lurked just beyond the light, threatening, waiting. Fear settled deep into Estchimah's brain and slowed her steps.

"I am choking," Estchimah cried. "Am I dying?"

The darkness moved, stifling, pressing against the light.

Twin Chiefs had placed a gift about the neck of Estchimah, a beautiful embroidered Sun Dance scarf.

"The scarf!" Estchimah cried. "I must tie the scarf around my waist!"

The darkness watched as the seeker tied the Sun Dance scarf, watched as the scarf became a Sun Dance belt.

Suddenly Estchimah perceived that the light had stopped when she had stopped.

"The light stops when I stop," she mused out loud.

The seeker took two steps backwards, watching to see if the light moved. It did.

"The light moves with me," Estchimah said, curious. "It has moved with each of my steps."

The seeker stood for a moment, waiting. There was no seeing beyond the light. The darkness beyond the tiny circle of light ended abruptly, as if it had met an impenetrable wall.

"This is impossible!" Estchimah thought. "Light cannot just stop and darkness begin. There is always a place in between. Why can I not see beyond the circle? What did Twin Chiefs tell me?

"Walk until you come to what will appear to be a fountain. Rest there."

Yes, that was it.

A hope lay just beyond the light, a hope in the darkness. Estchimah began to walk again. She expected to see the beautiful fountain with every step, but each step led only to the next. Would it be forever?

"It cannot be this far!" Estchimah said out loud.

The seeker's voice was an echo called back upon itself like imploding thunder.

The seeker stopped again, and the light waited.

"What was I to think about?" Estchimah asked herself, feeling panic reach up from inside her heart. "Twin Chiefs said that I should think about myself, about my way, but how am I to think when I am so lonely?"

Estchimah felt trapped, buried.

The seeker began to struggle with fear, but fear is an invisible foe when it is warred upon. It is a flood seeking a quiet place, and it will sweep everything before it.

But the flood is not an enemy; the flood is medicine water seeking to nourish. It is within us to discover the paths where the water will flow gently.

Estchimah trembled and became weak. She remembered Twin Chiefs' words. "Our hands shake because of fear and wonder. The medicine water flows within the streams of our lodge," he had said.

Estchimah sat down and rested, watching the light.

Estchimah began to speak.

"This dark hall. The light walks with me, the light knows me. Is there anyone else here? How could there be? Who would be here in such darkness with me? Why should I expect such a thing?

"What did the Buffalo Teachers say? I want to remember. I want to remember what the world circle sang to me.

"Should I think about the Sweet Medicine? I will think about my circle. I will think about the Power."

Loneliness became a force that Estchimah had to drag like the camp dog drags the heavy carrying poles.

As Estchimah began to walk, another question came from her heart.

"What did Twin Chiefs ask me to remember?"

"It is boredom that drives the mind into the clouds. The clouds absorb the mind, but the clouds wish for lightning and thunder," he had told her.

Estchimah stopped again. The light waited.

"What have I been thinking about?" She couldn't remember.

Estchimah began to panic. The great waters rushed against her heart. The water sought for a path!

Estchimah began to cry.

"Tears are an outward sign. Tears are reflected; tears are the ocean. The Mother Earth brings this rain to our eyes. Our hearts are spilling over; it is a dance of rain upon our face," Twin Chiefs had said.

"Look around! What has changed? What have we hidden from our inward eyes?"

The light did not move. The light waited. Then Estchimah remembered the rest of what Twin Chiefs had told her.

"The Buffalo Teachers once walked this way. The light moved with the Buffalo Teachers also. The ring upon Estchimah's finger was the ring of the Buffalo Teachers. It was the Dream Ring."

Estchimah dreamed this dream.

> The river was a torrent, a collapsed explosion of clouds suddenly fallen to earth into one fearsome surge to the ocean. The river grasped at the trees and boulders along its course to slow its frightful fall. The body of the water roared against the earth with the sound of a million thunders, but her voice was a weeping as she reached for the trees and rocks. With each explosion of rock torn from its place came a sharp sound of pity from the throat of the river. Helpless cries rang out each time a tree swung violently away with torn roots and disappeared into turbulent foam. A weeping of white sound trembled in the air the full length of the valley, the voice of the river crying for help.
>
> The great Mother, the Earth, heard the river's pleas and moved her body to catch her fall. It was a gentle movement. The river quieted within the soothing hands that now rocked

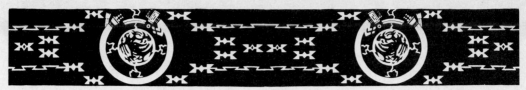

her like a child. The crying of the river quieted, becoming first sobs of relief, then murmurs of joy as she discovered her home.

Little Wolf blinked in wonder at what he had just witnessed. He had seen and heard it all from the place where he had begun his Vision Quest.

"This is truly a magical hill," he thought.

He had been just a boy when he visited that wondrous place, and the experience had grown with him as he had grown. The vision became the breasts of his new mother. He had been born into a new family. The vision had nursed Little Wolf until he was strong enough to play and walk by himself.. Then it had disappeared. But its milk had nurtured his growth and had become part of his entire being. Its song sang from deep within him, becoming a lodge of light that surrounded him. This dance of color painted everything he saw and touched.

Once he was playing along the river with the other children. Suddenly he saw a piece of rainbow that was caught in the trees.

"The rainbow lodge shines like gold within the trees," the children laughed, playing the game.

But Little Wolf heard another voice from deep within him say, "Gold is the sign of the East, and is our illumination."

Little Wolf frowned. The words were like a picture in his mind of a great sphere that shone brilliantly within its eastern side and was full of eyes that danced like fire.

"Seek," the eyes seemed to say.

"Gold is the color of the East," Little Wolf frowned.

"Gold is what?" The other children laughed. But they soon forgot, and so did he. He played and grew with his brothers and sisters.

One day one of the chiefs began to tell a story.

"It is the story of Holds The Circle and Two Slanting Arrows." The chief smiled as she settled herself comfortably on the ground in front of the children.

As Grandmother Deaf Woman told the story she began to draw upon the drum that sat in front of her. All the children watched in fascination as she began to draw, leaning closer for a better look.

As the old woman drew and painted she spoke of wonderful sunsets and medicine wheels. The story continued, and it seemed to become a turning star for Little Wolf. The eyes of fire took places within the circle and danced to the lodges of the six grandfathers. Two Slanting Arrows became a whirlwind of law that touched the moon and reflected within every tiny stone upon the earth. The winter became a jewel within the millions of bright gems painting each movement of thunderbirds' wings.

Suddenly Little Wolf realized that all the other children had left to play. He still sat looking at the beautiful horses the chief had painted on her drum, trying to remember the magical things he had heard. But he could not, no matter how hard he tried.

"Is there medicine in those stories?" Little Wolf asked as he rose to his feet to join the other children at their play.

"There is," the chief answered quietly. "There are powerful songs and medicine for those who listen."

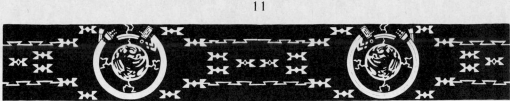

NOW ESTCHIMAH AWOKE within the patient circle of light and was neither afraid nor confused.

The seeker began to walk.

Estchimah took four more steps and saw the fountain.

She stepped into the circle of new light, a blood red light that came from the fountain. The fountain danced a children's dance, and within its own movement was a melody of time. This was a dance within a swirling force of power and brilliance. It held a promise so wondrous, so profound, that it became a song, an earth song.

All the paths of all the dreams came from every direction, meeting at the fountain. They met within the great water. The dreams, the rivers, danced up, sparkling.

Estchimah listened to all the voices of everything born. The fountain was singing. It was the song of the heartbeat, the song of the Sun Dance Drum.

The light from the fountain was like children's laughter.

The Buffalo Teachers had painted the morning star, the children's sign, upon the left arm of the seeker.

Estchimah followed this sign from within the sacred mountain out into the sunlight. Then Estchimah slept.

Estchimah awakened upon a great desert. She sat up and blinked. Her world had suddenly changed. The sacred mountain was far away now, hidden below the horizon.

"Was it only a dream?" Estchimah asked herself, standing up.

She began to walk. The sun was hot, almost unbearable.

"This is a beautiful place, but it is cruel. I must find the People," she thought.

As Estchimah walked she searched for even the slightest shade. She was almost at the crest of a large dune of sand when suddenly she saw a

carved and decorated stone. Curious, she touched the stone, running her fingers along its polished surface. Then she realized that she could decipher a portion of the message cut into it.

"We are dying," the message began.

She sat down, trying to piece together what remained of the inscription.

"We are gods dying," the writing said. "The people stand before the rivers and lakes but they do not see them as they are. Once we lived. Now we die."

"Did gods truly write these words?" she mused out loud. "Do gods die? And why would they bother to inscribe their deaths?"

She stood up and patted the top of the stone, the way you would pat the head of a child.

She rested her eyes as Twin Chiefs had taught her and slowly brought them into focus to scan the great distances. She turned in a slow circle, beginning in the south, but she could see nothing. Nothing but endless sand.

The west seemed even more desolate.

Slowly she turned north, and as she moved she had to blink and shade her eyes against the white-hot desert.

Then she faced the east and, turning, she noticed another stone, much larger than the one she now stood beside, and on that stone were more inscriptions.

"Water," Estchimah thought, "I must have water."

She took four steps toward the stone and screamed.

Estchimah had been watching her feet. If she had been looking farther ahead of herself, she would have seen the ancient temple with its massive statues and carvings. It would not have leaped up so suddenly from its sand grave, startling her.

"The desert is just like time," Twin Chiefs' words whispered in Estchimah's mind. "It can mold a trail and can make sculpture in front of

your eyes. The great winds meet in the desert and dance there. At one step it is one world, at the next it is another world. It protects, hides, covers, changes, and uncovers. It is the desert, it is the mind, it is time, and it is fantasy."

Estchimah thought about the city as she walked down into the deep canyon of sand.

"This is only one temple of the great city," Estchimah thought. Twin Chiefs spoke of this city, but what did he say? "In one day the city can appear and within that same day it can disappear." But didn't he say more?

The temple she now stood before was gigantic, magnificent! She measured the building by walking along its side and discovered that it was twelve thousand steps in perimeter.

"Is there water in this building?" she asked herself out loud as she sought for the entrance.

"Here, drink this," a guttural voice said from behind her. She turned and would have screamed again, but the misshapen hand that was stretched out to her held a water skin.

Trembling, Estchimah took the skin of water and drank.

"I am misshapen because I was born that way," the wild man said to her. "I am called Monster Beautiful."

"Is this your temple?" she asked.

"This temple belongs to no one!" the monster laughed.

"My name is Estchimah," the girl explained. "And I am lost."

"Follow me inside," the monster said, limping toward the entrance of the massive temple.

"I am afraid," Estchimah said as she followed.

"I am strong," the monster said, turning around and facing her. "I could easily overpower you, here and now, if I wished."

When they arrived at the entrance the monster reached just inside the door and brought out two tinder poles for torches. Next he pulled out his fire bow and turning arrow, fitted them together, and began to spin the arrow in the point of the torch.

"We will have light soon," the monster said as he spun the arrow.

"I am very afraid," Estchimah said. "I am afraid to go inside with you."

"You would become lost and be buried if I were not along," the monster said. Smoke began to rise from the tip of the fire arrow. Soon the torches were burning. The monster handed one to Estchimah.

"Follow me," he said.

They entered a treasure room.

"I cannot believe it!" Estchimah said, nearly breathless. "There is so much wealth, so much beauty!"

"There are four hundred rooms, each with more than this," the monster explained.

The room was heaped with gold plates, armor, helmets, spears, sword axes, gloves, vases, almost every treasure imaginable or possible to create. Each seemed to be more finely made than the next.

"I can hardly believe it!" Estchimah said in a high voice. "It seems impossible!"

"Look at the story marked out by the Dance Hammer on this great disk," the monster said, pointing to an ancient shield of gold.

"How big is that shield?" Estchimah exclaimed as she held up her light to the disk.

"It is twelve humans' height across," the monster answered. "What do you see?"

"There seems to be a story of a medicine person, or a priest, upon the shield," she answered.

"Read the signs," the monster said.

"How many people stand before us?" she read. "Your time means nothing. Come! Let us give you powerful gifts. Listen to our gods and become wealthy! Join us. We must go back to the perfect time, the time when all things were perfect. Fall asleep, come! The Great Creator walked among us and taught us perfect beauty. Come! Join us! Listen to our words. Ours is the word of God! Be saved! You must live correctly and join the perfect light. Let the word of god teach you. Come join us in our perfect circle. Walk our way, the way of god, and you will inherit perfect bliss. Be healed within our perfect way."

"It is beautiful," Estchimah said in awe.

"You are the priestess of this temple," the monster said. "Everything here is yours."

"I am rich!" Estchimah exclaimed in a joyful voice.

Estchimah remembered the words of Twin Chiefs. "You will never see your own circle," he had said. "I have seen people all my life who could never see what was right in front of them. They lived in the past, the past of their parents, the past of their priests and gods. They swam in stinking waters and saw them through the eyes of their grandparents. The lakes had long been dead, but they could not see it."

"I do not want this world!" Estchimah said, backing toward the doors of the temple.

"You can be the wealthiest person on earth," the monster said.

"No!" Estchimah yelled as she ran toward the entrance of the temple. "No! No! I want to live in my own time!"

"You are being silly," the monster said, following her. "You are making too much out of this. You are being a silly person."

"No!" Estchimah cried as she ran out into the light.

As Estchimah ran, a harsh wind began to blow and the sun began to fade. The sand stung her face and hands, but she continued to run.

Groping, almost blind, she found the side of the canyon of sand and began to crawl up it.

She scrambled frantically to the floor of the desert, trying to stand, but the wind forced her to take shelter under the robe she was carrying.

After what seemed to be forever, the wind softened and began to dance in smaller and smaller circles around her, until suddenly it ended its whirl of motion with quiet.

Cautiously, Estchimah peeked out from her robe and looked around. Sitting cross-legged in the sand in front of her was an old grandfather. He was filling his pipe.

"It was I who walked into the temple with you," the old man explained as he offered Estchimah the pipe. "It was my choice to show myself to you as a monster."

Estchimah began to cry.

"Be at peace, my child," the old man said, as he touched her shoulder. "Your grandfather, Twin Chiefs, sent me. He wanted you to confront the monster."

"I am exhausted," Estchimah said through her tears.

"Come," the old grandfather said, getting to his feet. "Come to my lodge and refresh yourself. Eat all you want and drink the cool water of the spring. The water is sweet, and it will heal you."

Estchimah followed the old grandfather to the valley of sand, and there within it was an oasis. There were four medicine trees in the oasis, and by each tree was a carved stone. The stone by the south tree was carved into a lion, and the lion was holding four painted arrows. To the west, by that tree, stood a carved bear and around the bear's neck, like a pendant, were four interlocking rings. By the tree of the north was a carved bull, and between its horns was a crescent moon. And to the east, by that tree, was a carved hawk, and its wings were like fire.

Within this perfect green circle of grass, flowers, and trees was a painted lodge.

Estchimah ate buffalo meat and berries of the earth and drank from the spring. After the meal the young woman spoke with the old man.

"Grandfather," Estchimah began, "tell me of the medicine."

"The medicine," the old man answered, "is in looking through the eyes of your sisters and brothers. We can see the entire universe within our minds. The earth, the sun, the moon, and all the planets, even the galaxies. When we learn to see through the eyes of our sisters and brothers we will then see through the eyes of the earth and the universe."

Estchimah yawned and tried to stay awake, but she grew so sleepy she could hardly ask the next question.

"What is this way?" Estchimah yawned.

"This way is a drum beat, a song. It is everything that is familiar," the old grandfather explained.

But Estchimah had fallen asleep and was within her dreams.

ESTCHIMAH SAW a golden lantern glowing far off upon the prairie. As she walked toward the beautiful lamp she saw that it appeared to be ribbed.

She hurried down into a soft valley and across it.

Would the magical lamp still be there? Would it be shining upon the prairie when she reached the other side?

When she peeked over the rim of the valley she looked for the light, but all she could see was a coyote smoking a pipe and painting a woven basket.

"What happened to the light?" she asked Coyote.

"Huh!" Coyote yelped. "Who? Where? What light?"

"The beautiful lamp upon the prairie," Estchimah smiled. She saw that the coyote was very frightened. "I have not come here to hurt you. You do not have to be afraid."

"Huh. Well," Coyote said and cleared his throat. "Huh, well, I am—I mean, I see."

Estchimah laughed.

"What light, ah, lantern?" Coyote said with a tiny nervous cough.

"The light I saw right over there," Estchimah said, pointing.

"That is the lodge of Willow Woman," Coyote chuckled. "Did you think that was a lantern?"

"Now I understand." Estchimah laughed. "I saw a teepee. It was very beautiful, all warm and golden, just like a lamp."

"Well, ah, I—you . . . I mean, I guess so. Who knows?" Coyote fumbled for words.

"What are you hiding behind your back?" Estchimah asked. "Come now, show me."

"Ah, it's, I mean, ah, what back? I mean . . ." Coyote stuttered.

Finally Coyote gave a long sigh and plopped a large furry bundle with great big eyes onto the ground. At the top of the round furry bundle were two large ears. The ears were wriggling.

"What is that?" she asked.

"Ah, a that, ah . . ." Coyote tried to answer.

"A That?" Estchimah frowned. "What is a That?"

"This, ah . . ." Coyote stuttered and coughed.

"I can see that it is This," she said, pointing. "But why is it called a That?"

Coyote frowned.

"That is a mystery!" Coyote said, suddenly gaining his composure.

"That is the strangest thing I have ever seen," Estchimah exclaimed. "I can understand why it is called a That, but calling This a That is confusing, isn't it?"

"It is," Coyote chuckled. "Very good. Now, why don't you be on your way? Remember the golden lamp? The lodge? I must finish my work on this basket."

Estchimah was about to leave, when suddenly the ears on the round furry That wiggled, and it spoke.

"This is not a That," That said, wriggling its ears.

"That is preposterous," Coyote chuckled.

"I do not even know what That means," That answered.

"What does it mean?" Estchimah asked Coyote.

"It simply means that that That is preposterous," Coyote laughed. "It is obvious, isn't it?"

"I am not one of those either," That objected.

"I am very confused," Estchimah said as she sat down.

"Don't sit on my basket," Coyote said excitedly.

"I am sorry," replied Estchimah. She tried not to smile as she moved to another place. "Don't sit there either!" Coyote howled. "You will sit on my other basket!"

"Isn't there anywhere I can sit?" she asked.

"Absolutely not!" Coyote said with finality.

"Coyote has seven baskets," That said.

"Seven?" Estchimah frowned.

"I always make seven," Coyote insisted.

"Sometimes he makes four," That said.

"Do you?" Estchimah asked.

"Only when it is necessary." Coyote giggled, then frowned.

"Why don't you go find that lantern?"

"This is very strange," Estchimah said, wrinkling her nose. "Very strange."

"Of course it is," That interjected.

"There is nothing strange at all!" Coyote objected. "Absolutely nothing!"

"Untie my ears," That demanded.

"Untie your ears?" Estchimah exclaimed.

"Nonsense," Coyote grumbled. "Don't listen to that That."

"Why are your ears tied?" Estchimah asked That.

"This That is always saying something like that," Coyote said, showing his impatience. "Pay no attention."

"Why are your ears tied?" Estchimah asked That again.

"Because that coyote is going to eat this That," That answered.

"Eat you?" Estchimah said in surprise. "I thought that you were a companion of that coyote."

"This is maddening," Coyote said, throwing his basket into the air. "That isn't a That at all, but it is rabbits."

"Rabbits!" Estchimah laughed. "Rabbits! You have rabbits in a furry bundle and tied by the ears—anyway, one seems to be."

"Exactly," that bundle of rabbits said.

"Let them out," Estchimah said to Coyote.

"I will starve to death!" Coyote howled. "Bones is all that will be left of me, only bones!"

"He has a whole buffalo to eat," That bundle of rabbits explained. "That buffalo is hidden in his coyote lodge."

"Let them out!" Estchimah said sternly to Coyote.

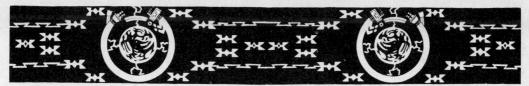

"I will make you a trade," Coyote explained. "I will give you these seven baskets I have made and one buffalo, hidden in my lodge, for this bundle of rabbits."

"Coyote is tricking you," That bundle of rabbits quickly said.

"How are you tricking me?" Estchimah asked Coyote.

"How?" Coyote asked in surprise. "Nobody ever asks a coyote that!"

"I am," Estchimah insisted.

"You have to answer," the bundle of rabbits said. "That's the law!"

"I know! I know!" Coyote fumed. "But this has never happened before. Give me time."

"Well?" Estchimah said.

"What's the use," Coyote sighed as he untied the ears of the bundle of rabbits. "The rabbits are out of the bundle anyway!"

Estchimah watched in fascination as one rabbit after the other hopped out of the furry bundle. One, two, three, four, five, six, then seven, but just as the last rabbit jumped from the bundle an eighth head appeared! It was the head of a very beautiful woman.

"Who are you?" Estchimah asked in awe.

"I am Willow Woman," the beautiful maiden smiled. "I am you."

ESTCHIMAH AWOKE alone the next morning with only the desert to comfort her. She set out again on her journey. As she walked she began to hear the desert whispering her song. The song grew and grew. A mirage rose in front of her eyes, whispering, and she listened. She heard these words.

"The Medicine Woman gave the name of Silver Comb and spoke to me of ancient campfires. 'Stir their ashes and see the rivers of moonlight. Watch the smoke breathe upon the embers of families who have seen the ebb and flow of laughter and tears, and have painted the earth drum.'"

Silver Comb spoke softly, telling Estchimah that some had called her a witch, and asking if she would mind staying long enough to help her build her fire. Estchimah did not understand until the Medicine Woman gave her a knowledge necklace made of turtleshell.

Silver Comb lived next to an old cottonwood tree. "Will you follow me?" Estchimah thought she heard her say. Around and around Silver Comb spun, until she became part of the confusion of Estchimah's mind. "Will you listen with your heart?" she asked. "The mirror shrinks before your eyes like a Medicine Lake that is drying away. And little puffs of dust are raised by the feet of playing children where once there was an ocean. You can cup the universe in your hands," Silver Comb said quietly.

"Such strange thoughts," Estchimah said out loud to herself. "What can they possibly mean? And where do they come from?"

"Do you always talk to yourself?" a voice whispered.

Startled, Estchimah turned to discover the source of the voice and saw a beautiful painted snake. The snake hissed and drew its long coiled body tighter into a circle. It raised its head, its eyes blazing red. It tasted the air with its blue forked tongue before speaking again.

"Peace, little sister," it whispered with a hiss, "It was I who wove the memory of Silver Comb within your mind."

"I cannot move!" Estchimah cried out, frightened.

"I will release you when you promise not to harm me," it whispered.

"Why would I want to harm you?" Estchimah squeezed the words through her teeth.

"Promise you will not harm me and I will release you," it whispered.

"I . . . I promise." Estchimah grimaced.

Explosions of violence and hatred tore through Estchimah's being. She reeled drunkenly and fell to her knees, clawing at the sand, as nightmares thrust themselves into her vision, sickening her spirit to the edge of oblivion. Then suddenly the spasm ceased. Estchimah's vision cleared. Her hands were around the slender throat of a beautiful young woman whom she appeared to have choked to death.

Estchimah loosened her grip and fell back numb with shock at what she had done. She staggered to her feet, blinded with shame and guilt, trying to rub what she saw from her eyes. But the beautiful young woman had not been killed. Her deception had been her way of teaching. She arose from the sand, encompassing Estchimah in her arms. She comforted her.

"I am Sweet Medicine," the young woman whispered, "and I live. You chose not to kill me."

LITTLE WOLF crouched by the tiny fire and pushed the twigs he had gathered into it, carefully trying not to smother what he had worked so hard to get.

"Everybody seems to have greater medicine than I," Little Wolf thought, adding more wood. "Alone! Alone! Always alone!" It didn't make sense.

He rubbed himself and stood up.

"Fire go out . . ." whispered in his mind, driving Little Wolf into a crouch again to feed his fire.

He pushed more twigs into the small flames. He watched, watched each glowing coal.

The wind gusted around the rickety cabin, pushing against the door. It creaked but Little Wolf was so intent upon his tiny fire he didn't hear it. Suddenly the door blew open, exploding against the wall. Instantly Little Wolf dived for his carbine. The gun roared into life the moment he touched it, hurling its thunder through the door. But there was no one there.

Little Wolf lay upon the cold damp floor, shaking and listening.

"The fire . . . See your . . . light," crept into Little Wolf's mind.

Startled, he looked around. Should he retreat further into the cabin? Should he race for the door? Get it over with?

A whimper escaped from his lips. His exhausted body didn't want to move, and his heart was faint with despair.

"No more want . . . fight. Want die," he thought. "Cannot move. No more run . . . everybody gone . . . want die."

The wind whispered in the pines outside the door, singing the *Shis-Shis* song. The fire began to crackle and dance, filling the cabin with its light. Nothing threatening moved.

Shaking, Little Wolf stood up. He held his carbine level. His hands shook pitifully.

"Why . . . they . . . not kill?" he thought feebly.

He stepped to the door. Nothing moved.

"Wheau—" His cry caught in his throat.

"The *Shis-Shis* song," his thoughts said out loud as he poked his rifle around the door. It began to rain again.

Little Wolf closed the door and returned to his fire. Warmed, he began to look at the lodge.

"Whiteman stinks," he thought as he looked around. "No comfort. No light. Their lodges shut out the light."

He put more wood upon his fire and he slept. Nightmares tore at Little Wolf's mind, searing his heart with cold pain. He saw the distorted scenes of butchered children and women. Over and over again he tasted the sharp stench of powder in his mouth as he killed and killed again the enemy that swarmed everywhere in his camp. A new hide for the Sun Dance Drum was staked upon the ground to stretch and dry. Little Wolf was hypnotized by its deformity because a dead child sprawled in blood upon it. He screamed in the nightmare again and again each time he recognized the face of his baby sister.

"Murderers!" he cried as he shot one of the hairy faces point-blank. Then he awoke. It was morning. He was shaking uncontrollably.

"Fever . . . probably die," he thought, then laughed. "Must find food. Will die, maybe." He laughed again.

Stiffly, painfully, he pulled himself up from the floor, using his rifle as a crutch. He banked the fire with the wood he had left and went out the door to hunt.

"The songs of the two-legged and the four-legged are not the same. But, my children, they are as alike within the same reflection as spring is to summer. One cannot exist without the other. Ask for this medicine song when you hunt." Little Wolf listened, remembering.

He prayed, saying, "I promise with a good heart that I am asking for my life, Great Mother. Speak to those of your children. Ask them to hear me because I am singing my medicine song."

He sat on his haunches and drew a holy sign upon the ground. It was a circle, and within the circle he drew the deer.

He spoke aloud to the grandfathers, saying, "I have heard your holy dance, and I have smoked with you many times, but now I have no tobacco. But I wear your Sweet Medicine above my eyes. These are the prayers my mother taught me. It is her moccasins I walk in. She is the sign of the earth, and I have kept her teaching. Look upon your daughter's moccasins, are they not hers? I am too tired and poor to hunt a long way. Send the deer to me."

He put his hands over the signs and spoke again, saying, "You will become part of me. This I promise. I will care for all of you. Not one thing shall be wasted. What I do not eat, my medicine brothers the wolves will eat. And cat also, and crow. I have learned this dance, and I walk this path. You will live within me, and I will remember your give-away to me when I Sun Dance. It is a holy song given to us by our Mother the Earth. I hear her song."

He then stood and faced the east saying, "Hear me, Maheo! I send my voice everywhere to you. I thank you for your sweetness. I know that you cause the life within all things, even our dreams. I see you everywhere even though I am blind. I hear you within my deafness. I talk with you today because I have witnessed terror. Which way should I go? Has the great hoop of the People been broken? Can there be a renewal? The Sacred Arrows have been spotted with blood. I have killed a human being. Send me where you will, and I will walk that path. I will search for the People."

Little Wolf began to walk. Then he saw her. She was standing in a small meadow, waiting. He fired and the deer gave-away that he might have food.

The fever came upon him slowly the next day, never quite enough to completely cripple, but enough to torture. Each day brought an inferno of pain that tore unmercifully at Little Wolf's heart until he was nearly mad. Hallucinations brought monsters to the lodge. They clawed at the bolted door, and the walls at times moved to crush him. He watched in horror as the floor rose up to smother his only friend, the fire. He cried out for mercy that day. The Mother must have taken pity upon him because she sent the wind to sing the *Shis-Shis* song until he fell into a healing sleep.

Finally it was the time when the plums were ripe, and all the growing beings gave signs that there would be an early winter. Little

Wolf worked skillfully and quickly on the gear he would need for his long trek to the Tongue River.

"The People will be hunting at the place of the Two Children's Trees right now," Little Wolf thought. "They probably have already heard that we are all dead."

He pulled hard on his bow, testing it.

"I wonder if anyone lived besides me? It's possible. All of them cannot be dead . . . I hope." He dismissed the thought.

He thought of his grandmother's words, "When the bees sleep it is a gift for the People. The bees walk the pollen path, and they dance with the flowers. They sing with Seven Arrows."

"Do they chase Seven Arrows and try to sting him?" the little boy had asked his grandmother. Little Wolf laughed at the memory.

"I'll chase you!" his grandmother scolded. She continued to gather her wood, complaining about her stiffening joints but continuing patiently with the story. "The bees do not seek out the People. They gather and wait for the time when the People are in need of the honey. They always sleep well because they know we will find them."

"I hope that our relatives, the bees, gathered much honey, grandmother, because my life may depend upon finding it this winter," Little Wolf said, setting his teeth.

Little Wolf knew that his journey would be long. The Pony Soldiers had forts now, to shield the hunting parties of whites who would be gathering together to take their stolen furs to the Great River. He thought out his route carefully because a person caught on foot would be instantly dead. He would have to circle far around the soldiers. It would take him forty-four days.

"Where's the balance in all this?" he wondered idly.

Suddenly something seemed to whisper *danger—danger*. Little Wolf felt his body tense even before his mind registered the warning. He jumped to his feet and looked around fearfully, scanning everything for any sign. Then he understood it. The birds had quieted. He grabbed his rifle, melted into the short brush, and waited.

Eight men rode into view and stopped in front of the cabin. He recognized one of the riders. He was one of the men who trapped the beaver. A knot coiled inside Little Wolf's belly, a spasm of hate and fear that almost made him retch. The men dismounted and led their ponies into the small corral behind the cabin.

Little Wolf had foreseen the possibility of surprise and had prepared for it in advance. Now he quietly gathered all of his gear from where he had hidden it. He desperately wished he could steal the

horses, but he knew that would be too risky for one person. They would have all the animals hobbled and guarded, especially here so far away from their main hunting camp.

He started down the mountain, keeping close to the cliff's face where its shadow was deepest. The descent was grueling because most of it had to be made in a stooped position. A person walking upright could be distinguished too easily from the four-leggeds.

"When the great-shoulder bear stands upright there is danger, my son," Little Wolf remembered.

He followed the thought further, almost asking the question out loud. "Grandfather, why has this way been given to the great bear?"

"The human being is more dangerous than any of the animals," his grandfather had answered, "but, my son," the old man added, smiling, "the Bear Teacher knew of the humans' need for others of their own kind, and the Power made it possible to recognize the People from all other beings."

Darkness was rising quickly from the prairie. Little Wolf stopped momentarily to look at the beautiful painted clouds over his head. There would not be any comforting fire tonight, but at least he had a warm deer robe.

"No moon to walk with tonight," he thought. "Tomorrow I will follow Little Creek until it is safe for me to hunt again."

The shadows were everywhere now, and he left his concealment for the smooth rolling prairie grass. He began to dog trot.

He ran and walked until the total darkness made it impossible.

"Care for your own circle of firelight," Little Wolf thought as he readied his night camp. Holding Lightning had explained that people can see only as far as the circle of light from their own campfire. It has been given to us from the universe, this Sun Dance Way. Our brothers and sisters can see our fire upon the prairie from very far away. It is the same teaching as that of the stars. It is the way of the Great Spirit. It is like Star Fire Water.

"It can also lead your enemies to your camp," the Chief, Jumping Dog, had said.

"True!" Holding Lightning had smiled. "True! But when there is a circle of many fires, who will be foolish enough to attack in the darkness?"

Little Wolf took some of the meat he had dried the week before and began to eat.

"I would have only one fire, and so I must have none," he thought before falling asleep.

The next morning Little Wolf found safety in a hidden valley. He worked hard in the following days. He needed the things of the human being. Much of his equipment was made expertly, but there were other things that he could not make so well. He made boots for the snow that would soon cover his world, and he would need moccasins to keep his feet warm. He had no leggings, no quiver, no hat. He worked from morning till night, then worked on by his fire until he fell to sleep exhausted. His work was not without its danger. He narrowly escaped with his life when he was suddenly attacked by one of the great bears. The bear had smelled the blood of an elk cow he was skinning and had charged without warning.

"Eat it! Thick head!" he yelled at the bear from a safe distance. "And I hope you choke."

Little Wolf came closest to death when an ancient tree snag broke, almost crushing him.

Twenty walking days were still ahead before he reached the Tongue River, where he hoped the villages of the People would be.

Then winter breathed all at once, covering the prairie with a new white robe, but food was still plentiful. It was that same day he discovered Dreamer Woman.

When he first saw the lodge he could hardly believe his eyes, but no amount of blinking made it disappear. There it was, stark and black, flapping in the wind like a strange wounded bird. It sat there alone, exposed and without reason.

The thought whipped into Little Wolf's mind, "No one would set up a lodge in such a place. No one but a madman. Is it a death lodge? Some horror I have not heard of?"

He dropped his bundle and began to circle the lodge, his rifle ready. The fearful specter grew in size as he approached, but its reason for existing where it stood still made no sense.

As he drew closer he began to understand why the skins were black. They were a collection of hides from many teepees that had been burned.

"But why put up a lodge in such an unlikely place?" his thoughts warned again. He moved closer. There were tracks leading down to the frozen stream and back, many tracks.

"Someone lives here! Impossible. Who? Where are they?" his thoughts asked, tumbling over each other.

He backed away slowly to a safe place and watched. Nothing moved.

"It appears to be a lodge of the Painted Arrows," he noticed.

He looked around again to make sure of what he saw. The prairie around him was nearly empty. Not enough wood to last the winter. There were not even enough trees. There were only the tracks to the stream and back. Not another track for hundreds of steps beyond the lodge, nothing. And no fire.

Throwing off his fear, Little Wolf walked deliberately up to the lodge door and opened it. He stepped inside, letting his eyes get used to its gloomy interior. Everything he saw was pitiful and ragged beyond belief. Then he saw a girl—asleep or dead he could not tell. He moved closer. Another ragged bundle began to move.

"Stand up!" he commanded, pointing his rifle.

A gray head appeared and moaned, then fell down again.

"Stand up!" he barked again, pushing away the robe with his rifle barrel.

Under the bundle lay a tiny, emaciated old woman. Little Wolf quickly pulled the robe back over the ancient grandmother and soothed her, patting her head as he would a sick child. He quickly examined the girl and discovered that she too was alive.

He ran back for his bundle, grabbed up what wood he could carry and hurried back to the blackened lodge. Quickly he lit a fire and began to heat stones to make soup. He unwrapped two extra robes he had carried with him and used them to make the little girl and old woman more comfortable.

When the stones were hot he placed them in his buffalo-skin kettle to heat the water. He did this again and again until the water began to boil. Then he added some fresh meat, dried berries, and herbs. Again he replaced the cooling stones in the kettle with hot ones and hung the kettle up to finish cooking.

He looked around the lodge. From what he saw he slowly began to piece together the story. The old woman, with the help of someone else, must have brought the lodge to where it now stood. But that someone else had either died or left them. The old woman hadn't been able to move the lodge further by herself, so she had done the best she could and had set it up alone. It had been their only chance for survival.

He tied a bundle of willows together and began to clean the lodge floor. The lodge must be kept clean if he were to save the two women.

"Dog bones! So they have eaten their dogs. That at least explains their being alive," he thought as he worked. "The soup must be warm— not hot, not cool—or they will vomit it back up."

He then turned his attention to the lodge skins. He tried clumsily to fasten them together where they had torn apart, but he only tore new holes.

Frustrated, he tested the soup again to see if it had cooled enough for them to eat. It had.

He would feed the little girl first. He shook her to awaken her. She would not open her eyes. He slapped her. She half opened her eyes and began to whimper.

"Eat!" he yelled at her, to keep her awake. "Eat!"

Slowly, after much coaxing and more slaps, she began to eat. She ate three or four mouthfuls and fell asleep again.

"Little by little. Feed the starving little by little. Now the old woman. I must keep waking her up to eat, both of them," he thought, now trying to arouse the old woman.

"Eat, grandmother! Eat!" he yelled at the old woman, fighting to keep her awake. "You know you must eat."

The old woman opened her eyes and smiled. Then, very slowly she turned her head toward the girl. He understood.

"You fed her all the dog meat," he said as tears filled his eyes. She would not eat.

The following day he carried the old woman from the lodge to the place where she would sleep forever under the snow.

Four days later the girl spoke for the first time.

"I know you want to know about your grandmother," Little Wolf said.

"Yes," the girl asked, "Where is she?"

"She has fallen asleep under the snow," Little Wolf answered. "She loved you very much."

He waited respectfully because he knew the girl would cry. He felt each heartbreaking tear and he remembered with her.

That evening Little Wolf returned from hunting.

"We cannot stay here very long," Little Wolf said, "The hunting is too difficult. We will have to move on."

"Where are we going?" Dreamer asked.

"To the camps of the Painted Arrow. They are living along the Tongue River," Little Wolf answered.

"I have no boots. Nothing," she said. "I am very poor."

"You are not poor!" Little Wolf laughed. "Look! I have made you new boots. Have you ever seen such wonderful skill?"

She laughed at the overly large and clumsy-looking boots.

"They are truly beautiful!" she exclaimed in joy.

"You are a great surprise to me," Little Wolf said, his smiles almost lighting up the lodge. "I saw you as a little girl, and now I see you as you are, a beautiful young woman. Are you very much younger than I?"

Dreamer laughed and touched Little Wolf's hand.

"I am fifteen winters—and you?" she asked.

"I am sixteen winters," Little Wolf replied shyly.

"What are we going to do with this lodge?" Dreamer asked. "It seems a pity to take it down. It's such a strange lodge. A very unhappy place, yet it has protected us."

"I know," Little Wolf answered. "This is the second strange lodge that I have been forced to live in. The other was the lodge of the white hunters."

"Tell me that story," Dreamer asked, so he began to tell her of the happenings that had brought him to her blackened lodge. When he had finished, it was Dreamer's turn to explain how she had come there.

"Our camp was destroyed as yours was. The main camp was not far from here. Little by little my uncle collected what he could from the old camp. Moving it bit by bit from the old site to this one. We were going to move within the protection of the canyon but sickness overcame him. Grandmother—"

"I know the rest," Little Wolf said. "Come! Let us prepare for our journey."

Seven days later, Dreamer and Little Wolf celebrated. A buffalo bull and a cow elk had given-away to them, and with these gifts they satisfied their hunger and gained protection from the winter's cold. They prepared all the meat they could carry and tanned the two large hides. The work was shared now, and the comfort of their moving camp grew. What skills one lacked, the other possessed. They had snow shoes now, and Dreamer had made comfortable back packs.

"How rich we are!" Little Wolf sang one night after their meal. "Even the winter seems to be warmer!"

Dreamer laughed with the happiness they both shared. "And it will be even more wonderful when we are with the People!" she sang.

THE SUN POISED at the southern horizon, watching. Then it swung quickly into its morning path. It was one of those mysterious days when the dream moves quietly at the People's side.

"What is this place?" Little Wolf asked, looking with a startled expression down into the gorge that had opened up suddenly in front of him. It had been hidden until they had come within just a few feet of its rim.

"It is the River That Sings With The Wind," Dreamer said, coming up to his side. "We could have been killed! My uncles have spoken of this approach to the canyon many times, and of its danger."

"The rise in the ground hides the canyon's rim until you're almost upon it!" he said angrily, "Why did you not remember?"

"I do not know," she replied, looking down.

"It is all right," Little Wolf laughed, "I was angry more at myself than you, because I was also told of this canyon."

"You were?" Dreamer asked, brightening up, "I guess we will both have to be much more awake."

"That is very true," a voice said softly behind them.

Little Wolf reached instinctively for his weapon, but a moccasined foot pinned his hand.

"Would you kill your uncle?" the voice laughed.

"Crazy Dog!" Little Wolf yelled with happiness. He turned to look at his uncle, but what he saw struck his heart in shock.

"I was tortured," Crazy Dog immediately explained with a twisted grin. "They burned me at the stake, but I lived."

Dreamer began to cry.

"Stop it!" Little Wolf growled with the old hate. "Stop it!"

"Tears are a way of speaking much, little brother," Crazy Dog said as he sat down, "It would be better if you cried also instead of tying your heart to cold stones."

"I—I," Little Wolf's voice trembled, "I . . ."

"I know you still love me," Crazy Dog said, taking Little Wolf's hand. "It is still me here under this ruined robe. I still bring you myself."

Crazy Dog's wounds needed attention, and the Wind River Canyon was the ideal place for his doctoring. Little Wolf hunted, and with back-breaking toil he and Dreamer constructed a lodge for their brother, Crazy Dog.

Little Wolf watched in fascination as Dreamer collected different roots.

"How do you know what to look for?" he asked.

"I will explain later," she said with urgency in her voice. "Go and get me seven sleeping prairie dogs; I will need their fat and liver."

Dreamer worked upon her potion, grinding, separating, cooking, and even chewing parts of it, and cooking it again until it was completed. Then she began doctoring her patient.

Crazy Dog responded to the treatment, and by the time of the Popping Trees he was beginning to show real healing.

"It's a miracle," Little Wolf said in awe. "A miracle."

"Who was it you walked with, little sister?" Crazy Dog asked Dreamer. "Your chief taught you well."

"It was my grandmother," Dreamer answered. "Her name was Buffalo Woman Comes In Sight."

"Will you go upon the war path?" Little Wolf asked Crazy Dog a few weeks later.

"The war path!" Crazy Dog laughed. "This is not my way."

Little Wolf's eyes narrowed as he looked at his scarred uncle. He felt something gnaw at his insides that he could not explain.

"Why so sullen?" Dreamer asked her husband as she entered the lodge. Little Wolf didn't answer.

"Pity and revenge are threatening the warmth within his heart," Crazy Dog said, looking at his nephew.

Little Wolf jerked his head up in surprise.

"That is not true," he said defensively. "I was wondering how it was that you—"

"Me?" Crazy Dog smiled, "You were feeling the war in your own heart, little brother. There is none within mine."

"How can you say that?" Little Wolf snapped. "It isn't human. You have to feel something!"

"I feel much, little brother," Crazy Dog answered quietly. "And what I feel is human. But if it is true what you say, then what is not human? Is it that our brothers, the animals, have no feelings?"

"I had a great-shoulder bear attack me without feeling," Little Wolf answered. "He had no compassion."

"Compassion?" Crazy Dog began. "It is not the same question. Do animals understand revenge?"

"Revenge?"

"Yes, revenge. Revenge is human. Compassion is human."

Little Wolf began to work nervously on his hunting spear.

"What is it?" Crazy Dog asked, leaning toward his nephew.

"What is it?" Little Wolf exploded. "War! I cannot help it!"

"Then begin with me," Crazy Dog yelled, "Kill me with your spear!"

"You? Have your awful pains affected your mind?"

"Yes, they have," Crazy Dog answered with an even voice. "It was I who brought the whiteman to our camp."

Little Wolf jumped to his feet, grabbing his rifle.

"Why?" he screamed at the man who still sat calmly.

"Would you hear my answer when your thunder point is burning in my belly?" Crazy Dog asked as he stood up. "Or would my nephew put his weapon down? It does not frighten me."

"You will need a good answer," Little Wolf said through gritted teeth, "because if you do not have one, I will kill you, my uncle."

"I brought them just as many of the chiefs brought them," Crazy Dog answered, "We sought for peace. We knew that we must talk. We heard of a great Spirit Dance and we wanted to dance with our whiteman relatives. It was to be a great dance. Our Lakota relatives were dancing, and many others. Walking Lightning, a powerful Medicine Man, told us of the way. 'It will bring us together with our relatives, the whiteman,' he had said. 'Because their Holy Spirit will be at the dance. It will heal our wounds.'

"We believed him. 'All the power that was lost will be found again,' Walking Lightning promised. 'We must put on new white robes, new medicine shirts, painted the new way upon the Medicine Wheel.' But what we received was more of their war. I brought them to our camp as the council had decided. They were to dance with us."

Little Wolf's hands were shaking so badly that he dropped his rifle. It roared when it hit the floor of the lodge, narrowly missing Dreamer, who was still sitting.

"Are you all right?" Little Wolf said, going to the side of his wife. "You're not hit, are you?"

"No," Dreamer said, taking Little Wolf in her arms, "I am all right."

"Forgive me, uncle," Little Wolf said through his tears.

Crazy Dog was standing. "There is nothing to forgive," he said as he picked up the rifle. "Here is your thunder iron. Take it."

"But . . . I—" Little Wolf choked.

"Take it!" Crazy Dog ordered, pushing the rifle into Little Wolf's hands.

Little Wolf, frowning now, meekly took the weapon.

"Stand up!" Crazy Dog ordered.

Little Wolf stood up slowly. A sudden apprehension welled up within him.

"What do you want me to do?" he asked, backing up.

"Kill me!" Crazy Dog commanded.

"Kill you?" Little Wolf blinked. "Why?"

"Because pain tears at me," Crazy Dog answered, stretching out his hands. "The pain is too much for me. Please, I beg you, kill me."

"By the Power, no!" Dreamer began to cry as she rose to her feet. "Please stop it. I beg you."

"Please, my uncle," Little Wolf pleaded. "Please do not do this to me. I cannot kill you. I cannot."

Crazy Dog sat down and hung his head.

"I—" Crazy Dog said as he looked up through tears, "I have pain of the body, little brother, but this pain is not as strong as the pain that is within my heart and mind. These are much greater."

"Crazy Dog, why are you doing these things?" Dreamer said, still crying. "Tell us."

"It was a hard path I chose," Crazy Dog began. "It was the way of the Coyote. It is the way given to me. These things are real and they are heartbreaking, but no matter how much it hurts I must teach."

"*Teach?*" Little Wolf said angrily. "You mean this was a game?"

"It is all real enough," Crazy Dog answered quickly. "I had to make you understand. That is why I put the rifle back into your hands. I needed the example of compassion."

"You mean the talk of killing you and the pain was not real? It was a teaching?" Little Wolf asked hoarsely.

"Little brother," Crazy Dog replied, reaching out his hands to Little Wolf, "are you so blind? Can you not see that I am in pain? And that my heart is breaking with these things?"

"I do not understand," Little Wolf said, shaking his head, "It is too much for me."

"He is trying to—" Dreamer said softly, turning to Little Wolf.

"Let him come to these things himself," the chief broke in.

Dreamer lowered her head and looked at her hands.

"What is it that is going on?" Little Wolf rose to his feet in anger. "You are both treating me like a fool!"

Dreamer started to speak, but the chief touched her arm, stopping her.

"By the horns!" Little Wolf exploded, grabbing up a warm robe and stomping out of the lodge. "Keep your conspiracy!"

It was noon and Dreamer was making their meal when Little Wolf returned.

"Who is this," he grinned, slapping Dreamer on her bottom, "making the meal at the lodge of Little Wolf? Is it a flower spirit that is lost in the winter?"

"It is," Crazy Dog laughed as he came from the lodge, "She was hiding in your medicine bundle all along and you did not know it."

"True, my uncle," Little Wolf smiled at his chief. "And she is very pretty too."

SPRING arrived one day with the explosion of the river coming to new life. Great blocks of ice pushed up and were crushed against the walls of the canyon, sending tremors the full length of the valley. The air was filled with the deafening sounds of the change of seasons. The thunder was not the sound of battle, but a song of relief. The ice gave way to what it had concealed.

"It looks as though we will have to move," Crazy Dog yelled to Little Wolf over the din of moving ice, "or we will get our feet wet."

"How long do you suppose we have?" Little Wolf hollered back.

"Before we go deaf, or before we drown?" Crazy Dog laughed, then added, "The river will be moving in with us by tomorrow."

"How do you know?" Little Wolf grinned as he walked up to his uncle. "Maybe the river will not put up with our snoring."

"I know because I hold many secrets," Crazy Dog answered somberly, "and I also know because I have seen the same thing over and over again for forty winters." Then he broke into laughter.

"We had better tell Dreamer," Little Wolf said, turning to walk the short distance to the lodge. He stopped short and began to laugh even harder.

"We are not the only great seers, uncle." Little Wolf groaned because he was laughing so hard. "Look, Dreamer has already done everything. While we talked she took down the entire lodge and has it ready to be moved."

"She must have started this morning even before the ice broke," Crazy Dog said in surprise.

"How did you know that the ice would break?" Crazy Dog asked Dreamer later, as he carried a lodge pole to their new camp.

"Great secrets," Dreamer answered shyly.

Crazy Dog lifted one eyebrow. Her answer was not enough for Little Wolf, however. He continued to probe. Finally, after their camp had been completely moved to higher ground, Dreamer answered.

"I saw rain in the mountains," she said. "It happens every season, you know."

"For forty winters that I know of." Crazy Dog began to laugh all over again.

"Why didn't we see that?" Little Wolf frowned. "I looked at the mountains this morning!"

"Because we were asleep," Crazy Dog grinned.

"Dreamer was awake before we were again!" Little Wolf moaned. "How does she do it? How does she always know before Crazy Dog and me when it is morning?"

"Great secrets," she teased.

"Great secrets?" Little Wolf frowned.

"Her great secret is that she is not as much of a sleepy head as we are," Crazy Dog laughed, picking up his hunting bow.

"Where are you going?" Dreamer asked quietly without looking up.

"I think it's about time I hunted," Crazy Dog answered, not turning around.

"I am sorry, my uncle," Dreamer said. "Give yourself a little more time."

"I am healed!" Crazy Dog said in his most jovial voice.

"How is it you can say no to Crazy Dog?" Little Wolf cut in harshly.

Dreamer smoothly rose to her feet and started off to the river, not answering.

"Wait!" Little Wolf said, following after her.

"No," Crazy Dog said, quickly grabbing Little Wolf's arm. "You have shamed her."

"Shamed her?" Little Wolf frowned. "How?"

"By taking away from her," Crazy Dog answered.

"How can I take away from her?" Little Wolf said angrily. "She is no Medicine Chief."

"Does she need to be a chief to command respect?" Crazy Dog answered. "Is it not possible for you and me to respect her word because she is a person like we are?"

"But—" Little Wolf fumbled for words, feeling he had made a terrible error.

"And was it not she who made the medicines that healed me?" Crazy Dog went on. "Were you wise enough? Was I?"

"Why can't I be right once?" Little Wolf asked suddenly through his clenched teeth. "Just once! Why are you and Dreamer so all-knowing? Am I nothing but an idiot?"

"Wait!" Crazy Dog commanded, quickly searching his mind for something to say. Anything that would give him time to recover from his surprise at Little Wolf's sudden reaction.

"Wait for what?" Little Wolf cut in tiredly, "For you to explain to me that I am even more of a fool because I am a fool. Isn't this an example of what happened the last time? Everybody sees before me, even the blind mole."

"I understand," Crazy Dog said, motioning for Little Wolf to sit with him, "We all feel that way at times."

"I have shamed Dreamer," Little Wolf said, even more resigned, "and I am ashamed."

"I have felt what you feel many times," Crazy Dog said, touching his nephew's shoulder.

"I have shamed Dreamer because I am stupid," Little Wolf went on without looking up, "and now you are about to begin all over again to explain to me just how stupid I really am. So begin. Tell me so that I will be illuminated."

"Why should I?" Crazy Dog said flatly. "Why should I waste words upon a man who is incapable of learning? Do you not see that which is right in front of you?"

Little Wolf laughed a bitter laugh. "I am stupid."

"Then let that be your first illumination," Crazy Dog answered. "But are you not also arrogant?"

Little Wolf frowned. "With whom? You?"

"Yes," Crazy Dog said coolly, "but more with yourself."

"You know that this is a waste of time don't you?" Little Wolf laughed. "Now I am stupid and also arrogant."

"Then let it be!" Crazy Dog cut his words sharply. "But if you seek another way, you will not be so unhappy. It is your choice."

"Seek another way!" Little Wolf said, getting to his feet. "How can a stupid man seek another way? He is too stupid!"

"Yeeoooeoh!" Crazy Dog yelled and laughed, jumping up and running outside. "!Yeeoheoh! My nephew is a ragged owl. An owl that feels sorry for himself!"

"Stop it!" Little Wolf growled. "Stop it!"

"Yeeoheoh!" Crazy Dog yelled even more loudly and began throwing handfuls of snow and mud at his nephew.

Angry, Little Wolf reached down, grabbing up as much snow and mud as his hands could hold. But before he could stand, Crazy Dog had filled the back of his shirt with cold wet snow.

"Yeeohow!" Little Wolf yelled, springing upright.

Little Wolf turned to throw his soggy missiles and saw his uncle standing with his hands upraised to the east. He was praying.

"I have a little brother whom I love with all my heart," Crazy Dog prayed. "He is stupid and arrogant and wonderful. Maheo, do you suppose he will ever see? Do you suppose he will ever learn? He is young and wants to know everything all at once. He has planted nothing but wants to see great gardens. He is powerful. You have given me this way to see. I am thankful that I can sit with this young man."

"Why does even the mole see before I do?" Little Wolf asked, sitting down beside his uncle, wiping the mud off his shirt and face.

"The mole sees very far," Crazy Dog smiled. "He is just like you, my nephew. His seeing is the great sign of the Earth Mother. It is the same when the People look within themselves. Look down deep within your own earth lodge."

"But the mole is blind," Little Wolf broke in.

"He is blind when he is out of the ground. It is the natural law." Crazy Dog grinned. "But it is also a Coyote Story. When the mole is within his natural surroundings he sees very far. He can even see through rock."

"These are strange signs you are painting above my eyes," Little Wolf said, frowning. "What do they mean?"

"Can you put your ear to the ground and hear the hooves of the buffalo when they are running?" Crazy Dog asked as he lit up his pipe.

"Of course."

"Those are vibrations. You see the buffalo with your ears, do you not?" Crazy Dog said, blowing a smoke ring.

"In this way I can even hear people running if they are not too far away," Little Wolf said, smiling.

"I know," Crazy Dog laughed. "It is a good way. Mole can see this way. But even better than you. In fact, he can see better than the eagle but only within and through the earth. He feels the earth. He knows your walk, the buffalo's walk, the worm's walk, and everything that moves upon the earth. It is even said that the mole feels the little waves of water along the rivers and lakes."

"Horns!" Little Wolf exclaimed.

"The mole is the medicine teacher for the bear," Crazy Dog said, grinning. "All the beings know this. Everyone, except for the People. How can you learn from this way?"

"We can talk with the mole," Little Wolf answered eagerly.

"But what does mole say?" Crazy Dog asked.

"I do not know," Little Wolf replied, frowning again.

" 'How do you feel?' mole asks." Crazy Dog burst out laughing. "How do you feel?"

"I feel stupid," Little Wolf said, wanting to laugh himself.

"We all say this," Crazy Dog said, leaning nearer Little Wolf. "But that feeling of stupidity is only the vibration. We are not truly seeing what we feel. If we speak with the teacher mole within our sacred earth lodge, the mole will tell us that what we see is our fear of being stupid. Our fear of being left out. And maybe the fear that something terrible is hidden deep within us. Perhaps something we thought we had carefully hidden. Mole knows of everything we have hidden within our earth lodges. Mole tells the Thunder Bear, the great Dreamer, of everything that is hidden. Mole wants to remind us that it is still there. The Dreamer Bear hears his teacher, and he in his turn speaks to all of us concerning these things. 'It has been said by my teacher,' Bear tells us."

"Such a strange teaching," Little Wolf said, wrinkling up his nose.

"It is a wonderful song," Crazy Dog laughed.

"Who teaches mole?"

"The Mother Earth," Crazy Dog answered. "She loves everything that is a part of her, and everything that is upon the earth is part of her. Everything that moves and grows. Even the air is part of her. Everything is separate, but everything is one with the Mother Earth. She provides the way for the People. She even provides their lodges, their earthly bodies. We are here to learn and to grow. You have heard this many times."

"And the sun?" Little Wolf asked.

"The great mirror, the sun, completes the Medicine Wheel," Crazy Dog answered. "The sun is the reflection of the universe. The sun is the mirror of the spirit. The central fire for the circle of all growing things. The sun has married the Earth Mother. The sun walks with her and is reflected within her waters. It is the way of the Sun Dance."

"It is true, my uncle. I have heard this many times," Little Wolf said, making himself comfortable.

"It is our healing," Crazy Dog said quietly. "But what has the mole within your lodge been singing? What has the Dreamer been saying?"

"Nothing I can remember," Little Wolf replied, sitting up.

"Nothing?" Crazy Dog spat like a cat. "Nothing? Look at me! Look at my burned body! Look at my face! This is what crawls inside of your nightmares! Can you hear the fire? Can you smell the blood?"

"Stop it!" Little Wolf screamed, shaking his fists, "Stop it or I will—"

"Kill me?" Crazy Dog yelled, grabbing both of his nephew's shoulders and shaking him. "What happened? What happened? Tell me!"

"I . . . I . . . let my little sister die!" Little Wolf began to cry. "Mother told me to keep her with me that day! I took her to my aunt's because I wanted to hunt."

"Say it all, little brother," Crazy Dog demanded.

"I can't seem to remember," Little Wolf sobbed. "I can't remember."

"The drum!" Crazy Dog pressed his words. "The drum! Why do you dream of a drum crushing you? You scream it out in your sleep. What about the drum?"

"She was lying in blood on the Sun Dance drum," Little Wolf cried. "Everybody was dying. I could hear my mother crying from her wounds. She was calling for my little sister! I clubbed a man who was standing nearest me. I kicked him. Then I ran. I ran. I must have grabbed his iron that speaks and his thunder points, because I still have them. I don't know, I cannot remember the rest."

"It has been said," Crazy Dog cried as he stood up. "Hear me, Little Wolf. Look upon the great tree. It is a summer tree that had its awakening time within this new spring. This renewal. You did not kill your baby sister. That old tree you have seen holds within its arms the remembrance. Like tobacco, the cured leaves were there waiting for the wind. The relatives have joined the song of the wind. Their spirits live there and love you. They understand. I see them dance along the ground, singing. I see them leap up from the earth and shake the tree, the Sun Dance tree. The leaves upon that great tree burst from those outstretched arms like beautiful plumes. And, my little brother, much of what you and I both saw were not old leaves at all. They were birds that flew away to make other nests for their young. And the old leaves fall to rest upon the ground like frail canoes upon quiet waters. Look! There is the songbird of the sun! They have returned from the south. They sing your mother's song and your baby sister's song. The Sun Dance drum has not been spoiled! Your heart beats. You have listened to the Dreamer!"

HUNDREDS OF MILES from Little Wolf's tiny camp stood the newly constructed but deserted Fort Church, whose sole occupant until recently had been one fat skunk.

No one knew why the fort had been built, and no one really cared except for the skunk and three very wet young travelers who had set out for the gold fields in Dakota Territory.

"It ain't much but it's dry in here," Calvin said as he wrung the water out of his soggy hat. " 'Pears to be the captain's quarters or somethin'. Looks plenty fancy to me."

"Beats drownin'." Pearlie groaned as she sat down on the only chair. "Where you s'pose we're at?"

"Hell, who knows," Calvin answered, "We could be anyplace. We're lost bigger'n all outdoors."

"I feel like I ain't et for a week," Evan scowled. "Why'd they build a place an' not live in it? Why do you s'pose they'd go an' do that?"

"God's the only one kin answer that," Pearlie yawned. "The gov'-ment is always fixin' to do somethin' and never doin' nothin'."

"S'crazier'n hell how we got all mixed around and come up lost," Calvin said, poking at his hat.

"What's that?" Pearlie asked, getting to her feet. "Kin you hear it?"

"What, for chrissake?" Evan laughed. "The coyotes talkin' to you?"

"No, by gawd. I heard somethin' movin' out thar. I mean it," Pearlie bawled.

Evan rose to his feet to open the door but was interrupted by a voice behind them from the only window.

"Don't turn around," the voice ordered. "Stay put."

The door opened slowly and a bearded face peered around it, taking in the room.

"Any more of you aroun'?" the man asked, poking his rifle into Evan's stomach.

"No, thar ain't," Evan answered, backing up.

"Whar you fellas off to?" the man asked, squinting.

"We were thinkin' of goal fieldin' it, but we got lost somewhar near the Ol' Muddy," Calvin offered.

"The Ol' Muddy!" The man roared with laughter. "Did you boys know you was pokin' around two hundret miles off to one side?"

"Two hundret miles off to one side!" Evan frowned. "Gawddamn me!"

"Jes' push your sidearms thisaway, if you please," the voice said from the window.

"Forget it, Bill. These mushhaids ain't gonna do nobody no harm. They's a bunch of runny-nosed cart chasers," the bearded man said, still laughing. "Come on in here an' get yourself dry."

"You boys get a fire agoin' in that place an' we kin eat," the bearded man said easily. "I betcha you're hungrier'n boat rats."

After the meal Evan told the story of how he and Calvin had heard of easy pickings in the gold fields for everybody and how they had decided to make the journey by themselves.

"So'z you struck out across the prairie," Bill sniggered. "Gawd, what no-good barrelhaids you are. Lordy!"

"Kin we make it?" Pearlie asked, speaking for the first time since the newcomers' arrival.

"Jumped-up Jerusalem!" Bill yelled, "That's a gawddamn woman, Barnaby. Gawds o' mighty!"

"You craphaids are travelin' with a woman?" Barnaby asked, unable to believe. "A real, live gawddamn filly. Gawd, you are a bunch of sourhaids. You'll never make it!"

"Why not?" Pearlie asked indignantly, "What's so all-fired wrong with that?"

"Looky here," Bill said in his most kind voice. "You got one rifle betwixt you an' twelve rounds of shot. You're dumber than an owl at a social, more ignorant than—"

"Put the reins on, gawddamnit!" Calvin said, getting mad. "Hell knows we ain't the fanciest, but we ain't no-accounts!"

"Looky here, boy," Barnaby said, leaning close to Calvin, "You're lucky. Sportin' all-fired lucky it was ol' Bill an' me who waltzed into your camp. Lordy knows you coulda been shot just for your young miss thar."

"But—" Evan cut in.

"But nothin'!" Barnaby went on. "You let me finish what I gotta say, by jingo. If you're sure you wanna tear your haids off tryin'," that's fine, but you gotta listen."

"That's iffen you wanna live," Bill added.

"Why you doin' this here for us?" Evan asked, frowning.

"Hells o' fire, boy," Barnaby roared. " 'Cause you're humans."

"That's right. You gotta right to live," Bill snorted. "Anybody knows that."

"What do you s'pose then?" Calvin asked.

"Jes' this," Barnaby answered, "You gotta zig zag from one injun camp to the next. They'll care for you an' feed you. Then when the time's right you kin finally scratch dirt for your goal." He scratched his head before going on. "Maybe a year or so from now."

"Injuns!" Calvin yelped, "Gawd, they'll lift our hair!"

"Lordy!" Bill snorted, "Your haids are like a frumped up bull in a sour bog. Thar's folks that shoot an' thar's folks that don't. Ain't you ready for that?"

"But we was told—" Calvin blurted defensively.

"You was told nothin'!" Barnaby sniggered. "You been listenin' to tall tales. Hell, boys, an' madam, them's real purty human bein's out thar—just the like of you and me, those injuns are."

"You mean there's not the fightin' an' killin' like we heard of?" Pearlie asked doubtfully.

"Sure thar is, you knothaid!" Bill grimaced. "Hell, you know better'n that. Thar's always those who's akillin' an' thar's always those alivin'. It ain't no different with injun folks."

"Thar's somethin' we ain't seein' here," Evan said suspiciously, "an' it's as clear as the smell o' the ol' skunk which lives hereabouts."

"Whatcha mean, boy?" Bill said, sitting up straight.

"I mean, you talkin' about goin' this way an' that, but not explainin' about the trail you're on," Evan said, coming out of his slouch. "What's your story? What're you doin' here?"

"We was, ah . . . kinda—" Barnaby fumbled.

"It's no crime to admittin' it," Bill said, turning to his companion. "We're lost bigger'n hell, same as you. We cut across the same way as you, but it *ain't* the same way as you. We're standin' maybe off to one side by fifty mile, an' that ain't a far piece at all.

"But you even look the part of injuns, the way you're covered," Pearlie said, intrigued. "What are you about?"

"We, ah . . ." Barnaby drawled. "We was—"

"We *was* injuns, by damn," Bill cussed. "We's part an' piece the same hide as they is. An' we're lookin' to stop the knockin' off o' our relatives by them thar no-good pelt grabbers, 'cause our folk are standin' in peace an' not fightin'."

"You mean you're totin' yourself on a peace mission or somethin'?" Evan asked, scratching his chin.

"You're damn tootin'," Bill snorted again. "We was run ragged by all the shootin' down o' our relatives. It's gettin' plumb wild crazy. An' it's sad, too."

"Gawd," Pearlie coughed.

"Looky thar, Barnaby," Bill said. "Looky thar, she's acatchin' a cough already. It's magpie business, I'd say, them arunnin' around lost. Whatcha say to that?"

"Sure," Barnaby answered, as he filled his pipe.

"What you got to do is get on over to our lodges," Bill said, turning to Pearlie. "Our folk will squeeze that cough outa you with medicine, an' you'll bed down with fine human bein's, our relatives."

"Or you can scratch your feet right up to your keghaids with trouble," Barnaby added, " 'Cause you're so ignorant."

"Then, by thunder, it's that ways for us!" Calvin hollered and danced around. "We's on the trail o' that goal agin!"

"I still ain't ready for the thought o' livin' with redskins," Evan pouted. "Seems there's a wind we ain't knowin' about yet, an' it feels like a puffy norther to me."

"Fall into your own badger holes," Bill snorted with disgust. "You keghaids are disgustin', ahatin' that way. It's gonna bend the ol' power wheel into a mess, that kind o' palaver."

"We ain't hatin'," Pearlie spoke up. "Evan's feared o' bein' hurt when he ain't even mussed a feather yet. No siree, not me, by jingo, I ain't ahatin' an' thar ain't no wheel gonna bend 'cause o' me."

"That's the girl!" Barnaby yelled, throwing his hat into the air, "You is on your way if I'm lookin' a straight course."

"Come on!" Calvin said, slapping Evan's leg. "Let's stomp up to the idear, less you got a better one."

"No, I ain't." Evan smiled, brightening up. "We're gonna raise some new dust!"

"Sure!" Barnaby said as he blew a perfect smoke ring.

"You'll be dancin' a new tune brighter'n Miss Pearlie's smile 'fore long," Bill yelped gleefully and giggled. "An' you'll dance 'roun a spankin' new pole with real purty human folk. You know, I got me a kid thar who's a jumpin'-up fine rascal."

"Yahoo!" Evan roared, "Yahoo!"

"Any of you kin read or write?" Barnaby asked.

They answered one by one.

"Nope."

"Nope."

"Nope."

"Ain't no cause for no shame," Barnaby smiled. "But it'd amade it amore easier."

"You could scratch a trail for 'em on a tear o' hide," Bill offered.

"Sure could," Barnaby said, reaching into a small bundle. "Now whar's that hide I throwed in here?"

"You're more careless than a suckling coyote pup," Bill scolded. "Here, take this one." He handed Barnaby a limp roll.

"Gawddamnit, Bill, that's our trail writ out thar," Barnaby cussed.

"We know whar the sun is, Barnaby. Ain't no use anyways, 'cause we're offen a bit anyways. Comin' aroun' we knowed the trail, an' alls we gotta do is remember," Bill insisted.

" 'Course," Barnaby agreed. "Now looky here." He began to draw. "That's the Ol' Muddy—"

"Why'd you jump up with the Ol' Muddy for?" Bill yelped. "Ain't no use noways. It don't cross no trail for 'em."

"Jes' thought they'd like to know whar the Ol' Muddy was, I guess," Barnaby said, screwing up his nose. "Least ways it don't make no mind whar I start, does it?"

" 'Course it does!" Bill argued, "You'd hafta scratch up the whole face o' the story on that scrap o' hide an' you ain't got a whole teepee side, you know."

"Guess you're right, Bill," Barnaby said, licking the piece of charcoal in his hand. "Pay no mind to that thar little dot which was the Ol' Muddy, but ain't now. You got to cut down the crick out yonder to that first big stand o' timber, then loop aroun' this here hill. Then run straight as a fox toward this here saddle in these hills yonder. Take up across this here big crick tharabouts an' move straight off north till you come to a big ol' prairie dog town."

"That's the biggest prairie dog town in the whole jumpin' world," Bill added. "Stretches out long enough to feed a hundret winter camps."

"You drag a stick line 'cross the prairie this aways an' head for that next set o' jagged sky, you know, mountains. Then you slip into this here draw."

" 'Sgood place for a camp 'fore you cross," Bill interjected, "an' thar's huntin' worth fine eatin' thar o' everythin'. That's if you don't scare away the whole jumpin'-up country with your coughin', Miss Pearlie."

"Then you scoot up along this here wall o' rock," Barnaby went on, "until you come to this here flat country an' 'zactly six days straight west an' you'll be there in a warm lodge."

"How many days all together?" Calvin asked. "I don' mean 'zactly, but tharabouts?"

"Nigh on to a month o' trottin' an' walkin', I'd say," Bill answered with a broad smile. " 'Less you hit more bad weather'n we did first week or so, an' ornery bars or runnin' herds an' stuff."

"You wanna look lively 'round these parts," Barnaby said, pointing to their proposed trail, " 'cause thar's a mess o' muddy patches that could drag you down to a pitiful crawl. An' right thar is whar we got lost for eight days."

" 'Sfunnier'n a crossed-eyed squirrel, that patch," Bill added. "We lost a good six pair o' moccasins'n thar, so'z you'd better step quick an' remember to foller these scratchin's 'cause it'll save you a might piece o' trouble."

"Gawd!" Calvin mused, "Gawddamn a' mighty!"

"What you thinkin'?" Pearlie asked, turning to Calvin.

"That's gonna be one hellfire long walk," Calvin answered.

" 'Course it is," Barnaby said as he relit his pipe.

"Whar's the gol-darn goal fields in all o' that?" Evan asked, pointing at the skin.

"Goal fields?" Bill laughed. "That's only the first little trip we told you 'bout. You gonna hafta trot a mighty piece more north than that to touch on them goal hills."

"Why'ncha come 'long with us?" Evan asked, turning to Barnaby. "You think you could do that?"

"Nooo siree!" Barnaby answered, screwing up his nose. "We got us a mess o' peace-makin' to do or we won't sleep a wink for our relatives an' their care."

" 'Zactly!" Bill said as he pushed up the coals in the fire. "We probly'll run straight up your backside though, slow an' dumb as you all is, on our way back."

"Why're you so sure o' our bein' so dumb?" Evan asked, showing his anger.

" 'Cause you are!" Bill answered, looking Evan straight in the eyes. "You're flat jackassed stupid to make that walk! 'Specially with Miss Pearlie thar."

"We knowed that this piece weren't no cakewalk!" Evan shouted, "an' I was against Pearlie comin' along, but her brother thar talked it all up into this here scheme."

"Goldamnit, Evan, you know better'n that!" Calvin said, his face showing confusion, "You know sure as hell we couldn't have left Pearlie to work herself to death an' we ajoy-ridin' 'cross to the goal fields. You agreed pure an' straight."

"Looky here!" Pearlie said, getting to her feet and putting her hands on her hips. "You're both makin' out like I'm a dog on a rope, draggin' my heels. Christ-o-roarin'! It was me found this here dry place, an' it was me pulled you from breakin' your neck, Evan. And—"

"An' you'd better make peace with one 'nother quick!" Barnaby broke in. "Bill an' me is leavin' come mornin' straight to the peace-makin', an' you can come along or whip up the trail I scratched out thar."

"We're shippin' 'er up, ain't we, Evan?" Calvin asked, turning to his friend. " 'Cause I know Pearlie wants to dig into the goal fields. Whatcha say?"

T HUNDERCLOUDS RUSHED across the sky, washing themselves in the light of ten million cedars that glowed like brilliant red candles in the setting sun.

Startling gold blended with every hue as rivers of lightning flashed from the dark water-laden clouds, crackling in the air in the same voice as the forest fire.

For one brief moment, before the driving rain poured itself into a cloud of steam within the fire, the earth seemed to pause and look. It was in that instant that everything stopped.

Billions of diamonds rose up along the curtain of rain shimmering with the fire of the earth and the sun. Rainbows leapt up from their hidden places in the cloud and mountains to dance quietly, just before the soothing water churned into an ocean of exploding foam in the valleys.

"It has been said that our faces were first painted with the same fingers of lightning we now see in those mountains," Crazy Dog said, his voice echoing the distant thunder. "We see these things every day and blink in astonishment at the power of it, but what we see is only the surface of the great water."

"Touch me with an explanation, Crazy Dog," Dreamer said, turning around to face him. "What I have just seen makes me tremble inside."

"It is like a story," Crazy Dog answered, "and it is the same with the beauty we have just witnessed, including the awesome burning of a whole mountain. The learning is all around these things like a bright circle."

Dreamer watched Crazy Dog, waiting.

"You can still hold your fantasies within the wonder of the time you were a little girl, can you not?" Crazy Dog asked.

"I can." Dreamer smiled.

"It is this time that is called The Time Of Dreaming The World Awake! The symbol of learning is the Maze. You wander as a guest of your world within the wonderful Maze. It is like a great magical garden where you are the principal person. You are protected there. You are the shadow of light of the flowering tree.

"Did you dream of a wonderful, almost magical lodge, and was there a lover waiting within that lodge for you?" Crazy Dog asked, his face as bright as a boy's.

"Truly, it was almost like that!" Dreamer said shyly.

"How old were you? Can you remember?" Crazy Dog laughed.

Dreamer smiled. "Very young. I guess I was six or seven. I do not remember."

"I dreamed in this same way," Little Wolf added. "I can remember, now that you speak of it. I too dreamed of a beautiful woman I loved and made love to."

"I remember the beauty and magic of those dreams," Dreamer said. "I was so young, even silly."

"You were not silly!" Crazy Dog laughed. "You were dreaming the world awake! You dreamed what the world was to be like. You were remembering the future with the power of the past, a past that reached back into ten millions of suns.

"Little girls dream of a man as their lover, as little boys dream of a woman; this is a good circle.

"The child walks within two realities, the reality of the dream and the reality of the law within their new world. This time is the transition between the total world of the dream and that world we call the awake. The child is like the tadpole, neither egg, young frog, nor adult frog. Like the tadpole, the child swims within the medicine world until it is introduced into its new world.

"The human creature is an animal with the power of mind. No other creature possesses this gift as fully as the human being does.

"Many children dream of flying. That is their dream, but their dream is struck down cruelly by adults around them who know of nothing else than the ground upon which they walk. No other creature experiences this but the human being. The animals are fixed within their worlds, but not the human. The human being dreams of flying, of burrowing into the earth, of swimming under deep water and leaping into the stars! Humans are the weakest of all the animals, and yet the most powerful because of their minds.

"Children view the world from the South, the place of trust and innocence. They begin their walk from the place of the great red road.

"You, Dreamer, dreamed of making love to a man. You dreamed of that reality. It is the same with Little Wolf. Cruelty and thoughtlessness on the part of the adults within the camp of any people can cause the child's dream vision to blur, and the dream can become a nightmare! But even worse than this, the child will eventually cease to dream at all. Many adults have forced their children to accept their own dreams. This is no different from rape. Adults who force their realities upon their children cause pain and suffering and destroy the power of the child's dream. The little child can only cry.

"Many children have to hide their dreams from their parents and from all other adults—even from other children—because of the traditions and taboos that exist as law among them. These people are trapped within their own ignorance! They are not wise, introspective, illuminated, or trusting. They are slaves to their own devising, their own laws.

"Yet children cannot hide their dreams for long. No one can. Dreams are a driving force of life. Strangely enough, they are the awakener. However, more often than not dreams are twisted into grotesque realities that roar like lions among those Peoples who have crushed their children. Their camps become a gray empty world of fantasies that have been accepted as realities but that have little to do with true realities. Wars are an example of this. War parties seek plunder and they kill others who are not like themselves. War parties are extensions of twisted dreams.

"The crushing of the dream comes dressed in many robes and it wears many faces. If the child sees that its family is cruel or superstitious, it too becomes caught within this way. Children walk within mimicry. It is their way of learning. Too many times adults teach their children to dream only in certain accepted ways. They do this because they have not the minds to understand the power they see before them. It is important for adults to understand this mystery."

"A society of people must be sensible," Little Wolf argued. "Reality is reality!"

"Is it?" Crazy Dog laughed. "I am sure the first people who dreamed of being warmed by a fire built from their own hands were ridiculed and feared. A dream spoke to them of what could be accomplished with the use of fire, but when they suggested it to others in their camp, punishment was brought upon them. This use of fire was outside the camp's laws. The other people believed the reality that the fire would burn up everything. Hadn't this happened before? They said that they would be burned trying to hold the fire. Wasn't this also a reality? No, my son, these things you speak of as realities exist only within the people themselves, not outside of them."

"What then should be the way of the People?" Dreamer asked.

"The way of the People is to perceive within the innocence of the child." Crazy Dog smiled. "The child does not want to be different from its parents. If the mother and father do not let the child know that they too have dreams, the child will feel crushed by its own difference and ignorance. The child will feel separated from those people it loves and depends upon. And of course if the child continues to dream, it will begin to hide its dreams. But if the child's family speaks of its dreams, the child will share with them and there can be a learning. Dreams can be realized in this way. They can become part of the People, a new awakening.

"Truth between every person within the family is the proper way. Children can only speak within their own understanding. Their questions are, more often than not, ones that are silent. The civilized parent will answer out loud the silent question. If this is not done, the child learns to become a liar like its parents, for the greatest lies are the things that are not said. It is no secret that the little boy is jealous of his father. The chiefs have taught this, and no one should be surprised. The little girl is jealous of her mother; this also has been taught.

"Children are not mindless. Answers can be given to them. When they are very young, an honest but simple answer is enough. But when the child is older a more complete answer is needed. The child will see that what it feels toward its mother or father is not uncommon. This will quiet the heart of the child.

"These emotions are only a very small part of the many things the child must understand in order to feel like a complete person among its brothers and sisters. The child must understand that its mind can produce any dream. That dreams have no boundaries. It is a challenge to any person to learn how important the gift of dreaming is. The challenge is to bring the dream into reality as a gift to the People. Every dream is either a question or an answer to a question that is needed among the human beings.

"The world is a real dream. All things upon our world are a totality of all our dreams together. The world is exactly how we want to see it. Not individually, but as a World People."

"War is no dream," Little Wolf said bitterly.

"It is possible that war has become a dream for you," Crazy Dog replied. "But I ask you, is there reason in the terror the human knows as war? Does it solve anything? Has it ever solved anything? Does it protect anything?

Little Wolf sat sullenly, refusing to answer.

"Is it possible we can do nothing concerning war?" Dreamer asked.

"That is a foolish question," Little Wolf growled, "As foolish as all this talk about dreams!" He began to laugh loudly, straining to control himself. "A madman's talk in the face of hard reality!"

"If there were no soldiers, there would be no armies," Crazy Dog said evenly. "And that is what we face, armies! Many kinds of armies that are acting out a role of death. Not as defenders, but as destroyers!"

"But they exist!" Little Wolf scowled.

"They exist! I never said that they did not," Crazy Dog answered. "Did I say that they were not real? But what of their reality? What does this say to you? Isn't it possible there can be another way?"

"Of course there can!" Little Wolf fumed. "But not with talk of them being a dream! You cannot dream away a war!"

"As a whole People we can," Crazy Dog said quickly. "We as a People create war. It is not some force outside ourselves that creates it."

"How does it all begin?" Dreamer asked nervously.

"It is taught," Crazy Dog answered.

"We are taught, all right," Little Wolf laughed scornfully. "We are taught by everything! Our parents, our brothers and sisters, and even the animals teach us to kill!"

"But only the human plots murder," Crazy Dog said emphatically. "If the animals wanted to kill us, we would have perished from the face of the earth a very long time ago. If the animals were to become warriors, determined to destroy, we would not last one summer. The animals show the human beings another way, the Give-Away. Is this not different?"

"Agreed!" Little Wolf scoffed angrily. "So you are saying that we, the human beings, are mad! But no dream talk can heal madness!"

"Can't it?" Crazy Dog laughed. "Is it not talking that helps to create war?"

"Talk!" Little Wolf laughed. "You are surely mad, my uncle."

"Mad! Am I?" Crazy Dog smiled. "I would be truly mad if I were to be part of a war party that sought the death of a People I have never seen or known. If someone within the camp of the People were to be murdered, the hearts of the People would be inflamed to revenge themselves. But if they decide to proceed as a war party against the People who have hurt them, then and only then would their passions have to be put aside. You are unable to discipline a People who are inflamed with passion. No, the paradox is that the heart is not listened to. A war party is a cold and calculating thing. It must not have passion, only determination. This is brought about by talk. Talk organizes a war party. Talk teaches the patience to kill."

"Strange," Dreamer said with emotion, "You mean that the soldiers who attacked our village felt nothing?"

"They felt, my daughter, but they had no passion of the heart," Crazy Dog answered. "Because when the heart speaks, it always speaks of recognition. When the heart speaks, each face becomes recognizable as a brother or sister. No, the heart must be covered with determination so that it cannot speak. Then the man or woman can kill without feeling. The faces of their victims blur. If the heart speaks, it cries out in pain and it pleads for compassion."

"How is this possible?" Little Wolf frowned.

"If you mean the terror of war," Crazy Dog explained, "it is the collective fear of a People. If you mean the myth that is taught that war solves problems, then . . ." Crazy Dog stopped speaking and held his hands to his mouth.

"Please answer," Dreamer said, suddenly feeling afraid.

"I cannot," Crazy Dog answered. "Because you know. We all know the answer. It is our reality. It is our dreaming awake. If our dreams include the brutality of war, then it exists."

"How do you know these things?" Little Wolf frowned.

"Because of the Vision Quest Of The Rainbow Lodge," Crazy Dog answered.

"Tell us!" Dreamer said, excited.

"When I first heard of the Rainbow Lodge I became afraid," Crazy Dog smiled. "I had always been afraid of peyote, and I thought this would be my teacher. I thought this because the Medicine Woman who taught these ways was also the Keeper of the Lodge Of Vision Medicines. Her name was Woman Who Paints All The Colors Of The Give-Away. I sought only for power in those days." He brushed a wisp of hair that blew in his face, remembering. "I had brought a dance back with me from the mountains. It was the dance of feeling the power places of the earth. But I was more confused than illuminated with the gift, so I approached the old woman for guidance.

" 'I have brought you this pipe, grandmother,' I said, offering her my pipe.

"She began to laugh, which made me very nervous. I asked her why she was laughing, but she only laughed the harder. This went on for a very long time until I had no more patience for it. I rose to my feet, disgusted.

" 'This is an ugly thing you do to me, grandmother,' I said. 'I have offered you this pipe with sincerity.'

"I had hardly finished my words when I saw her crying. Perplexed, I tried to console her, but she would not have it. She pushed me away.

I looked around behind me where Medicine Rock Of The Fire was sitting. I meant to ask for advice, but what I saw caused my blood to freeze. Medicine Rock Of The Fire had become a giant toad with a beak and talons. I was so frightened I became sick."

"By the Power!" Little Wolf coughed.

"Things like that can discourage you," Crazy Dog said, smiling, "but I was determined to continue. Not because I was suddenly brave, but because I knew little else to do.

" 'Why have you come here?' the old woman asked.

"I almost wet my pants when she spoke, because I was so busy watching the toad. I began to babble. I just could not get out an intelligent thought no matter how hard I tried.

"Suddenly the old woman turned into a coyote right in front of my eyes. It was too much for me. I fainted away as smoothly as an otter going for a swim."

".Are you teasing us?" Dreamer giggled.

"No, I am not," Crazy Dog said. "It all happened just as I have said. When I awoke, the old woman was sitting smoking my pipe with Medicine Rock Of The Fire.

" 'We accept your pipe, grandson,' the old woman said. 'Come to my lodge tomorrow morning before the sun.'

"The next morning, shivering, I waited for my teachers, but nobody came. I fidgeted for a while and then I decided to start a fire to keep warm until they came. I found some wood and took out my carrying coal, which I kept in a small turtle shell. I was about to light some dry grass, when I heard a voice.

" 'Why do you build a fire? Shouldn't you be blessing the wonderful new morning? Giving thanks to the four grandmothers who sit with you in this holy place?'

"I turned but could see no one.

" 'I was cold and I will give thanks,' I answered.

"But before I could finish what I had begun to say, the voice spoke again, saying:

" 'Do the trees, when they first bud, speak to you of the spring?'

" 'I—' I began but was interrupted by the voice that seemed to come from everywhere, saying: 'If you cannot see me, how is it that you think you see the world?'

" 'The world . . .' I stammered.

" 'And Seven Arrows, who dances, braiding your hair. Where have you hidden your powers? Has your sacred pipe been shattered against the stones of the Sacred Mountains? Look at me!'

"I did, and I saw Medicine Rock Of The Fire sitting about four good steps from me.

" 'How . . . how did you do that?'

" 'How is it that you could not see me?' Medicine Rock Of The Fire asked.

" 'Or me,' the old woman said, suddenly becoming visible right at the side of Medicine Rock Of The Fire.

"I sat down trembling.

" 'Please, my uncle,' I said, 'do not become a toad today.'

"He rose laughing to his feet and greeted me with a hug. The grandmother hugged me too and made me comfortable on a buffalo robe she had brought with her. It was completely white."

"The robe from the Medicine Bull!" Dreamer said in awe.

"How is it you know of this robe?" Little Wolf asked, turning to Dreamer.

"The robe was given to the camp of my grandfather," Dreamer answered. She turned to Crazy Dog. "You were taught by my grandmother! But you called her Woman Who Paints All The Colors Of The Give-Away. That is not the name by which I knew her."

"She had many names," Crazy Dog answered.

"You mean that the old woman I buried beneath the snow was a powerful Medicine Woman?" Little Wolf asked, surprised. "Could there not be another white robe, another old woman?"

"She was my grandmother," Dreamer insisted.

"If your grandmother was so powerful, then why did she die? Why did she not work some great medicine to save you both?" Little Wolf asked.

"She did," Crazy Dog answered. "She called you to the lodge where Dreamer was dying."

"But the old woman died," Little Wolf persisted.

"Like any ordinary human," Crazy Dog said quietly.

Crazy Dog lit his pipe before continuing.

"I fasted for four days," Crazy Dog began again, "and I was kept awake all four days. The old woman and Medicine Rock Of The Fire had taken me into a deep cave where there was absolutely no light. Sometimes, it is hard for me to remember completely everything that I found there within the Rainbow Lodge. I experienced tremendous fear, but the Medicine Woman was my constant guide and comforted me. After a time, which seemed to me to be days, I thought I was beginning to see in the dark. I could make out shadows. Many strange things danced in front of my eyes. Then suddenly I could see the Medicine Woman and Medicine Rock Of The Fire. I could see them clearly. Little by little there were many other things I could see. To their backs was a beautiful bright sunlit prairie. Many of the beings were there. There were buffalo, elk, deer, horses. There was everything there. And everything seemed beautiful except for one thing."

Crazy Dog stopped and hung his head for a very long time before continuing.

"There was something terrible there that killed the animals and withered everything it touched. It had no form. It caused terror inside me that cannot be described.

" 'What are you seeing!' the old woman asked with urgency. 'Quickly, tell us!'

" 'It is horrible!' I said, shaking in fear. 'Terrible! Please grandmother!' I begged. 'Help me!'

" 'What you see is the combined dreams of hate and violence of all the People,' the grandmother answered.

"She clapped her hands hard and everything became dark again. I began to scream. I did not stop until I saw Medicine Rock Of The Fire. He was holding two torches, one in each hand. I was unable to walk and had to be carried out of the Rainbow Lodge by Medicine Rock Of The Fire and the Medicine Woman."

"I can almost see it!" Dreamer said, her voice shaking.

"Everyone can," Crazy Dog answered.

"In the following days I learned the way of the passing the hand in front of the eyes from these two chiefs. It is a way in which anyone can be put to sleep while they are awake, even you. And in these times when you are asleep-waking I can cause you to see anything or to see nothing."

"Impossible!" Little Wolf exploded. "No one has a power to do that!"

"What do you see in your hand, Little Wolf?" Crazy Dog said, looking straight into Little Wolf's eyes. "Is that not Seven Arrows?"

"Seven Arrows!" Little Wolf exclaimed in astonishment, staring into his hands.

"Speak with him," Crazy Dog commanded.

As Little Wolf began to speak, Dreamer turned to Crazy Dog. She was about to question him, but Crazy Dog interrupted and commanded her to do the same as Little Wolf.

"Seven Arrows!" she exclaimed in delight. "Crazy Dog! Look! It is Seven Arrows!"

Then Crazy Dog clapped his hands, and the images in the two young people's hands disappeared.

"If everyone within a camp decided to do so together, they could change the entire world." Crazy Dog began again. "This is what the Medicine Woman told me. 'It is a teaching,' she said. She told me that many terrible things happen within our realities and our dreams, but we, as a People, have the power to change these things."

"How?" Dreamer asked.

"Tell me," Crazy Dog said with a smile. "Tell me of the most horrible thing your mind can devise."

"Horrible?" Little Wolf blinked. "You mean like starvation?"

"We can see starvation as horrible," Crazy Dog explained, "and we can whine at its reality, but there is another way. It is the way of dreaming awake. We can begin to change this terror, this thing we know as starvation, if we begin to understand it. And the most direct approach is the best."

"How?" Little Wolf asked.

"It is for those who are full and rich to give to those who are hungry. Is this not what our Mother Earth has taught us?" Crazy Dog smiled.

"But would not hunger still exist?" Dreamer asked.

"Not if everyone gave," Crazy Dog answered. "Because the Mother has promised that there will be enough for everyone."

"But could there not be more people than there is food upon all of the earth?" Little Wolf said, sweeping his hand around him to emphasize his words.

"There is balance to learn, my children," Crazy Dog answered. "Is it not true that if all the People were to Sun Dance together that understanding would be brought amongst them? And that they would learn of their own reality? Is there reality when the camp becomes so encumbered with itself that it cannot feed its children? Is it not better to do as the camps do now and limit the birth of children to our ability to provide them with the gift of food?"

"Then it is indeed true that we can change our realities," Dreamer said softly.

"WELL, HOSS'S NECK, we're lost bigger'n a puddle in a flood," Calvin said in his cheeriest voice.

"You had to go aroun' lost in your haid, thinkin' up every wrong jump, goldamnit!" Evan growled. "An' I figger we're 'bout daid."

"Stow the palaver," Pearlie said, getting to her feet and brushing herself off. "We're all fixin' to close ourselves into a shearin' pen if we don't quit our yappin' like we was all daid. We gotta set ourselves straight, an' I mean it."

"Listen to the boss achewin' like she's arunnin' a tight ship, would you!" Evan mocked. "An' the crew droppin' over the rail like sea scale. Christ!"

"You're not cuttin' any sure moves yourself, Evan, by jingo!" Calvin laughed.

"Lookit yourself, for chrissake!" Evan said, sitting up. "You's goin' flap-jawed in your haid sure as wind. Why is it you always goes trompin' under deck when we're fixin' to belly up?"

"Gawd, I dunno!" Calvin laughed. "Guess it's 'cause I'm a bit foggy aroun' my ears, Lordy knows."

Pearlie sat down on the flattest stone she could find and began to draw in the dirt with her foot.

"If we could get near to them goal fields, I'd be shuckin' these ol' rags an' buyin' me somethin' dry an' clean, Lord knows," Pearlie said, half out loud.

"An' I'd be sinkin' a nail or two into a good latch for my cabin door, sure as lightnin'. An' fixin' me a bed as you or nobody else ever thought about. No siree! It'd be the most finest," Calvin giggled.

"I'm gonna get me the fanciest hoss that ever dropped, by gawd!"

Evan said as he rolled onto his back. "An' the fanciest ever goldamn guns an' boots."

"You know it's funnier'n hell how we ain't seen not one goldamn human bein' this here whole trek. Not one! 'Cept them thar two fancy map scratchers," Pearlie mused.

" 'Course! Anyone'd know thar ain't one damn livin' human ever would come to these parts. 'Less they was jackasses like us," Evan crowed.

"Maybe we's the only humans left on the whole earth," Calvin said, squinting at the sun. "Could be, you know."

"Thar ain't even a injun!" Pearlie said, a little worried. "S'pose we're off to one side so far it ain't possible for anyone to live?"

"Talk like that ain't worth its value in flies!" Evan answered. "We ain't gonna die. By goldamn, we ain't!"

"I'm scared, Evan," Pearlie said without looking up. "You said yourself we ain't got but one shot left an' that ain't gonna feed us for long."

"I still says we could kill ourselves a rabbit, by damn," Calvin said.

"We've built traps an' run ourselves raw tryin' to bait one of 'em, goldamnit Calvin," Evan protested. "Quit that talk. Thar ain't no way we're gonna even cripple one of them critters. True fact is, we gotta catch and eat us more of them bitty ground critters what lives here."

" 'Sdisgustin'," Pearlie said, trying to smile, "These here prairie dog critters have been our whole livin' for too long. We gotta rustle up some human food 'fore long or roll over."

"Fetch aroun' more twine, you jughaided mules!" Calvin grinned, "We has gotta fix us 'nother one o' them them catchin' loops for a ground critter or we ain't gonna eat today."

"My goldamn drawers is gonna pile down aroun' my knees iffen I gives more o' my trousers for a twine loop," Evan growled. "Knife off some o' your own rags."

"We's all tattered," Pearlie said, getting to her feet. "We gotta go human huntin' or we're gonna land up stiffer'n dried gut."

"Human huntin'?" Evan laughed. "Now how is that one shippin' out? What's the good cap'n gonna do? Jes' round the bend an' pull the slack up ona human?"

"You're damn well shootin' I am," Pearlie huffed. " 'Sbetter'n sittin' on my backside like you're always doin'."

"Rein in there!" Calvin said as he squinted at the horizon. "Ain't that a forest fire yonder?"

"It is, by damn!" Evan cussed. "An' it's eatin' up our trail quicker'n a starvin' cat kin lap up milk. Lordy gawd! Now what are we gonna do?"

"What do you mean?" Pearlie asked, coming up to the two men.

"I swear!" Evan bawled. "Looky there. Can you tell which way that thar fire is gonna run?"

"No! The wind's ablowin' ever which way," Calvin said, "up an' around these here hills like scared geese. Lordy, it could be here quick. We need a crick, an' right now!"

"Thar's one yonder!" Pearlie yelled, running. "I seen it when we was tryin' to loop up a groun' critter this mornin'."

"Run, by gawd, run!" Calvin yelled.

"Gawd, don't go haid-foggy agin—not now!" Evan roared as he ran.

"Looky thar!" Pearlie yelled as Evan came running up to join her and Calvin at the small creek. "That thar thunderhaid done sopped up the fire!"

"Sure did!" Evan laughed as he threw his battered hat to the ground. "We run ascared for nothin'."

"Come!" Pearlie said with determination. "We is goin' human huntin', an' right now."

After almost five hours of walking, they were just about to sit down to rest when Evan tripped over Calvin's heels, knocking all of them sprawling into the dirt.

"Why don'tcha watch whar you're walkin'?" Calvin bawled. "You're clumsy as a sick sea gull."

"Clumsy! You . . ." Evan roared. Then he yelped in fright and grabbed for the fallen rifle. "Get here!" he ordered, diving head first into a thicket. "Those is injuns!" he said, pointing to where Dreamer and Crazy Dog stood watching.

"Injuns!" Pearlie cried, turning around in confusion. "Whar?"

"Right behind you!" Evan yelled from his hiding place, "Get in here! Both o' you!"

"Thar ain't no room in thar nohow, Evan!" Calvin yelled, looking around for concealment.

"Throw out your thunder iron," Little Wolf said quietly from behind Evan, "or you will be one dead whiteman."

"Lordy gawd!" Evan cussed, "He's got the drop on me, bigger'n hell!"

"Better do what the man asked, Evan," Calvin laughed.

"How you know what he said?" Evan roared. "You know injun?"

"Any fool knows when he's afixin' to be shot," Pearlie said. "And besides that, these here is humans. Jes' what we was needin'."

"Humans!" Evan growled as he threw down the rifle and stood up, "Lordy gawd!"

Calvin was still giggling.

"Gawd. Oh, Jesus Christ!" Evan cussed. "We's in whoppin' big trouble and probably fixin' to get skinned, an' you're goin' foggy agin!"

"Can't help it," Calvin giggled. "Ever twitch o' big trouble an' I laughs. Surely it will one day be my end, I know it."

"What shall we do with them now that we have them?" Little Wolf asked Crazy Dog. "I still say we should leave them before one of them kills one of us. Look, one of them is a madman. He stands there laughing."

"The girl is very frightened," Dreamer said, turning to Little Wolf. "Let me try to speak with her."

"No!" Little Wolf said through his teeth. "They are dangerous! They killed my family!"

"What will you do with them then, little brother?" Crazy Dog asked quietly. "Shoot them down when they have no weapons? Crush their skulls? Cut their guts onto the ground? And why? Will this bring back your family? Will it do any good?"

"They should be punished!" Little Wolf grimaced.

"These puppies?" Crazy Dog asked. "Look for yourself. Look at them. They are young and lost. Hungry and ragged. They are not warriors or we would not have heard them. They are clumsy children. Go ahead and shoot them down if you wish. I have spoken."

"But," Little Wolf said, hesitating, "what shall we—"

"We shall take them home," Dreamer said as she took Pearlie's hand. "We shall adopt them."

"Pick up your weapon," Little Wolf said as he pointed at the rifle that lay upon the ground. Then he turned his back and followed Dreamer.

"We isn't daid, by gawd!" Calvin said as he picked up the rifle.

"These mus' be the injun folks what them peace-makers was talkin' of," Evan said, scratching his head.

"An' those goal fields are right over them thar hills!" Calvin whooped and laughed. "An' that bright shiny stuff is 'bout to jump our way, sure as rabbits."

A few days later, when they had reached a good camping spot, Crazy Dog and Little Wolf, with help from Calvin and Evan, put up a lodge. Dreamer and Pearlie began work on new garments to replace the tattered clothes worn by the three newcomers.

Little Wolf tried to shy away from the newcomers but was having trouble because of Calvin.

Calvin seemed to insist on following Little Wolf, even to a point that embarrassed Calvin once when he followed him into the brush.

"Something needs to be done!" Little Wolf whined one day to Crazy Dog. "The Laughing One follows me everywhere. I cannot even go to the brush to relieve myself without him following. What should I do?"

"Be a hunter," Crazy Dog answered. "He is but a little boy."

"He is twice my size!" Little Wolf protested.

"But he is only a little boy," Crazy Dog went on. "And he wishes to learn. Teach him to hunt. Help him. Encourage him and teach him our language."

"By the Power!" Little Wolf exploded. "I will do it, but you must discover what the Laughing One means when he points everywhere and repeats the word 'gowl' over and over. He is causing me madness with his insistence. Do you suppose it is something he wishes to discover? Some power or something?"

"Gowl?" Crazy Dog frowned, repeating the word. "Gowl? I will try, little brother."

The following evening, Crazy Dog spoke with Little Wolf about their new family again.

"How was the hunting today?" Crazy Dog asked as he filled his pipe. "Were you successful with the Laughing One?"

"I cannot believe it!" Little Wolf said, shaking his head. "The smallest child in the People's camps knows more of hunting than Laughing One. He is helpless, yet he is very beautiful about his ways. Except for the one time he almost killed me."

"Almost killed you?" Crazy Dog said, lifting his eyebrows.

"Do you want to hear about it?" Little Wolf laughed.

"Of course!" Crazy Dog smiled, feeling Little Wolf's mirth. "What happened?"

"You will not believe it!" Little Wolf laughed until the tears began to roll down his face. "How completely this one is a clown!" He roared with laughter again. "His feet are his worst enemy. Everything trips him! Even the smallest prairie dog hole!"

Crazy Dog joined in Little Wolf's laughter.

"I was teaching him how to walk quietly and carefully, but he was so intent upon me that he fell, the first time, head over heels straight into the river!"

Crazy Dog shrieked with laughter.

"I then motioned for him to walk the opposite bank of the river so that he might scare out the elk there to my side. I carefully explained it to him by drawing pictures in the sand and signing. He shook his head and grinned and I thought that he completely understood me, but of course, that was not true at all!"

Little Wolf deliberately stopped to increase Crazy Dog's attention before continuing.

"Well?" Crazy Dog asked. "What happened?"

"He disappeared into the river trees and stayed disappeared."

"Disappeared?" Crazy Dog blinked.

"Completely and totally without a sound," Little Wolf grinned. "Of course, I thought that he had tripped again and probably broken his neck. I began to search out the problem when suddenly there he was! Running for his very life straight for me, waving his arms wildly and shouting, and right behind him was a shoulder-bear. I thought he would run past me so that I could kill the old thick head, but no—he tripped! And of course, he grabbed me for support when he fell. I fell, and the thunder iron roared. Through the dust I saw that the thunder iron had killed the bear."

"Lucky!" Crazy Dog said, wiping his forehead. "Lucky, very lucky! The medicine protected you."

"I could barely move because of my fright," Little Wolf went on, "but do you know what he did then?"

"I cannot imagine." Crazy Dog frowned. "What?"

"Instead of touching the ground in thanksgiving, he shook my hand in greeting!" Little Wolf laughed. "And he was laughing so hard he could barely see!"

"Strange!" Crazy Dog smiled. "He is a strange one."

"And you?" Little Wolf smiled. "How did my uncle do with the other puppy? Did you speak with him?"

"I did," Crazy Dog said seriously, "but my story is even more strange than yours."

"I can easily believe it," Little Wolf said as he made himself comfortable.

"I offered the gold haired one a smoke and we sat together," Crazy Dog began, "and everything went smoothly until I stopped signing and spoke out loud the word 'gowl.' At first Gold Hair only blinked, then he jerked slightly. I said the word again, but this time he frowned. I repeated the word again and he grinned from ear to ear. I pointed, as the Laughing One does when he says the word, and repeated it again.

'Gowl,' I said, pointing, and Gold Hair jumped straight into the air and threw his hat upon the ground. He danced and whooped, then suddenly sat down again and frowned."

" 'Gowl?' he asked, pointing to where I had pointed, still frowning.

"I supposed that I had not complimented him, so I jumped to my feet as he had and threw my buffalo hat upon the ground, and I whooped and hollered 'gowl' just as he had, but he acted frightened and almost jumped out of his own skin."

"Then what happened?" Little Wolf probed when Crazy Dog fell silent.

"At first nothing," Crazy Dog replied. "He sat there, and I sat there, just looking at each other. It was obvious to me that I was getting nowhere, so I drew a circle upon the ground and made him understand that this was our camp circle. He blinked and frowned when I had completed my drawing. He pointed at the circle, then to our lodges, all the while shaking his head. Then he drew a straight line into the circle in the same direction that I had pointed when I said the word 'gowl'. I felt that something was wrong, so I stopped for a puff on my pipe to give myself time to think. I thought and thought, and he sat there frowning. Then I received an idea, and I drew three more lines to the other great directions. I pointed to the line in the circle to the north, and I touched my head. Then I pointed to the line to the south, and I touched my heart. I pointed to the line to the west and I closed my eyes. I opened them wide when I touched the line to the east, and I made the sign of the eagle."

"Then 'gowl' must be the same sign as the four grandfathers!" Little Wolf smiled.

"No," Crazy Dog frowned, thinking. "I do not think so. Somehow I think it has something to do with rocks, or maybe their use, or a teaching from them. Because he, Gold Hair, hefted a rock in his hand and said the word again. Has the Laughing One mentioned the word again?"

"All the time," Little Wolf said with a sigh, "and he has pointed everywhere in every direction possible."

"For awhile I thought maybe 'gowl' was their home. The one they left when they wandered upon the prairie," Crazy Dog said as he refilled his pipe. "But each time I drew a lodge or a pony-fort lodge, Gold Hair would shake his head another way and become upset. No, it is something else. Something very important to them."

"It must be a power within the medicine of a spirit," Little Wolf said, getting to his feet. "I hope we can help them find it."

"These are strange lost children," Crazy Dog said, looking up at Little Wolf. "I will try again. What will you do with your hunter?"

"We will begin again in the morning," Little Wolf sighed. "But this time I will begin as if he, Laughing One, were only nine winters old."

"WE'RE RUNNIN' up against a talk fence, Calvin," Evan said as he poked at their cooking fire, "Them injuns ain't squared off in their thinkin' ways 'bout goal, or they ain't lettin' it slip."

"Thar's a slip comin' aroun' quick I'm thinkin', Evan boy, 'cause we're gettin' close for sure now on understandin'," Calvin said, sounding unsure. "You know somethin'?"

"What?" Evan asked.

"These folk are human, surely. I ain't sayin' they ain't dumb as sheep, no siree I ain't, but they is sure fancy in their helpin'," Calvin said.

"That's clean an' sure, I'm thinkin', but no-ways are they throwin' us a line 'bout that goal." Evan yawned. "We is gonna hafta roun' the corners off this puzzle quick or decide to set a spell."

"I been helpin' us a whole jump closer," Pearlie said as she sat down by Calvin. "These here folk is right smart 'bout livin' ways, an' I'm sure as a sawed line they know nothin' 'bout goal nohow."

"Lordy gawd!" Evan almost shouted. "That's no jump closer! Christ, Pearlie! You jes' smothered my whole wish, sure as flint!"

"You meanin' it?" Calvin said, unable to believe. "These folk never heard o' goal?"

" 'Course I ain't sure to puttin' a rope aroun' it, but I'm bettin' close it is," Pearlie answered. "What would they use it for? They ain't chasin' any thoughts o' buyin' nothin'."

"They could use it for danglin' pieces," Evan cut in. "They know 'nuff for that. Looky straight, ain't they got them necklaces hangin' aroun' their necks? I mean all them wearin' danglies."

"That's a true huntin' man, that one," Calvin said, changing the subject. "He's a smooth hand, sure as wind, when it comes to bringin' in food."

"Anybody can larn that," Evan sneered. "Huntin' is huntin' an' it comes eazy as eye-ballin' it."

"This 'un don't stomp aroun', no siree!" Calvin laughed. "He is the fanciest whatever what brung down critters. Yes siree."

"Bringin' down critters," Evan scoffed. "What's so all-fired 'bout bringin' down critters? Any fool kin larn that. What we're needin' is goal! Goal beats stompin' aroun' twixt trees, scarin' up critters for vittles."

"That's it!" Calvin said, jumping to his feet, beaming from ear to ear. "We's goin' into that business o' hide stretchin'! Thar's plenty o' goal in that, big as you please!"

"That's a damn good idea!" Evan laughed. "An' we could poke 'bout till we knowed whar the goal fields were, sure! We ain't gonna pull up hungry here, no-ways, an' it's comfortable too!"

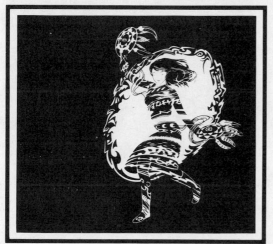

THE BLACK LODGE

POWER FLOWED like the water of ten million dreams into Estchimah's body, and she was healed. With her being renewed, Estchimah looked into the eyes of Sweet Medicine.

"What happened with me?" she asked with her eyes.

"Time knows all things, because time is within all humans," Sweet Medicine answered in a whisper that was all the music of all the winds of the earth. "The terror you were experiencing exists within you and within time. Terror and violence were brought into being. These are powerful forces within all humans.

"All things, plants, animals, everything except the human, must act with violence, but not the human. Violence is an awareness every human knows, but because the human has awareness he also has choice.

"The human, of all the beings, is the only one capable of choice. It is an act of decision among humans who raise their hand in violence. No other being is capable of such a conscious act.

"I am joyous that you choose for me to live. My heart is full because you choose your mind and not brutality.

"The starving brutalize each other. The gardens of knowledge are full, and the fruits within them are sweet. Many people are starving to death. These people brutalize themselves and others, but this does not have to be. The gardens have been walled in with the stones of ignorance.

"So when you become hungry, my child, search for the wild food. It has always been right in front of you. It is within you. Every question you ask is a step into fullness and completeness. Those things that are within the walled gardens are only relatives of the wild food. They were all taken from my greater garden. All the seeds come from my circle.

"Would you like a song painted within your eyes?"

"A song?" Estchimah asked, wondering.

"It is a journey we can make together. In this way it is possible for you to see into the heart and mind of your earth family. You and I can see those things that have been chosen among the People," Sweet Medicine said.

"How is it we can do this?" Estchimah asked.

"Look into my eyes," she whispered.

Estchimah brought her face close to her Mother the Earth, as close as a kiss, and saw her imagination.

"Imagination has no form," she thought, as she was drawn into the transformed world she now saw. She would have spoken another thought out loud, but she could not, because her voice began to transform into pictures of silence.

"You have brought yourself into The Place Of The Muses," the voice of Sweet Medicine said within Estchimah's mind. "You are casting the signs before you upon the polished mirror of the foundation of everything physical.

"This place you have created with me is familiar to you because this is where your dream of the day marries with your mind. It is a joyous place, as you know, because this is where you are born; the beautiful child of the mind.

"If you should hear laughter, it is I. We shamanesses are always happy when we make medicine. Laughing causes us to become invisible, and that is one of our ways of telling a story. We are always within a story, aren't we?

"Now, before we tell each other the story, we will contemplate the Muse.

"The first Muse reminds me of when About To Be Adult asked her teacher why she had not been given a medicine painting to reflect upon equal to that of her brother, whose name was Young Eagle Learning To Fly.

" 'Are you ready?' her teacher asked.

" 'Yes,' she answered. 'I have asked the question, haven't I?'

" 'Then show me the seed of corn I planted in your garden,' the teacher said.

About To Be Adult thought about the question all day, and when night came upon her she went to the dream room where her teacher was sleeping.

" 'It is everything I have learned,' she said.

" 'But what is that?' the teacher asked. 'Show it to me.'

"She pondered the question all her second day, and when night came upon her again, she again went to where her teacher was sleeping.

" 'It is here and not here,' she said. 'I can see it and I cannot see it.'

" 'You have only shown me yourself,' the teacher answered.

'The third day she thought and thought again concerning the painting, but this time as she thought she also weeded in her mother's garden. She waited until dark and went to see her teacher again.

" 'I am transformed from what I once was, just like the corn,' she said.

" 'I can see the transformation, but where is the seed?' the teacher asked.

"The fourth day, as she reflected upon the painting, she noticed for the first time that her teacher was sitting in her mother's garden. Curious,

she went into the garden. She wished to ask a question, but the closer she came to her teacher, the farther away the teacher seemed to be.

"On the afternoon of the fourth day, About To Be Adult approached her teacher, who was sitting in the shade of a cottonwood tree, and placed her hand into her teacher's hand.

" 'You, my mother, my teacher, are the seed you wished to show me. You taught me to be exactly like you,' she said to her mother.

" 'I am that seed, even though you were born from me,' her mother answered. 'And it is true, no matter how I tried to teach you to be yourself, I always taught you to be me. The only image I had was of myself.'

" 'I have the teaching of the garden,' About To Be Adult said. 'And that teaching will show me my own path. I have looked within the story, and I saw the water of the sacred lake within my heart, and I also saw the image that is a reflection of me.'

" 'Then you are of a different clan,' her mother said, smiling. 'And you have learned to teach yourself.'

"This, as I have said, is the first Muse. However, we should by now be reminded that to complete one circle is to begin another, because everything has its twin.

"While we are within the mind everything is possible, and nothing is impossible. Simple, is it not? What I am saying has the magic of learning, if you will listen to your own thoughts.

"Humans resist learning because they are afraid of not knowing. When we are children we structure the world to learn, and now we are upon the trail of discovering how to untie those roots.

"The human being is the earthly symbol of the sacred tree in animal form. This tree is called the Tree Of The Shaman And Shamaness, or the Animal Tree.

"The Animal Tree represents human growth and learning. There is as much tree above the ground as there is below. The tree we see above the ground is called the Sun Lodge Tree. It represents the half of the mind we understand as being awake. The tree below the ground, which we know as the roots, is called the Moon Lodge Tree. This represents the half of the mind we experience when we are dreaming, our sleep dreams and also our daydreams."

Estchimah listened raptly. Sweet Medicine continued . . . "The Sun Lodge Tree is our conscious mind, and the Moon Lodge Tree is our subconscious mind—the shadow mind.

"The Medicine People tell us we are the principal person in each of these two lodges. However, one of us is male and the other is female. These twins are one principal person but have two minds.

"In the beginning, the chiefs tell us, when we are seedlings, we are completely dependent upon the roots of the sacred tree. All of our power comes from the roots. The roots are the eyes, ears, voice, and mind of the young seedling. But when the tree is adult this is reversed, and the roots are completely dependent upon that part of the tree within the sunlight.

"That portion of the tree that is below ground remembers all. Its memory goes beyond itself, its roots, into the total of the earth. But that portion of the tree that is above ground remembers only those things it needs to grow.

"If the roots do not nourish and provide for the tree above ground, the tree will die. And if the tree above the ground does not nourish and provide for its roots, again the tree will die."

Sweet Medicine smiled a mischievous smile and began again.

"A shaman named Buffalo Teachers told me that the Sacred Tree Above The Ground had to have a model, an image, to learn. But he went on to say that the Tree Below The Ground always transforms every model or image into the power of the earth. The paradox of this unravelled my

braids. I was still confused when Buffalo Teachers took me to the camp of a shamaness named Medicine Tree Below The Ground. She had invited Buffalo Teachers and Buffalo Teachers had invited me.

"I remember the day when Buffalo Teachers and I rode up to the lodge the shamaness had prepared for our meeting. It was a place in the northern part of the country where four rivers came together. The names of the four rivers were the Everyday Singing River, Sun Dance River, Painting Signs River, and Changed River. These four rivers flowed together to become what is known among the nations as the Medicine Wheel River.

"Buffalo Teachers and I jumped down from our horses and made ourselves comfortable in front of the lodge. I was sitting beside Buffalo Teachers, when suddenly I realized that I was naked. I had prepared the clothes my grandmother had made for me for the occasion, but in my excitement, after taking my sweat bath, I had forgotten to dress.

" 'You have lovely braids,' the shamaness said to me when she came from her lodge. "But wouldn't you be more comfortable with a robe? It can become very cold here during the night, and the meeting will last until morning.'

" 'I will give her clothes,' an old woman said, as she came from the lodge. 'She is my granddaughter.'

"Shaking, I carefully rose to my feet to receive the clothes my grandmother held out for me. I was shaking with fear and emotion because I knew that I was receiving the clothes from the dead. I tried to speak to greet my grandmother, but I could not utter a word.

" 'And here is a bright new robe of the sun,' the shamaness said as she put the robe into my hands. 'By morning your body will have changed your grandmother's clothes into a living painting.'

"The shamaness then disappeared into her lodge with my grandmother.

"My adventure continued, but now is the time for you and me to look in at the second Muse.

"There were twelve great tents that stood in a circle upon the prairie, and each of those tents was protected by a guardian.

"There were many paths leading from every direction to the tents, but almost everybody who approached those tents did so by the Way of the People.

"Some of the People had already approached one or another of those great tents, and it was they who prepared anyone who sought for power there.

" 'Sit in the middle of those tents and prepare yourself for one of the powerful dogs that will rush at you from one of the tents," they said to His Name and Her Name, who were brother and sister.

" 'What will happen if we should run when one of the dogs charges us?' His Name asked.

" 'You will have failed,' the instructors answered.

" 'If we prepare ourselves and do not run, how can we gain the power from one of those tents?' Her Name asked.

" 'Follow the dog that charges you back to one of the tents,' the instructors answered. 'Go into that tent and you will have the power within it.'

" 'How will you know if we have that power?' His Name asked.

" 'You will lead a fine horse back here to the People,' the instructors answered. 'That is how we shall know.'

" 'What if we should question the dog instead of following it?' Her Name asked.

" 'Then you will have opened all the doors to all the great tents,' the instructors answered. 'The dogs and all the powers of all the tents will charge upon you, and you will be destroyed.'

"His Name sat down, right there in that circle, and began to talk to his sister about what they should do. Her Name took her brother's hand, and they began to talk.

" 'It is forbidden!' the instructors yelled to the People, and the People arrested His Name and Her Name and put them in separate lodges. The People guarded those lodges by watching them very carefully.

"The only ones that would visit Her Name and His Name in their lodges were two very ragged crows, and these came because they knew that they would be fed.

" 'What is in those tents that is so terrible?' Her Name asked the crow that visited her.

" 'There are twelve tents, as you know,' the crow answered. 'One is white. It is a tent of wisdom. The second is black. It is a tent of introspection. The third tent is red. It is the sign of the blood of the People. The fourth tent is blue. That tent is the sacred tent of imagination.'

" 'But what does that mean?' Her Name asked.

" 'We must eat or otherwise we would disappear,' the crow answered.

"His Name asked the same questions and received the same answers from the crow he spoke to.

"Her Name and His Name were brought from their enclosures on the day appointed by the People, and they were led to the entrance of the circle of tents.

"His Name and Her Name walked silently to the center of the circle of tents and sat down.

" 'It is forbidden that we should speak to one another,' Her Name said to her brother, 'but my love for you is more important than my fear,' and with this she told her brother what the crow had said to her.

"His Name smiled at his sister. 'You are brave,' he said. 'You have given me the strength to speak also.' And with that he told her what the crow had said to him.

"Their own power roared between them, and the boy and girl each saw the other as a fearsome, snarling dog.

"Both, without the other knowing it, gathered all their strength and said together, without the other hearing it, 'Why am I afraid of my sister, brother?'

"And what was between them fled into the tents, and those tents were transformed into beautiful lodges.

" 'Come and hunt in each lodge,' twelve thunderous voices said all together from each of the lodges.

"His Name and Her Name rose to their feet, trembling, and began their visit of the lodges. The sun moved backwards, reversing the days, until twelve years had completed themselves backwards, and then the sun reversed itself and moved forward twelve years. The People who watched did not see this, because it happened in one day.

"His Name and Her Name returned to the People, but now they had two powerful rainbow circles about them, like two Sun Dance belts.

"They rode, each of them, a powerful horse with a bridle of gold. And they moved among the People with gentleness and care because they saw that the horses of the People were really only emaciated dogs.

"You and I are constructing the clothes of the shaman and the shamaness. Muses are painted or beaded on the shaman's clothes. On the clothes of the shamaness are the reflections of these signs. They are husband and wife. On the loincloth of the shaman is the tree painting which portrays a beaded snake beneath the roots of the tree, and an eagle in the branches. On the shaman's spirit shirt is painted a beautiful rosebush, right over his heart.

"The shamaness carries a beautiful shield and a wonderful drum. She

does this because she knows of all the healing herbs. It is in this way they sing together.

"The shamaness stands with her arms upraised, encircled by the trees. She is praying to the mirror each of us holds within our sacred lodge.

"The millions of flowers upon our Mother the Earth are her words of prayer. She is saying:

" 'Bless and care for my children physically, mentally, emotionally, and spiritually.

" 'Paint rainbows in their minds and hearts.

" 'Bring the Sweet Medicine,

" 'The flame of the lodges,

" 'And my children will gather

" 'In the light of the council circle.'

"This shamaness sometimes is called White Buffalo Woman, or Silver Comb.

"Her husband, the shaman, is always calling some kind of meeting together. He does this because he enjoys it.

"He wears a buffalo cap with two black and white horns on it. He does this because it makes him feel good.

"He is always sitting around and saying things like:

" 'Within me is a spirit.

" 'That spirit then must know me.

" 'I am talking to myself.

" 'My spirit self is speaking to the universe.

" 'The universe is talking to me.

" 'I am telling my spirit what I see.

" 'We are dancing to the sun.

" 'We are dreaming with the moon.
" 'Around and around the Muse tree.'

"The Sun Dance Chiefs tell us that the signs of the shaman and shamaness are written everywhere upon the earth.

"I now found myself within the laws of the Kachina, also known as the Heyoehkah, the Contrary. My own People speak of this as the Crazy Dog. Others of our brothers and sisters have even more words for this teacher. The name Kachina has been given by the People of the South. The People of the West call the teaching the Tree Mask Dance. In the East it is called Walking With Old Man Coyote, and in the far North it is called Wolf Roads, and The Ice Light Curtains. Through these different names the People see many kinds of beautiful moccasins.

"Before I think about these teachings I usually find a very comfortable and beautiful place within my mind. It is from there I dance with these things.

"Dance with me now into a wondrous world where everything is beautiful. Many people know this world as the World of Enchantment. Sometimes it is also called the Place of Imagination. Everything is possible within this miniature circle.

"This Children's Maze is the world of the Kachinas. There are two gifts given to children from this world: fantasy and the image.

"Bringing The Dream Into Reality is the name of the shaman of this very special world. The name of his wife, the shamaness, is The Breath Spirit Woman Of The Law.

"Every human invention upon our earth has come from this world. The gods were born in this world, and so was the use of fire. This world is the place of creativity. The laws of the community, the laws of the camp, the laws of the spirit, and all other humanly contrived laws are called the Kachina.

"Children know of this world before they know themselves or any of their

earthly family. There is no force on earth as great as that of the teaching of the Kachina.

"The Sun Dance chiefs tell us that a People can call forth the incredible of incredibles, and powers whose mirrors could burn the galaxies, or be the gentle sweet corn, if those People hold sacred the Children's Maze.

"Modern inventions, so called by the old within a camp circle, are old medicine hats to the very young. To the young, those inventions are already ancient. Children set those medicine hats upon their heads matter-of-factly. They expect them to work. After all, don't they work? But remember also that these same children sit at the edge of discovery.

"The children are our inventors because they are our poets. It is the children who reach into the special world and bring forth the magic of discovery. They do this sometimes when they are very young, and sometimes when they are grown men and women. However, remember this. It was in the Fountain of the Children's Maze that they first saw the dance of the Kachina.

"The Kachinas dance around the tiny growing tree. The Kachinas are dressed as the rain, the sun, the moon, the growing things, the dream. They are dressed like everything.

"Now I think it is time we looked into the third Muse.

"There was a person whose medicine was a gold cat, and his name was Walks Upon Ice. He was given four horses that were magical. Each of them held certain powers. Walks Upon Ice gentled the red horse to ride, even though it was the horse that breathed fire and roared as the thunder. Walks Upon Ice did not have to use a bridle because his horse responded to the slightest touch. The other three horses did not have to be haltered or led, because they always followed wherever the red horse went.

"The first time Walks Upon Ice spoke to his mother and father about the horses, he noticed that they seemed to ignore him.

" 'Did you not hear me, mother?' he asked his mother. 'I have four very powerful horses and I have gentled one of them to ride.'

" 'What kind of nonsense talk is that?' his father scolded. 'What is a horse?'

" 'It is something like a cat and something like a dog, but much bigger, almost as big as a buffalo,' Walks Upon Ice explained. 'And its hooves are not split. They leave tracks that are like tiny moon's tracks wherever they walk or run.'

" 'That is almost as good a story as the one that crazy old lady, Rainbow Woman, tells,' his father laughed.

"That night Walks Upon Ice could hear his father speaking to his mother, quietly but sternly. That was the first time the boy had heard his parents quarrel, and he knew it concerned him. It was frightening.

"The following morning his mother spoke to him.

" 'You must not speak of those things, those horses,' his mother told him. 'You must work hard and learn to be a great hunter. The other boys are—' she stopped, fumbling for words, '—are gifted in ways that you are not. If you ever want a wife you must learn to be the best of hunters.'

" 'It is because I am not pretty like the other boys, isn't it?' Walks Upon Ice asked with a trembling voice.

" 'You are beautiful to me!' his mother said, hugging him.

"But even as his mother hugged him, Walks Upon Ice knew that she was lying.

"Walks Upon Ice did as his parents asked, and tried very hard to conform to the camp he lived within. But whenever he became lonely, and that was much of the time, he would go out to where his horses waited for him.

"He learned to hunt, but he never was the greatest. No woman or girl would look at him. He became lonely and embittered. Soon after this

even his beloved horses began to disappear, and all he was left with was his dream.

"Four years went by. Walks Upon Ice's loneliness grew, and his dream faded into obscurity. He tried almost everything he could to become more popular, but nothing seemed to work.

"Then one night Walks Upon Ice dreamed, and in his dream he saw the night sky filled with crescent moons. He followed them like a hunter follows tracks.

"He asked many people what they thought about his dream, but they only laughed or turned away from him in disgust.

"Then one day his mother visited his lodge.

" 'I have heard people whispering about you and your dream,' she said to her son. 'It is a beautiful dream, my son.'

" 'Do you know what the dream means?' he asked his mother excitedly.

" 'I do not know,' she said, lowering her eyes. 'I stole that dream from you when you were still a boy.'

" 'You stole the dream?' he asked, perplexed. 'How?'

" 'I have forgotten what the dream was,' she replied emotionally. 'But it is not too late. Follow the dream.'

" 'I am too old to follow such a thing now,' he said in sorrow. 'And who will hunt for you now that my father has died?'

" 'It is true, my son. I will be hungry, and I probably will even have to beg, but you must follow your dream!' she said with tears in her eyes.

"Walks Upon Ice left his camp and followed the crescent moon. It was all he had, his only guide. He walked alone upon the prairie. He was even more lonely than before. He searched and walked for twelve moons, through many camps. He experienced pain as he had never known pain, but he also experienced the joy of the person who learns of many circles.

"During the twelfth moon he sat down and looked back along his trail, the one he had come along since leaving his camp.

" 'Such a tiny world,' he said out loud to himself.

"Of course he meant the tiny world he once lived within. His new knowledge did not make Walks Upon Ice arrogant, because hadn't he envied those people in that very tiny world?

"Walks Upon Ice became a very powerful person, and he walked a good path. One day while he was out hunting he saw some marks upon the ground in the shape of tiny moons.

"It was here, within the heartbeat of self-prophecy, that Walks Upon Ice finally understood the dream.

" 'I must make medicine,' Walks Upon Ice said, as he untied his drum from the travois his dog had pulled for him.

"He began to sing the four songs of his own personal vision. They were songs he had taught to himself.

"As he sang, Walks Upon Ice became completely encircled by horses. He remembered his dream and began to braid a rope, just as he had imagined it when he was a child.

" 'These beings are different,' Walks Upon Ice said, with happiness filling his heart. 'Different than what I imagined them to be as a boy. They do not breathe fire and smoke, and they do not have wings, but I recognize them!'

"He caught up one of the horses with his rope and tried to ride it, but it threw him into the dust. He tried three times before sitting down disappointed and exhausted.

" 'How am I going to ride them?' he asked out loud to himself.

" 'Lead these beings into the river, then ride them,' a beautiful woman said as she walked into his camp. 'The beings will not be able to throw you off in the water. It is within this way you will gentle them.'

" 'Are you a spirit of the prairie?' Walks Upon Ice asked, surprised at this beautiful woman who now stood before him.

" 'I am not a spirit.' She laughed gently. 'My name is Painted Lodge Law. My heart sang with love for you when you visited the camp of my mother and father. My mother's name is Rainbow Woman, and my father's name is Red Man's Prairie. Do you remember them?'

" 'I remember them,' Walks Upon Ice answered. 'Did I also meet you?'

" 'You did.' She smiled. 'But you did not understand my signs. I thought you did not like me and I was very sad. My mother told me that you loved me, but that you did not understand my signs because you had closed your heart. She told me that you had embraced loneliness. You had closed your eyes because you were afraid to trust.'

" 'No one wanted me.' Walks Upon Ice frowned, remembering.

" 'That is only one half of the circle.' She laughed with her eyes. 'I saw many very beautiful women near you, and I know that many hoped you would notice them.'

" 'Me?' he exclaimed in surprise.

" 'The people you first lived with built an invisible wall around you,' she answered with kindness. 'But it was you who maintained that wall because you believed it protected you. But that same wall also blinded you to the many other people who showed you wonderful signs of love.'

" 'I believed it was pain that drove me to seek my dream,' Walks Upon Ice said, as he touched her hand. 'Pain can be the awakener, but pain is not a song that can be followed by the seeker. Does the hunter seek to bring pain to the buffalo that will be the food for his body? No, he does not. Pain is the physical spirit that asks for healing. I had pain with me as a comforter because I feared there would be no dream. There is no pain in the circle of death. Death gently touches every tear, and it is the nature of death to end anguish. The human knows this, and many times kills the dream in order not to feel pain.

" 'This is a balance I have learned. It is a balance important to everyone, because pain is a sign of life. If I feel pain, then I am alive. I will heal pain because it calls out for healing when we seek the dream. I am able to see even more than this now that you are with me, Painted Lodge Law. I also see now that to substitute the dream is to kill it. It is easy to follow a substitute dream, because it has no feeling and no life. It is life that sang to me as I followed the trail of my dream.'

" 'I have a dream also,' Painted Lodge Law explained. 'The dream that is within my eyes is not a force that would steal you from your trail.'

"Walks Upon Ice laughed. 'It has been a curious circle. I began my walk feeling like a caterpillar. I hoped for the wonder and color of feeling as a butterfly, but this image I saw in the eyes of the People was not me. When I began my second walk, the image I saw of myself was that of a maker of Ice Lodges. My mind held whatever People I met close to me. It saddened me when I saw the lodges I gave to the People melt in their hands.'

" 'Those rainbow lodges became water for a thirsty People,' she said.

" 'My third walk was within the image of a terrible warrior.' Walks Upon Ice laughed with joy as he took both of Painted Lodge Law's hands into his in the sign of marriage. 'I would ride down over the People, especially the People I had been born among. I wanted to destroy the tiny world they lived in. I wanted to free them with my power. The dream within your eyes helps me see into my power and dreams. We will ride together to the camps of the People. We will give them these beings, and it will make them strong.'

" 'Have you given these beings a name?' she asked.

" 'I will call them horses—spirit dogs,' he answered.

"This dream story has within it the teaching of the rivers of the sacred tree. The shamaness was speaking within the story of Walks Upon Ice as a teaching for us. It tells us that the Reflection Tree has two great rivers. The Sun River nourishes the tree from the physical universe. But she

sang to us from the source of the moonlight, the Sweet Water River. The Dream River is a fountain to slake our thirst. The Intellectual River is a river of lightning. Both nourish the principal person in our lodge bodies.

"I will bead a necklace for you to wear when you dance with this teaching," Sweet Medicine said to Estchimah.

"Humans honor the restless voice of the vision as a beautiful woman who slowly disrobes before their half-opened eyes of understanding. Her cloak falls as silently as a wish down beyond the earth she stands upon, down into the jeweled room where the holy spring nourishes the dream. Naked, she steps lightly into our remembrance to bathe. We accept her with tenderness into the water of imagination. We watch her swim and feel the sensual joy of her perfect beauty. Love becomes a bright mirror, and we lift her to its surface to be touched with gossamer thoughts.

"She smiles, dances, and sings a melody we dreamed about when we first heard of creation. Suddenly we see our own image and we begin to cry. Will our image twist itself into a frightening mask again? Will we scream as we shatter the awesome reflection? Not this time! Never again!

"This time we will dance with ourselves. We will listen as the shamaness speaks of signs that have been only half-drawn among the ruins. These half-drawn signs we can now complete."

THE VISION slowly faded, and Estchimah was now looking deep into the eyes of young Sweet Medicine once again. She blinked and shook her head.

"There are others who know of the Medicine Wheel and who teach concerning the way!" Estchimah said in surprise.

"There are," Sweet Medicine whispered softly.

"I know that you are my mother," Estchimah said, "but you appear to be young enough to be my sister. It is something that is difficult for me."

"I am younger than you," Sweet Medicine said in a whisper, "and I am truly both."

Estchimah looked down at her hands for something to say, especially about her love for this beautiful Sweet Medicine, but she could think of nothing.

"I love you," she said looking up. But all she saw was the evening mist within the valley. Sweet Medicine had gone as quietly as she had appeared.

"Peace," Estchimah said quietly. "Peace, my beautiful sister."

As Estchimah began to walk she saw a tiny sweet sage plant. She picked four branches to remember Sweet Medicine by, because this was her sign. As she tied them to her waist she saw a little girl about seven steps from her.

"Greetings!" said Little Girl. "I have been sent by the old man with whom you fought upon the great desert."

Little Girl laughed and jumped upon a stone. She now stood as high as Estchimah.

"I am change, as you are change. Everything is change. It is the way of the universe. Come. Let us go into the valley," Little Girl coaxed. "I know the way."

"Wait!" Estchimah said, running after the girl. "Where are we going?"

"We are going to the city." Little Girl laughed. "Come. Don't be so slow."

The young woman and the little girl bounded into the valley like two playful deer.

Little Girl and Estchimah camped four times upon the great plain called The Place of Coming Together before they reached the city. The last four days had been a happy and wonderful time for Estchimah. When they reached the gates of the city she did not want to go in.

"I do not want you to leave," Estchimah said as she sat down.

"I will stay as long as you want me to," Little Girl offered. "What would you like to do?"

"I do not know," Estchimah said nervously. "I cannot stay here because I have no food."

"Do you wish to return to the plain?" Little Girl asked. "You can hunt for food there as you did before."

"No," Estchimah said uneasily, "I cannot do that. For some reason I do not wish to go back." She sat for a moment, then added quickly, "Come with me into the city."

"I cannot enter the city," Little Girl answered. "I cannot retrace my steps. I must go ahead. I must follow the light."

Estchimah looked up in surprise.

"Follow the light," she said, remembering. "Now I understand. I have grown to love you very much, little sister. Thank you for caring for me."

"It was you who cared for me," Little Girl smiled. "I have always loved you as you love me."

As THE SEASONS passed, Calvin and Pearlie became more and more a part of their new world, but not Evan. Evan seemed not to care, not because he didn't want to, Crazy Dog believed, but more because he seemed unable to change.

"He has difficulty with the language," Crazy Dog said one day to Calvin. "You must have patience with your brother. Teach him as you would a little boy."

"He does not care to learn," Calvin protested. "I think he dislikes our camp."

"No, I do not believe that," Crazy Dog explained. "His heart keeps him from sharing our camp. He dreams of other things. Other places and other people. This is a hard way, my son. He believes that this world he now lives within has less reality than the other world he dreams of. Four winters have passed since you sought the place of the yellow iron. Our sister, Pearlie, has married Painted Cloud and we now have a camp of seven people. Yet our brother Evan still seeks the yellow-iron place. This is why he speaks the tongue so poorly, and the reason he seems to be far away even as he sits with us. It is because his imagination lives in another place. It lives in the world of the yellow iron."

"Did you speak with him concerning these ways when you talked with him yesterday?" Calvin asked.

"I did," Crazy Dog answered. "But it is hard to talk with a man who is asleep here and awake in another place. He would leave our camp if he could, but he is afraid."

"Afraid?" Calvin asked. "Evan afraid! That is hard to believe. He is a very brave man!"

"He is a very strong man," Crazy Dog explained, "and has a strong heart. But he is also afraid. He believes that if he seeks out the place of the yellow iron he will not find it. 'Why do you want this yellow iron?' I asked him. He answered that with it he could get many fine horses and much more. 'But we already have horses,' I said, 'and many fine things,' but he would talk of it no more. I then tried to speak with him concerning his dream, but he became angry and left me."

"Should I offer to accompany him to the place he seeks?" Calvin asked with concern. "Then maybe he would not be afraid."

"Then you would be chasing his dream," Crazy Dog laughed. "Do you wish to pursue his dream?"

"No, I do not, but—" Calvin tried to find the right words.

"It is his seeking, not yours," Crazy Dog said as he added some wood to their fire. "Where is that place of the yellow iron? Do you know?"

"It is probably in the whiteman's camps, as Painted Cloud has explained," Calvin answered.

"Is it, my son?" Crazy Dog asked. "Is it? Or could it be something else?"

"What do you mean?" Calvin asked, showing his confusion.

"Perhaps the place of the yellow iron will never have reality for our brother Evan," Crazy Dog said with seriousness. "Dreams of this kind have little to do with reality. The place of the yellow iron inside Evan's heart leads him into a magical dance. Like a rainbow, it is there but not there. It is possible that he will pursue his dream with all his heart and become bitter at not finding it."

"You confuse me, my uncle," Calvin said. "Could you give me another example?"

"You are a hunter and you understand the ways of hunting, so I will begin there," Crazy Dog said. He drew a circle upon the ground. "Do you see this circle that I have drawn? It is the Medicine Wheel. To the North is the dream and to the South is the reality. They balance our harmony within our understanding of the universe. To the West is death and to the East is life. Now let me ask you. Is life real? Is death real?"

"They are," Calvin answered.

"But, my son," Crazy Dog pointed to the circle, "where do these things meet? Or is there a meeting?"

"What do you mean?" Calvin asked, frowning.

"The beings upon the great prairie give-away to us so that we might live. Death furnishes the food so that there might be life. And life is a dance that moves into death. It is a teaching."

"Fire!" Calvin exclaimed. "Your teaching causes me to grow dizzy."

"Do not try to understand it all at once, my child," Crazy Dog laughed, "because these things take many years. Let its song grow within you. These things are the same when we consider dream and reality. When you are hunting the white tailed deer at the river, do you ignore everything around you?"

"What do you mean?" Calvin asked, perplexed.

"I mean do you ignore the signs?" Crazy Dog smiled. "The trees, the sounds, the smells, the place you walk within?"

"That would be impossible," Calvin quickly answered. "A hunter must see and feel everything. It is the way of the hunter."

"True," Crazy Dog laughed. "But think how often we hunt other things without truly experiencing what exists around us. You understand how tragedy would befall the hunter who is not attentive to his surroundings when he hunts the prairie beings, but many of us ignore all the signs around us—the realities—when we hunt for love. Consider how many of our brothers and sisters hunt for the spirit. Dance with me concerning this search for power. Do we see or understand the realities of these things?"

"You mean that the realities change around us as we hunt these different things?" Calvin blinked.

"Is not the prairie different than the river? The mountains different than the plains? And what of the hunting in the winter or the summer? And are there not different realities to move among, to dance with? Are there buffalo on mountain peaks? Does the bighorn sheep live underground with the moles? No, my son. Learning to hunt within the night is as powerful within its teaching as learning to hunt within the day. When we hunt the invisible we must dance within that world. We must look closely at our invisible surroundings. There are worlds within worlds, and each one is unique. Each one is a wondrous adventure. These worlds are all around us all the time!"

"*Heyeeeow!*" Calvin yelled. "It staggers my mind!"

"And our brother Evan?" Crazy Dog asked, leaning close to Calvin's face. "What of him?"

"He is in between," Calvin said quickly. "He is not hunting. He is not seeing his reality. But what should he do?"

"Seek for himself," Crazy Dog answered. "He must seek to perceive that which is around him. He must learn to Sun Dance with everything that will enter his lodge. In order to do this he must speak with the Mother Earth and the forces that surround him. He must go upon the Vision Hill and begin his Quest."

Everywhere is the mystery. The earth turns within the wonder of worlds in the movements of worlds until the wind dances in front of our eyes. Like the flower at the feet of its relatives who are the forest, we think we discern between light and dark as the shadows move about us. We make fire from the forest's bones, knowing that the exchange of songs has been retaught to our magicians. Like the horns that are beaded in patterns on the myth robe, we reach out touching our memories of all the holy places.

"THE FOG HAS caused our hunting to become dangerous," Little Wolf grumbled, "and winter moves upon us quickly."

"Where is our brother Calvin?" Painted Cloud asked as he leaned against the shade arbor beneath which Little Wolf sat.

"He insisted upon hunting at the place of Two Lightning Strikes this morning," Little Wolf answered. Apprehension showed in his voice. "I do not understand it."

"He received a medicine sign," Dreamer explained without looking up from her work. "He felt it singing all around him yesterday. He came to me asking about the healing herbs and the way of the medicine."

"He is no healer," Little Wolf grumbled. "He is a hunter."

"Are you so sure of your brother's path?" Dreamer smiled, now looking at Little Wolf, "or is it that you will be lonesome hunting without him?"

"It is very dangerous for him to be alone," Little Wolf scowled. "The herd of buffalo that grazes in the Two Lightning Strikes is very large, and they will be nervous with this fog."

"It is a very dangerous thing, my brother." Painted Cloud agreed.

"It has worried me too," Dreamer admitted, "but he asked me to keep you from going after him."

"He is still just a boy about many things," Little Wolf growled.

Dreamer laughed. "You remember each of his mistakes as much as you remember his successes. That is why you worry."

"There are so many things that are just feeling," Little Wolf said with worry. "It is very hard to teach these things. The best of the hunters will tell you so."

CALVIN CIRCLED wide, keeping well downwind from the milling herd. The fog covered the floor of the prairie from hill to hill like a luminous white lake. Bobbing here and there like brown leaves were the shadowy forms of the buffalo. The deep thumping growl of the bulls fell in upon the sounds of a thousand hooves as they swished and stamped in the tall wet grass. A tree in the middle of the clear white cloud trembled and swayed as the animals brushed against it. The tree seemed to Calvin to dance, waving its upraised arms and moving with a startling resemblance to the shamaness in the purification ceremonies. Calvin blinked the mirage away as he moved closer, hunting for the bull he had seen in his dream.

Suddenly four blue grouse whistled shrilly into the air to Calvin's left. The sound of the birds' flight sent a shock completely through his body, momentarily paralyzing him with fear. Calvin touched the ground at his feet in thanksgiving and blessing, then turned and looked around wildly at another new sound to his right. It was a bull, a young warrior that challenged him by pawing at the ground and charging in short explosive bursts.

Calvin raised his lance for the charge he knew would come, and began softly to sing his medicine song.

"Ahey a nonea ahey
Tsistsis ahey ya ha
Echo hey a nah."

"We will touch each other. We will touch the bright circle. You and me," he now sang out loud.

The bull grunted and charged from the cloud of fog, but veered sharply to the right just before it collided with Calvin's lance.

Calvin sang again and touched the ground with both of his hands, then patted his stomach and head with the earth's blessing.

The bull charged again, only this time it did not stop. Calvin drove his spear deep into the bull's neck and shoulder. Within the same second he dove headlong to one side, but he was not quick enough. He was slammed sprawling into the dirt.

The bull looked at him and seemed to wait. It backed and pawed the ground. Calvin reached for his second spear and prepared himself again.

"Thank you, my brother," Calvin sang. "Thank you for allowing me to have my spear. I will remember your name forever."

The young bull roared and charged again.

D ANCING TREE is my name!" Calvin cried as he filled his pipe. The tears were streaming from his eyes. "Maheo! Hear me! I send my voice everywhere to you. I am talking to you for the first time. I am thankful."
Dancing Tree left the broad prairie valley and caught up his horse.

E VAN BROODED about the camp. He tried to keep busy, but no matter how much he did, he seemed to have time on his hands; time he did not know what to do with. He saw Pearlie coming from the river with water, and he stopped her.

"How have you been, Evan?" she asked, as she put down her bucket. "Were you at Thunderchief's camp again?"

"Step on that damned injun chatter, Pearlie, an' palaver in human talk," Evan said as he sat down beside her.

"It is too hard for me to talk in the old way, Evan," she said with kindness. She laughed. "It is even funny for me to hear it now. Isn't that strange?"

Evan stood up and walked away without answering. He returned to the camp just long enough to bridle his horse and to collect his gear. Crazy Dog saw him packing and walked up to him.

"You are finally leaving us to seek out the yellow-iron dream, aren't you?" Crazy Dog asked. "You are going away?"

"Yes," Evan answered sharply.

"Your family will miss you, my son," Crazy Dog said, his face showing his worry. "Would you care to take along with you a little of my medicine?"

"No," Evan frowned. "You keep onto you medicine. You keep all. I no want."

Evan jerked his horse's head around and left the camp.

"I HAVE A NEW NAME!" Calvin said as he reined his horse in and leaped from its back. "My name is Dancing Tree! Do you hear that? It is Dancing Tree!"

"Dancing Tree," Little Wolf said softly. "Then you have sung your song!" He laughed and hugged Dancing Tree.

"It is wonderful!" Crazy Dog said excitedly. "I feel the power all around you. It feels good to know this new man."

Then everyone began to cheer and laugh.

"What of your vision?" Little Wolf grinned. "Tell us of every sign."

"I will," Dancing Tree answered, smiling, "but first, where is my brother Evan? He must know of these things. I have been searching for a very long time for a way to talk with him about his unhappiness."

"He has left us," Crazy Dog answered sadly. "He left this very morning."

"Did you try to stop him?" Dancing Tree asked.

"No, my son, we did not," Crazy Dog answered.

"Did no one try and stop him?" Dancing Tree cried.

"No one," Little Wolf said. "Let him seek his own vision, little brother, just as you have."

"But he has no family!" Dancing Tree exclaimed. "He will be alone!"

"He has a family, my son," Crazy Dog said as he touched Dancing Tree. "He knew that we cared for him, but our caring turned his stomach. We are not his People. His People are in the place of the yellow iron."

"It is true," Pearlie said through her tears. "We are all afraid for him, and we all feel the way you do. I do not know why, but it was important that he leave us."

"It seems so strange," Dancing Tree said, sitting down. "It seems twisted and unclear."

"We are strange beings," Dreamer said as she sat down beside Dancing Tree. "You are the hunter of the buffalo, and our brother Evan is a hunter of the yellow iron. What feeds you starves your brother. And he may return, our brother, because he knows that he has a home with us."

"YOU HAVE BROUGHT a child to me," pouted Rose Bush, the dwarf, "and all of his medicine is worn backwards!"

"They have come from a very distant place," the old woman scolded. "Do not be so impatient with them."

"I must leave you at this camp," Dreamer said, turning to Dancing Tree. "I will stay as long as you wish, but I must return to Little Wolf."

Dancing Tree looked around nervously, trying to make up his mind, when suddenly the dwarf jumped on his back and began to ride him around like a pony.

"Go, you silly brute!" the dwarf laughed.

Startled, Dancing Tree flung the tiny man from his back to the ground, but the dwarf rolled expertly and leaped like a frog into his small lodge.

"Is he mad?" Dancing Tree sputtered.

"No, he is not mad," the old woman answered, then added sharply, "Will you have this young woman stay here to protect you? Or perhaps you wish to leave with her?"

Dreamer's horse backed, throwing its head. Dreamer soothed her mount with a pat but said nothing, waiting.

"Go!" he said too loudly. "I will be back in the camp soon."

Dreamer turned her horse without a word and raced away in a cloud of dust.

"Sit down with me," the old woman said gently. "My name is Silver Comb, and I live here alone with the shaman, Rose Bush. The evening will be upon us soon, and I wish to begin immediately."

Dancing Tree watched nervously, annoyance showing on his face, for the dwarf to spring suddenly on him again where he sat.

"Why are you so nervous?" Silver Comb grinned. "Are you afraid of the shaman?"

"No!" he answered, scowling. "But I am not used to people leaping on my back!"

"Why are you so angry with me?" Silver Comb asked gently. "I have not jumped on your back."

"I am sorry, grandmother," Dancing Tree said, calming himself. "It is just a bit strange."

"Strange?" Rose Bush repeated the word. He stuck his head out of his tiny lodge that had seven arrows painted upon it. "Strange?" he asked again before disappearing inside.

"Do you see this flower?" asked Silver Comb, ignoring the dwarf. She placed it in his hand. "This is what you will search for tonight."

Dancing Tree examined the flower.

"But you will not pick the flower," she instructed him. "Find where it lives and speak with it."

"Speak with it?" Dancing Tree frowned. "Concerning what?"

"Maybe it will speak to you of the manner in which you will die," the dwarf smiled from his lodge door again.

"And you will make a fire," Silver Comb said, continuing to ignore the shaman. "A tiny fire, just big enough to roast a portion of the deer that will give-away to you tonight."

"If you are able to see it!" the dwarf laughed, poking his head out again.

"But first you must take off all your clothes and purify yourself in the sweat lodge," she continued. "The shaman prepared it before your arrival."

"But how did he know that I was coming?" Dancing Tree frowned.

"Mystery! Mystery!" Rose Bush laughed. "Is it not possible that I saw you coming?" He disappeared in his tiny lodge again.

"Come on out!" Dancing Tree said, jumping to his feet. "Come out and talk. Stop your playing like a child!"

"Do you wish to change our custom?" Silver Comb asked, laughing musically. "Besides, Rose Bush is not in his lodge."

"I just saw him go into it," Dancing Tree said, still angry.

"Then look within his lodge," she laughed.

Dancing Tree walked to the small lodge and bent to his knees to look inside. He turned around quickly, looking behind him and scanning the whole camp. He stood up and returned to Silver Comb and sat down.

"What did you see there?" Silver Comb asked.

"A tiny owl!" he answered, shaking his head. "Just an owl. It was sitting at the back of the lodge, and it blinked when I looked in."

"An owl?" Silver Comb said, scratching her head and looking puzzled. "I wonder where Rose Bush has gone?"

Dancing Tree moved uncomfortably, not answering.

"Shall we continue?" Silver Comb smiled.

"Yes," he answered flatly, shaking his head. "Yes. Let us continue."

"Make a wreath of sweet sage for your head, wrists, ankles, and waist," she went on, "and sing your song four times before you enter the sweat lodge. I will have a pipe waiting for you when you return."

After Dancing Tree finished his sweat bath he swam in the small stream that ran beside the camp. He dried himself with the soft tanned deer hide that had been left for him and walked the short distance back to the camp. The dwarf and Silver Comb were sitting at the fire in front of the old woman's larger lodge. He noticed that they were whispering together. They stopped when he approached.

"Did you have a nice swim?" Silver Comb asked as Dancing Tree sat down.

"Yes, I did," he answered, looking around.

"What are you looking for?" Rose Bush asked, wrinkling up his nose.

"My pipe," Dancing Tree answered, "You said you would have a pipe waiting for me. Without it I cannot finish my song with the grandfathers."

"It is there right in front of your eyes," the dwarf answered, and pointed to the ground in front of Dancing Tree. "It is a magical pipe, and it will disappear with your last smoke."

Ignoring Rose Bush, Dancing Tree stood and spoke to the four great directions, touched the earth, and asked for blessing from Maheo as he pointed the pipe to the stars. Then the pipe began to vanish in his hands just as Rose Bush had predicted.

"Horns!" he said, jumping back as if he had been stung, "What—? What?"

"Go and do as I instructed you," Silver Comb said, pointing at the broad valley that lay below them.

"Ah, I—" Dancing Tree said, floundering, almost stepping into the coals of the fire.

"And stay out of trouble!" Rose Bush laughed.

From habit, Dancing Tree picked up his bow, quiver, lance, and knife.

"Do not take your lance," Rose Bush ordered from where he sat.

He stood his lance carefully beside an ash tree and began to dog trot.

The night was rising swiftly from the valley, reaching for the tops of the highest mountains.

"It will touch hands with the stars soon," he thought as he ran in the moonlight.

The earth around him was peopled with every being natural to the valleys. Dancing Tree saw their signs everywhere. He stooped for a closer look at the tracks of an elk that had crossed the stream.

"The grass has not even stood back up yet," he thought. "It must be watching me from across the stream."

He ran on a little further, then he stopped. A strange sick feeling was growing deep within his stomach, threatening to choke him. He retraced his steps and the sickness slowly began to dissipate within him.

"What is this?" he thought, fighting his fear down.

He began to circle to his left toward the stream, carefully taking notice of his feelings.

"Do not run frightened from your feelings, my son," Dancing Tree remembered Crazy Dog saying, "because it is power you feel. There is no spirit of bad or good. There is only power. Power does not circle these things of bad or good. Power is power. Power can build and the same power can destroy. Power can open and power can close. Both are the same with power. Power can also absorb. But do not fear power, because your spirit will guide you. Your spirit feels. You may feel a sickness. Avoid it. Go around it, but do not be frightened. But more importantly, bless it. Stop. Touch the earth and bless those places."

Dancing Tree circled wide around the place of power, stepping carefully, letting his feelings guide him. When he was certain he had avoided the place, he stopped and touched the earth with both hands, saying, "Sweet place, wondrous place, I send my whole heart within your wonder. Accept my offering. It is like a pipe of peace. I have

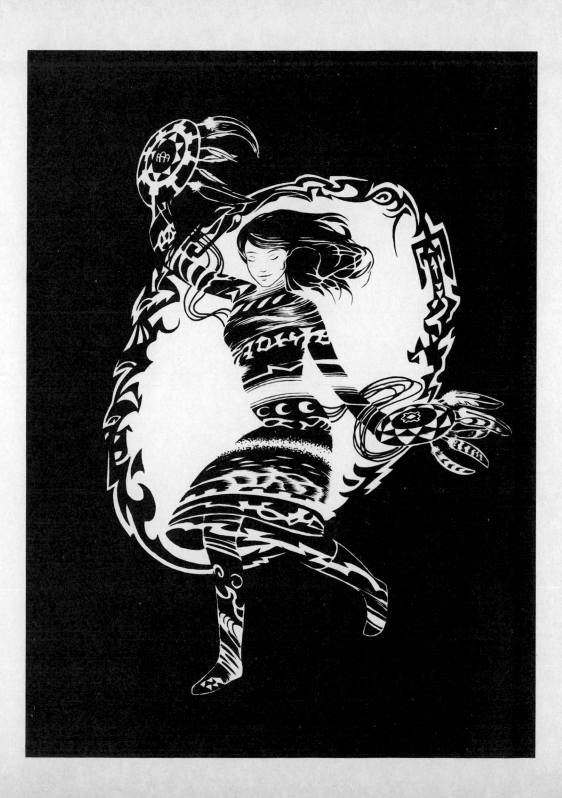

respected you. I have recognized you, and I have walked around your unhappiness. I offer you what I can. It is the painting of Sweet Medicine. I recognize you as a sacred place and I will walk accordingly, remembering that you have touched me. It was I who felt your unhappiness, and it is I who speak to you now. My name is Dancing Tree. Peace to you and your wholeness."

He turned his back to the place of power and began to walk, but he could not. Something still seemed to be wrong.

"What is wrong?" Dancing Tree asked, turning around. "What more can I offer?"

He turned again and stopped. He knew that something was still undone.

He spoke again and this time he sang, but it did not seem to help. Within his fourth try Dancing Tree was becoming angry.

"I must go!" he said out loud, angrily, and then he saw the flower. Pity for the place of power overwhelmed Dancing Tree so strongly that for a moment he wept.

"Forgive my anger," Dancing Tree explained. "I am young and foolish. I did not mean to hurt you more. I will build my fire in remembrance of you for four days, remembering you with gentleness. These things of gentleness are my sweet dreams of love. Now I will approach within your circle with trust of you because Silver Comb, the Medicine Woman, spoke to me concerning the flower that grows within your holy circle."

He touched the earth and touched himself with the blessing in thanksgiving; then he began his walk into the circle.

A flood of nervousness began to engulf Dancing Tree's body as he walked toward the flower, and he stopped again, trying to remember what Crazy Dog had told him.

"Be at peace after you have made medicine," Crazy Dog had said. "Trust the power. It is never the same when you enter the circle of the power. You may see things, hear things, smell things, and even feel fear. But be of a strong heart because it is the power speaking. Be respectful. Walk respectfully. Do not try to catch or hold the power, or it will destroy you. Do not try to use the power. It is the way of the People to become part of the power. Speak to the power of what is in your heart. Do not try to deceive yourself, or the power will feel sick and will try to drive you out of its holy circle. Find something that grows within the circle, and speak with it concerning your thoughts and feelings. Look closely at your thoughts, little brother, and seek to understand them. It is in this way that the power can speak with you."

Dancing Tree sat down in front of the flower and began to think. His body was shaking almost beyond control, and fear rose up in his heart to the point of terror.

"Pearlie," he suddenly thought. "I want to make love to Pearlie."

He fought the thought away, not listening to it. Tremors began to grip him, and he rolled over on his side clutching at his stomach.

"Pearlie," he thought again, "I want to remove her dress and to touch her."

He struggled to sit upright.

"Yes!" he yelled out loud, "I do want to touch her!"

Suddenly he felt a calm. The wind blew softly, and the flower danced in front of his eyes.

"Why not?" he thought, "That feeling is not unnatural. I wonder why I fought against it so much?"

"You are bad-good," he heard another voice say quietly in his mind, "Touching your sister and seeking this girl-woman for your mate."

"That is true," Dancing Tree said out loud. "I am lonely for a wife-mate, but I have not found one."

"You experience much loneliness," the voice whispered. "Speak to your sister Pearlie of your love. You both will learn of many things. You will grow within a closer place with her. It is healing."

"You mean I should seek marriage with her?" He frowned.

"You desire this because you are lonely," the voice said softly. "She has her husband; you have no wife and are lonely. Search for your own love. This way is more full. Discover your own wife-mate," the voice echoed over and over again until it disappeared.

"It has moved away," Dancing Tree thought. "The power has moved within another circle."

He stood up feeling the burden of his loneliness. It was true, he knew, but the problem seemed unsolvable. He had tried to find a wife many times, but had been discouraged every time. The rejections left him feeling ugly and foolish, and one day he had stopped searching.

Now he shrugged his shoulders and began to walk. He walked idly, caught up in pity for himself, and did not, at first, hear or feel the presence to his right.

He had stopped and was looking up at the moon when suddenly something touched him on his right shoulder. He jumped, grabbing for his knife at his belt, but was knocked unceremoniously onto the ground.

"What! Who?" he croaked as he looked around wildly from where he sat, but he could see nothing.

He quickly rose to his feet and in a crouch raced for an open meadow. He slunk down close to the ground, waiting. He knew that whatever had attacked him would come after him, and he would have a chance of seeing who or what it was.

He breathed slowly, letting his breath quietly in and out. His left hand touched the ground to feel the slightest tremor, and his eyes expertly watched for movement. Every one of Little Wolf's teachings of the hunt came alive within Dancing Tree, so that the hunted could become the hunter.

Silently, just above a whisper of the wind, he began to move within the shadows. He sang the holy song in his brain to mask the sounds of his mind as he began to brush the sweet sage from the medicine bundle he carried, to mingle the smell of his body with that of the earth.

Then something touched his shoulder again.

A tiny sound of despair escaped from Dancing Tree's throat as he prepared himself for death. Spasms of shock raced through his mind as he scanned the meadow, but still he perceived nothing.

"Peace," he said, getting to his feet. "I am prepared."

Nothing moved.

"I am prepared?" he thought. "For what? And why?"

"Who are you?" he said out loud.

"I am a shadow," he heard his mind answer.

"Am I doing this to myself?" he asked out loud, turning around and looking frantically about himself.

"Am I doing this to myself?" the thought echoed back in his mind.

"This is nonsense!" he said hoarsely. "Am I going mad?"

"Going mad!" the voice whispered more loudly. "Nonsense! Going mad!"

Dancing Tree screamed. His eyes rolled back in his head, and he began to run. He ran a few yards and stumbled. He crawled on his knees, crying.

"Why are you crying?" a voice asked behind him. "You confused my voice with yours."

The voice was so gentle and sweet that it immediately brought Dancing Tree back to his senses. He felt suddenly ashamed. He, the hunter, had panicked. He had even left his bow, quiver, and knife where he had dropped them. He turned around slowly and saw a radiant deer.

"My brother wishes to give-away to you," the deer said with a melodic voice. "He waits for you just beyond the trees."

"Are . . . are you real?" Dancing Tree asked, unable to believe his eyes or ears.

"You are dreaming," the deer answered. "You have fallen asleep with your pity. Wake up and be a hunter."

Dancing Tree awoke. He was lying just a few feet from where he had previously stood within the circle of power.

He stood up and brushed himself off. The full moon was now over his head, illuminating the valley with its bright light. Remembering the dream, he strung his bow and began to walk.

He crossed over the stream. Just as he broke out into the meadow he saw the deer. He drew his bow carefully and sent the arrow to the deer. It fell quietly.

"Thank you, my brother," he said, coming up to the deer. "I promise that you will be cared for. You will become part of me. I will live because of you. I am humbled with your courage. Your teaching is great, and it heals my heart."

Dancing Tree was busy preparing his food over the fire he had made, when suddenly he noticed that he had company.

"You were standing to the left side of your brother, the deer," Silver Comb said gently as she sat down across the fire from him. "And the bowman stands at your left, also."

"Who is the bowman, grandmother?" he asked.

"The bowman is death," Rose Bush answered as he made himself comfortable. "Death is always at our left. And you have spoken with the bowman tonight while you dreamed."

"The wondrous deer!" Dancing Tree exclaimed in surprise. "How did you know?"

"I did not know that death showed itself as a deer," Rose Bush answered, "but I knew that you would dream."

"How?" he asked, perplexed.

"Because we told you to sleep before you left our camp," Silver Comb answered.

"How?" he repeated, his voice almost a squeak.

"It does not matter," Rose Bush said and laughed. "Those ways are the ways of the shaman. It is a teaching. But know this, little brother. I did not tell you to speak with death, I only told you to dream."

Dancing Tree could only stare.

"We are here upon our Mother Earth to make peace with our brothers and sisters," Silver Comb said. "It is our growing and our learning."

"And it is the way of the People," the shaman added. "Many people bring disharmony upon themselves, because they follow paths that have been made by others. It is hard for us to seek our own way, my son. All of us would have it that we were told how to live and who we are."

"You overwhelm me with all this talk," Dancing Tree said. "Have I not tried to learn of my own path?"

"Have you?" Rose Bush asked, leaning one elbow on his knee, "or are you walking the path of Little Wolf, Crazy Dog, and Dreamer?"

"I . . . I do not know," he faltered, trying to understand the question.

"How many days have you been with us?" Silver Comb asked.

"One, of course." Dancing Tree answered emphatically.

"You have been with us two days," Rose Bush said with kindness. "We put you to sleep immediately after Dreamer left our camp. And we talked together. We asked concerning your life and its many roads to our lodge doors. Then we commanded that you forget what you had told us."

"Am I dreaming this, too?" Dancing Tree blinked. "Is this real? I am confused."

"You are not confused," Silver Comb smiled. "It feels good for you to pretend you do not know whether you are dreaming or not. You know. We all know. The only time we truly become confused is when we act out the role of not knowing. Remember when you were just a boy?"

"Yes," Dancing Tree answered.

"You played out many of these roles. You experienced your world through these different ways. It is a holy way with children. They can, through play, become many things. But it is dangerous for adults to continue these ways. They will become blind and will die to themselves."

"Die to themselves?" Dancing Tree asked. "What do you mean?"

"Children know of the spirit and the many faces of life, because the power still surrounds them," Silver Comb explained. "But many adults cling to this way even after the power has moved away from them."

"Why?" Dancing Tree asked with concern.

"Because they do not want to be responsible to themselves or to the world they live within," Silver Comb answered. "They beg to be told how they should live their lives. And so they die. They see nothing but the path dictated by someone else."

"They ignore even their death," said Rose Bush. "But worse, they ignore themselves. They can be instructed to do anything when they are asleep within the paths that are not their own. They will justify even murder if they are told to do so."

"Is there no answer to this problem?" Dancing Tree asked with fear.

"The Power of the Universe and of our Mother Earth is kind, my son," Silver Comb smiled. "Many things are laid across the path of these people. They are put there for many reasons, but the most important of these is the changing path medicine."

"I do not understand," Dancing Tree said. "Can you give me an example?"

"Yellow iron called your brother onto his own path," Silver Comb answered.

"It called to him and he went," Rose Bush quickly added. "But that is not to say he will discover his own path."

"It is not," Silver Comb agreed. "The answer, of course, is the Vision Quest. All people must seek their own identity. It is only in this way that they can discover their path."

"You mean a person's path of speaking with the spirit?" Dancing Tree asked.

Rose Bush laughed. "All ways of speaking with the universe lead to the same place," he said, still laughing. "No. We are speaking here of the search for yourself. Everyone knows of the spirit and its identity with the creation. The Creator is the Creator. We all know this. But who are we? Surely we are not the Creator! Why have we been placed here upon our Mother, the Earth, within limitation? Why do we not understand balance? Why are we so quick to walk in another's way? Why are we so difficult when it comes to understanding each other? Why must we teach one another?"

"It is truly strange," Dancing Tree grinned.

"I have the power to change it. Would you care to be a dwarf like Rose Bush?" Silver Comb asked quickly, cutting off Dancing Tree's laughter.

"A dwarf?" Dancing Tree sputtered, "Ah . . . I—"

"Or a woman, like Silver Comb," Rose Bush laughed.

"You . . . I mean—" Dancing Tree fumbled for words.

"Do you find our lodges unattractive?" Silver Comb asked gently.

Dancing Tree sat immobile, unable to speak or move.

"Or would you care to have us give you the form of a very handsome man who could sway any woman he saw?" Rose Bush quickly added with a serious voice.

"Think before you answer," Silver Comb said with mystery in her voice. "Would you have that handsome body, that perfect face? Suppose we were to grant that to you."

"Could you do that?" Dancing Tree asked, now smiling. "Could you give me that?"

"Of course," Rose Bush yelled, jumping to his feet. "But it would destroy forever our beautiful son Dancing Tree! Would you will your own death for that!"

"My death?" Dancing Tree sputtered.

"Your death," Silver Comb added. "Because you would die the same as if we were to drive your lance through your heart. You would no longer be yourself!" she said in her loudest voice.

"You would be no more!" Rose Bush said, sitting down again. "You would be someone else."

"No," Dancing Tree said, feeling emptied, "No, I would not."

"And would you have us give you a path that is not your own?" Rose Bush smiled as he patted Dancing Tree's hand.

"No," he answered.

"Come," said Silver Comb. "Come back to the lodges and sleep. You must be very tired. Tomorrow we will begin again."

The next morning Dancing Tree awoke to discover that he was sleeping alone. Everything was gone, people, lodges—everything. The only signs that anyone had ever lived upon the spot were the circles where the lodges had stood and where the fire pits had been.

His first reaction was to drift back into sleep, but his eyes soon popped open with the realization that he was truly alone. He sat up wondering what to do.

"I must be dreaming," he laughed. Then he scowled, correcting himself. "I am not asleep."

He looked for his bow and quiver. They were gone, and so was his horse and lance.

"They have taken everything!" he muttered to himself, feeling that he had been tricked. "Would they steal my horse and bow?"

His thoughts made him ashamed, and he looked down at his hands. "Why would I think such things?" he scoffed. "I am a hunter."

"Are you?" his thoughts asked. "What does that mean? That you can feed yourself?"

Angry, he threw off his thoughts and began to look for signs upon the ground. It would be almost impossible for anyone to lose him, and he knew it.

The tracks of the horses led down to the stream, just as he had suspected. He waded into the stream and looked up at the branches that dipped toward the water. Nothing was disturbed upstream. Not one tiny break of a branch or mark from dust or horse. He looked downstream and there were the signs. A tiny broken limb and then another. He followed. Soon he saw a few strands of horse hair that had caught on another broken limb. He walked, watching for the place where they had left the stream bed. Rocks would be their only chance of hiding where the horses would leave the water. He rounded a bend, and then he saw nothing but rocks. Rocks lined the entire stream for as far as he could see.

Dancing Tree knew that they would not necessarily have left the water at the first possibility, so he began making short circles in and out of the stream. He looked for chipped stones. There were none.

He continued down the stream, watching for signs.

Finally Dancing Tree stopped. He remembered what Little Wolf had said one evening when they were making arrows.

He was a clever teacher, Dancing Tree remembered. He spoke of tying large pads of buffalo skin about the hooves of his horse. The hair side was out.

"And they left absolutely no signs," he said out loud as he ran back.

This time he circled wider onto the soft grass and earth. Then he saw the prints.

"Those two are clever," he thought as he followed the tracks. "I am going to have to be awake."

The tracks led up and into a large valley. Suddenly the tracks disappeared.

"They have brushed them out with pine boughs," he thought as he made a wide circle, "And they could have doubled back."

They had. There were the tracks leading straight back to where he had come from, but this time they were up against the hills. They were easy to follow and he began to jog, making sure to keep them in sight. They went right back to the stream.

He made a wide circle around the stream and saw no more tracks.

"Then I was right the first time," he laughed. "Those two are truly clever."

Again he followed the stream, this time watching very carefully for any signs. Then he rounded a bend and there they were, sitting beside their fire and eating.

"Good morning," Rose Bush said, handing Dancing Tree a bowl of sweet berries. "We thought you would never get here. Did you sleep late?"

"Did you think we had deserted you?" Silver Comb asked as she added some meat to his berries.

"No," he lied.

"Why did you lie?" Rose Bush asked quizzically. "Was there something that made you ashamed?"

"How did you know that I lied?" Dancing Tree frowned.

"Because if I were to wake up and discover that everybody had left and had taken everything, I would have been suspicious and upset. I probably would have been mad, too. And I know that I would have felt deserted. Or do you frequently wake up and discover that the whole camp has moved away, and that they have taken everything, including the lodge you were sleeping in?" He roared with laughter. "You don't want me to jump on your back again and flog your rear, do you?" He laughed even harder.

Dancing Tree laughed until the tears came into his eyes.

Then suddenly he noticed that he was laughing all by himself. He sobered as quickly as if he had been struck and looked at the two people who sat silently across from him.

"We spoke together of your problem last night," Rose Bush said evenly, "and we discovered that you cannot possibly—" He stopped and frowned, then blurted out, "You know what I mean."

"It is difficult," Silver Comb added seriously. "But if you learn how to conduct yourself like a shaman we can get somewhere with you. Do you wish to become a shaman?"

"Yes. I believe so," Dancing Tree said with a sinking feeling in his stomach.

"Can you memorize certain songs?" Rose Bush asked.

"I believe so," Dancing Tree answered.

"And conduct yourself in a strict manner according to the rules of being a shaman?" Silver Comb asked.

"Yes," he answered.

"Do you want to become a shaman in the sense that Rose Bush is a shaman?" Silver Comb asked.

"Yes. I believe so," he answered.

"Believe so!" the dwarf yelled. "Do you, or do you not?"

"Yes! I do!" Dancing Tree said, almost yelling himself.

"You must work hard," Silver Comb said, "because you must walk directly in the same path as that of Rose Bush if you wish to succeed. Are you certain you wish to?"

"I am certain," Dancing Tree said with finality.

"You will also have great power," Rose Bush said. "Are you still certain?"

"Very certain," Dancing Tree smiled. "It would be a great honor."

"He still wants to die," Rose Bush said, turning to Silver Comb. "Now he wants to become exactly like me."

"It is truly a shame," Silver Comb said, shaking her head in sorrow. "But I guess if he insists we should make him over in your exact image, power and all."

"Wait!" Dancing Tree gulped.

"And maybe we could mold him into a good puppy to put in our pot when the dog ceremony comes along," Rose Bush said, looking serious. "What do you think?"

"Wait!" Dancing Tree yelled, waving his arms.

"I think he would make a good Crazy Dog," Silver Comb said, ignoring Dancing Tree's yelling. "He is so eager to let us do anything with his life."

"Wait!" Dancing Tree yelled, his voice growing hoarse.

"Do you wish to speak?" Silver Comb asked suddenly, turning to Dancing Tree.

"By the Power, yes!" he croaked, "I want to be myself."

"Then begin by speaking the truth." Rose Bush smiled. "Why should you lie? Do you believe that if you are yourself you must lie?"

"What lie?" he stammered defensively.

"Are there so many you cannot remember them all?" Rose Bush said, pressuring him.

"No. There are not," Dancing Tree stammered. "I have told a few, but I do not lie all the time. Which lie do you mean? It must not be too important, otherwise I would remember it."

"There are important lies and unimportant lies?" Rose Bush asked, looking surprised.

"No, there are not. I mean, yes there are," Dancing Tree said angrily. "You know that as well as I do."

"I do not," Rose Bush said sharply. "Why should you lie at all?"

"Sometimes it saves embarrassment," he said. "You know."

"Sometimes it would serve to hide your fear of something," Rose

Bush said evenly, "not your embarrassment. Why should you be so afraid?"

Dancing Tree sighed, then said, "Yes, I am afraid that the people whom I love and want to be friends with will not understand. That is why I lie."

"But are those people your friends, who force you to be so afraid?" Rose Bush asked. "Should it not be true that your real friends understand?"

"Not many do," Dancing Tree said. "Very few."

"Do you believe we would not understand?" Silver Comb asked.

"No, I believe you would understand," he answered.

"Then did you feel deserted?" Silver Comb asked again.

"Yes," he answered, "I felt deserted and tricked. And I thought you had even stolen my horse and hunting tools."

Tears glistened in his eyes as he spoke, and he tried to hide them. When he looked up he saw that Rose Bush and Silver Comb had tears in their eyes also. He looked down, ashamed.

"I . . ." he choked, "I am truly sorry, my chiefs."

"Do not be sad," Rose Bush grinned, touching Dancing Tree's arm, the tears still in his eyes. "We are crying from joy. You are becoming yourself, and it is wonderful."

"I am?" Dancing Tree said, grinning through his tears. "I am?"

"You truly are," Silver Comb said, hugging him.

Later, after they had washed their faces in the cold stream, they all went for a walk.

"The rocks speak of many things," Rose Bush said, pointing to a large cliff face. "Some of them are very holy."

He grabbed Dancing Tree's hand and led him to the place to which he had pointed.

"Look," the shaman said. "Do you see those pale marks upon the rock?"

"Yes, I do," Dancing Tree answered as he examined them. "What do they mean?"

"Do you see the sign of the Sun Medicine Hat on this drawing?" he asked, pointing at a figure that held an object in each hand.

"That sign on the person's head is the Sun Medicine Hat?" Dancing Tree asked.

"Yes. And those objects in their hands are two Sacred Arrows," the shaman said, smiling. "The signs tell a story. This sign represents a turtle that is eating the People. It symbolizes a tradition that does not help the People. Instead it kills them. The person with the Sun Medicine Hat taught them concerning the circle of wholeness. See it there?" he pointed.

"Who was this person?" Dancing Tree asked.

"This principal person has many names, my son." Silver Comb offered the answer, "Our People have given the teacher the name of Sweet Medicine."

"Or Seven Arrows," Rose Bush added.

"And these flowers here," Silver Comb pointed, "are used for the healing of sore throats. They make a very good tea."

"Everything seems to hold a power," Dancing Tree said with awe.

"Everything within and upon our earth is a gift given to us," Rose Bush laughed. "But most of the time we merely stumble over our gifts instead of letting them teach us."

"It is true," Silver Comb joined into the laughter. "We are only beginning to learn."

Dancing Tree laughed too.

"Do you know why we had you follow us today?" Silver Comb asked as they sat down in the shade to rest.

"I thought about it, but for some reason I did not ask," Dancing Tree grinned. "I probably forgot about it because I thought it would be something that would embarrass me."

Just then Rose Bush, who had disappeared for a moment, returned. "Today, when the sun is at its zenith, we want to take you to a place of power," the shaman said as he sat down. "Do you know why we had you follow us?"

"I already asked him while you were in the brush," Silver Comb laughed.

"No, I do not know," Dancing Tree laughed.

"Because there is a shadow following you," the shaman said matter-of-factly, "and we wanted it to know that you could not be fooled."

"A shadow?" Dancing Tree frowned. He could feel the nape of his neck crawl. "What do you mean?"

"What is the matter?" Silver Comb asked, sensing Dancing Tree's discomfort.

"I do not know," Dancing Tree answered, "but when Rose Bush mentioned a shadow I felt very uneasy."

"Curious," Rose Bush frowned. "Why should you be afraid of a shadow? Do you think it can harm you?"

"I suppose so," he answered.

"But there are shadows everywhere at night," the shaman said quizzically. "Why are you not afraid then?"

"I guess it was because you said that it was following me," he answered.

"But it always follows you," the shaman laughed. "I was speaking of your own shadow."

"Mine!" Dancing Tree exploded into laughter.

"Yes," Rose Bush grinned. "Your shadow is the same as all the others, you know."

"But why would I want to show my shadow that I could not be fooled?" Dancing Tree laughed.

"Because when you are at the holy place your shadow will try to fool you," the shaman grinned.

Dancing Tree suddenly sobered.

"Within those tumbled stones over there," Silver Comb said pointing, "the shadows will begin to dance. And that dance will go into forever. Your shadow will try to take you into forever with it because it loves that lodge. It does so not because it wishes to harm you. It will be acting naturally as shadows are supposed to. And it will try to trick you into following it because it will believe it is helping you."

"Wheeeo!" Dancing Tree yelped. "What should I do?"

"Each time you feel that you are becoming lost, look at this," the shaman said, handing Dancing Tree a coyote's tail.

Then all three climbed to the edge of the valley where the place of the tumbled stones began, but Dancing Tree went on alone. He walked and walked, seeing nothing. The stones shone blinding white in the noonday sun.

He walked some more, wondering what he was supposed to see, especially since there were no shadows, when quite suddenly he felt the panic that accompanies being lost.

"I am lost!" he cried, stumbling onto his knees.

He tried to blink away the swirls of darkness that swam in front of his eyes, but they persisted.

He looked down to see what he had stumbled against, and in glancing he saw the coyote's tail. Immediately his eyes began to clear.

"I was seeing shadows!" he said in surprise. "But I thought they would be shadows of the stones!"

There did not seem to be any reason for him to walk further, so he sat there, wondering what it was he was supposed to learn. The shadows began to dance in front of his eyes once again.

"Their patterns are beautiful," he thought as he watched, "and they blend into one another almost lovingly."

It was not long before he thought he could see deep inside one of the shadows. It seemed to go on forever. Worlds and still more worlds of shadows danced within the shadow he now looked within.

"Beautiful," he thought to himself. "Just beautiful."

"Look at the tail!" A voice cracked as sharply as a rifle behind him.

He turned and saw a shadowy form not too far away. He looked into it.

"It's beautiful," he said out loud. "Very beautiful."

"The tail!" the shadow's voice roared. "Look at the tail, you young fool!"

Slowly, like swimming beneath the water, he looked down at the tail he held in his hands. His vision began to clear.

The panic of being lost began to grip him again, and he looked up and saw the shaman.

"Come!" Rose Bush commanded, "You have seen enough."

As they walked back down into the valley to where Silver Comb was waiting, the dwarf was grumbling.

"I knew we were too hasty with you," he grumbled. "It is lucky that I followed you."

"Did he see the shadows?" Silver Comb asked when Dancing Tree and the shaman sat down in the shade.

"Did he ever!" the shaman growled. "He was off to forever."

"But we told you to look at the tail when that happened," Silver Comb said. Worry showed in her voice.

"I am sorry I worried you both," Dancing Tree said. "From now on I will be more awake."

The following day at the morning meal, Rose Bush repeated the question he had asked the day before.

"Why do you suppose we had you follow us?" he asked as he refilled his bowl with berries he and Silver Comb had gathered that morning.

But before Dancing Tree could answer, Rose Bush pointed to a place on a nearby hill.

"Do you see the large grassy place upon that hill?" he asked, wiping his chin.

"Yes," Dancing Tree said, turning to look.

"The pines grow on every available place upon that hill except there. Did you notice that?" he asked. "I am going to give-away that place to you. It is yours," the dwarf laughed, "It is your Vision Place. You will dance into forever there just like the shadows."

"Your Vision Quest will begin tonight," Silver Comb said, touching Dancing Tree's hand.

"Tonight?" Dancing Tree sputtered.

"No one ever feels they are in readiness," Rose Bush smiled. "I think I must have decided a hundred times before I finally just did it. It is much like jumping into a cold lake for a swim."

"It was worse for me," Silver Comb blushed. "Fear kept me from going upon my Vision. I was very delicate." She laughed. "I thought I would certainly be a tasty meal for the shoulder-bear."

She stopped speaking and looked down at her hands. Then she looked straight into Dancing Tree's eyes.

"But even more frightening than that," she said, still looking deep into his eyes, "I was afraid of being caught by strange men while I was alone." She looked down at her hands again. "I had already given myself willingly to a few men. Three. Each time I was left frustrated, hurting. I could have spoken to my mother or my aunts of the problem, but for some reason I did not. And I carried the problem around with me until it began to change its face. Its face became ugly. I had nightmares of being taken against my will. Then one day I blurted all of it out in rage to one of our oldest and wisest Medicine Women."

" 'You want to punish yourself because you feel you are the one at fault,' the Medicine Woman answered. 'It is a teaching for you.'

" 'A teaching!' I remember screaming.

" 'A teaching,' I heard her say through my sobbing.

"After awhile the old grandmother calmed me and we spoke together.

" 'I only am satisfied when I touch myself,' I said to her, 'and my dreams become more and more complicated. I even dream of having a young horse. What should I do?'

" 'Of course,' the old woman answered me. 'Dream of having a horse, a tree, a frog, even an owl. It makes no difference. Do not be afraid of these.'

" 'No?' I asked.

" 'No.' She smiled. 'I remember being with ten dream giants one after the other when I was about twelve winters old,' she laughed. 'These dreams cannot hurt you unless you ignore their meaning. And I know you do not ignore this,' she added quickly, before I could speak. 'You are uniquely yourself, my daughter. These things are only a teaching. You do not have to be afraid. Now listen,' she went on, leaning closer to me. 'Many men and women alike do not understand the many ways of touching within love. They have to learn. It is not all magic, you know.' She laughed. 'It is learned, also.'

"She was right, of course," Silver Comb said, laughing. "Because as soon as I was over my fear I began to learn. My learning did not take place in one day, either." She laughed again. "I married soon after that, and true to the old woman's words I had to teach my husband. Then and only then could I find fulfillment. And I went upon my Vision Quest."

"And you were not afraid?" Dancing Tree asked.

"By the Power, yes!" Silver Comb laughed. "I was petrified! I still thought I might be eaten by a grumbly old shoulder-bear!"

"I see," Dancing Tree said quietly.

"You see what?" Rose Bush asked.

"The importance of Silver Comb's teaching," Dancing Tree answered.

"You do?" Rose Bush's words cracked like a whip. "Can you know the pain she suffered?"

"I pained with her," he mumbled.

"No one can ever fully know another's pain, my son," Rose Bush said evenly. "People always act for a reason. No matter how obscure it may be, there is always a reason. That is why you lie."

"Lie!" Dancing Tree exploded, "Are you telling me that I am a liar again!"

"Yes," Rose Bush said, hardly above a whisper. "Yes, I am."

Dancing Tree sat angrily.

"What is there to say then!" he said through clenched teeth.

"Nothing, I guess," Rose Bush sighed. "Nothing."

Dancing Tree rose to his feet and paced back and forth, talking to himself. He kicked at a piece of wood and sat down again, slowly.

"There has to be!" he yelled.

"Has to be what?" Rose Bush answered.

"An answer," Dancing Tree fumed.

"An answer to what?" Rose Bush asked.

"An answer to why you insist upon calling me a liar!" he roared.

"Do you want the answer?" Rose Bush asked calmly. "Do you believe there is but one answer?"

"What do you mean?" he asked, a little more quietly.

"What about the time Crazy Dog asked you if you had ever stolen, and you lied?" Silver Comb replied softly.

"I—ah, it—I mean," Dancing Tree flapped like a wounded bird.

"You told us yourself," Silver Comb said, showing him her hands.

"You had no right to pry!" Dancing Tree said with resignation. "None!"

"You came to us," Rose Bush said quietly, "We did not seek you out. You agreed to sit at our council."

"I had no idea that you would put me to sleep and pry," Dancing Tree fumed.

"Would you have decided not to seek our council if we had warned you?" Rose Bush asked.

Dancing Tree hesitated.

"Consider your answer," Silver Comb said, getting to her feet. "We can stop right now if you wish."

"Wait," Dancing Tree shouted as Rose Bush also got up to leave.

Silver Comb and Rose Bush stood waiting, saying nothing.

"I want to learn," Dancing Tree said, nervously clasping and unclasping his hands.

Silver Comb walked to Dancing Tree and sat down beside him.

"You stole Thunder Chief's shield and medicine bundle and threw them into the river," Silver Comb said softly as she put her arm around his shoulders.

"I did," Dancing Tree answered, feeling empty.

"You wanted to make love to Thunder Chief's beautiful wife," Rose Bush said as he sat down, "so to punish yourself and to punish Thunder Chief, you threw his shield and medicine bundle into the river."

"Do you remember Thunder Chief sending for you soon after that?" Silver Comb asked.

"Yes," Dancing Tree said, his eyes showing his fear, "I remember."

"Thunder Chief followed you the day you threw away his shield and medicine bundle," Rose Bush added. "He watched you throw them away, even though he believed they were his greatest possessions."

"He did?" Dancing Tree said, feeling sick.

"He made medicine at that place for you, Dancing Tree, because your friendship meant even more to him than the shield and medicine bundle. He wept for you at that place."

"Would it not have been far better if you would have had the courage to mention your feelings towards your friend's wife?" Silver Comb asked.

"I could not," Dancing Tree choked, putting his head down.

"You are a very brave man," Rose Bush said, touching Dancing Tree's head, "a powerful hunter, and yet you did not have the courage to speak the truth to your brother, Thunder Chief. Is this not a teaching for your own quest for yourself, my son?"

"It is," Dancing Tree answered, unable to lift his head.

Silver Comb gently raised Dancing Tree's chin.

"We respect you, my son," she said, looking straight into his eyes. "You do not have to be afraid. It is a teaching for your own growing upon this, our Mother Earth. We love you."

"We do!" the shaman said, coming to Dancing Tree's side. Standing, the dwarf barely reached the top of Dancing Tree's head. "Your problem is even smaller than me," he grinned.

"You have wrestled with bigger buffalo," Silver Comb smiled, "Come wrestle with this tiny one."

"When Thunder Chief sent for me, I was afraid," Dancing Tree said, taking a deep breath. "I was afraid of my friend. I thought he would kill me. That is why I did not answer his request for me to visit his camp."

"And it was the same act that put a barrier between you and Crazy Dog," Rose Bush said. "You thought Crazy Dog was prying, but all he wanted was for you to look at your problem."

"And all because I was running away from fear," Dancing Tree said, letting out his breath.

"You have lied so many times that you have forgotten," Silver Comb said. "It has driven you away from your own path."

"It has complicated my life so much that it has been difficult keeping it together at times," Dancing Tree laughed.

"True," Rose Bush said, dancing around in a small circle. "But now you are going upon your Vision Quest."

That evening, before Dancing Tree began his walk to his sacred place, Silver Comb asked if he would sit with her for a short song.

"What is your song, grandmother? I will need it," Dancing Tree smiled.

"You will need nothing but yourself. You need only respect yourself," Silver Comb corrected him sternly. "My song is a gift, not a crutch. You are not crippled. Be true to yourself upon this Quest as you seek the holy mirror of the Vision. It is a gift from our Mother the Earth and the Power of the Universe. Breathe your thanksgiving and renewal into these gifts. Be brave and touch everything you can that is yourself. You will experience a new sunrise within you, which will brighten your night into sweet harmony. Keep holy your circle, and let it touch as much as you can. I have spoken."

"Here is your robe," Rose Bush said, offering him a pure white robe.

"This is the holy robe of the Medicine Woman!" Dancing Tree said with awe.

"Wait!" Rose Bush said, taking back the robe. "You do not understand."

"What?" Dancing Tree asked, feeling more strange than he had ever felt in his life.

"You are making too much of this robe," Rose Bush said. "Here, sit down with me."

"This robe is no more holy than any other robe," Silver Comb explained. "It is just a robe. A robe to keep you warm."

Rose Bush laughed. "Would you have exclaimed in the same way if I had given you that ragged robe you put under your bed last night?"

"No, I would not have, because—" Dancing Tree answered.

Rose Bush interrupted him. "Whatever we honor is holy! If I were to have given you that old ragged robe it would have been the same. Because this is your time of the Vision. Would you not respect the robe that kept you warm?"

"I would, with this new understanding you have given me," he grinned.

"Good," Rose Bush laughed. "Here, take this scraggy old white robe with you. It might keep you warm. It has warmed many other people."

"And now it is time I gave you my song," Silver Comb smiled.

Rose Bush handed her his pipe. She smoked to the four directions, saying in the way of her medicine, "My mother, we walk backwards into the lodge of the contrary and sing the upside down language of everything we have forgotten. We move among the stars like reflections of light upon the pools of understanding. We blink at the tiny cracks of darkness that bring the fresh winds of remembering."

"Strange," Dancing Tree exclaimed. "What does it mean?"

"Strange!" Rose Bush teased, "There you go again, trying to figure it all out before you've been there!"

"Go!" Silver Comb said, slapping him on his rear.

FOUR DAYS LATER he returned. After they had welcomed him, they moved camp. Silver Comb led them to a sheltered meadow. "This place is called the Two Medicine Lakes," the shaman said.

"It is very beautiful," Dancing Tree said from his horse.

"We will set up our camp here," Silver Comb said to Rose Bush as they dismounted.

"Are you sure you do not want me to help you raise your lodges before I go?" Dancing Tree asked.

"No, we do not!" Silver Comb smiled. "Do not get off your horse."

"And do not turn around and look back when you leave," Rose Bush said.

Silver Comb walked to the side of Dancing Tree's horse and touched his hand.

"We can always be found, my son," she smiled gently. "Be of a strong heart and remember that which you have learned. Think about us sometimes. It will feel good."

"And remember to say hello to Old Mother Crows Nest when you see her," Rose Bush grinned.

"I will," Dancing Tree said as he kicked his horse into a run.

As he rode he remembered a place called Four Springs, where he decided to make his evening camp. Dancing Tree loped his horse in order that he might get there before nightfall.

No sooner had he reined his horse in at the springs than he noticed that someone had drawn a sign upon the one large cottonwood that grew there. He slid from the back of his horse and studied it. The picture was of four circles: one north, one south, one east, and one west. Drawn through each circle was an arrow. The tips of the four arrows met, forming a star.

"It must represent a name," he thought as he took his gear off of his horse.

He began to ready his meal when suddenly he heard the braying of a donkey in the distance. He grabbed his shield, bow, quiver, and lance in one swoop and ran to the top of the knoll where he had placed his sleeping robe. From this position he could see in all directions for a distance of two looks.

The rider he saw coming toward him rode slowly and deliberately.

"It is either a child or a woman," he said out loud.

He ran down the slope to where he had hobbled his horse and caught it. He leapt to its back and kicked it into a run, racing to a small plateau not too far from the spring. From there he could see if more riders followed. He pulled his mount to a stop and stood as high as he could to see as far as possible.

"No one else comes," he said out loud to himself as he patted his mount, "only the one rider."

From his new vantage point he studied the approaching visitor. It was still impossible to say whether it was a child or a woman. The rider stopped and took a white cloth or hide from a carrying bag behind himself or herself—Dancing Tree still could not tell. The rider carefully wrapped the cloth or hide around the neck and began to sing. The song finally told Dancing Tree it was a woman. She began to walk her little donkey again towards his camp. Dancing Tree rode into the valley to intercept her.

When he reached the bottom he waited. She was close now, and he could see that she was an old woman.

"Greetings, mother," he said as she came abreast of him.

She never once even slightly looked at him. She continued to ride and sing. Curious and a bit apprehensive, Dancing Tree turned his horse in behind her and followed her to his camp, where she dismounted. Then she turned around slowly, still singing, and began to loosen four beautiful blue grouse from where she had tied them on her saddle. She stopped her singing once she had retrieved the grouse, and she began to clean them.

Dancing Tree dismounted and unsaddled both her little donkey and his horse. After he had hobbled both of them, he returned and sat down. She had already skinned the grouse and fastened them on the fire spit.

"You were very slow getting here," she smiled as she sat down.

"You were waiting for me?" Dancing Tree asked in surprise.

"Dreamer and Little Wolf gave-away and held a dance in our camp for you five suns ago," she answered with a smile. "I am here to paint your eyes."

"Do you have a name?" he asked and smiled.

"My name is South Horse Woman," she answered as she turned the grouse. "And your name is Dancing Tree."

"I have been with the dwarf called Rose Bush and the Medicine Woman called Silver Comb," he explained.

"Rose Bush is not a dwarf," she said matter-of-factly. "He only chose to show himself to you as a dwarf."

"He isn't?" Dancing Tree said in surprise. "And I suppose Silver Comb was other than what I saw her," he laughed.

"How did you see Silver Comb?" she asked, looking at him.

"As an old woman," he answered.

"Sometimes she shows herself as a very young woman," she said as she pushed more wood into the cooking fire.

"She is old, isn't she?" Dancing Tree asked, sitting up.

"Very old," she answered.

"You people are amazing!" Dancing Tree smiled.

"I hear two sounds when you say that," she said, turning on her heel and looking into Dancing Tree's face. "What do you mean by 'you people'?"

He sat there, ready with an answer, but he hesitated. She waited.

"Somehow . . ." he said, looking down, "I meant that you were different." He hesitated again. "I mean, I somehow . . . I separated myself from the People for a breath of one thought. I like you, and I want you to like me. You will have to accept me as I am."

"I accept you," she said with curiosity showing in her voice. "I have no idea if I will like you. That remains to be seen."

"I do not want to lie, not to myself nor to you. I have learned that," he stammered. "I somehow set you apart from the people I came from. You know, the white hides, I mean skins, ah, people. I have never done that, not once since I became one of the People. It is honesty I offer you. That is what I meant. I do not want to lie to myself. It has brought me pain and blindness in the past. Rose Bush and Silver Comb taught me that."

"I see," she smiled and she turned back to the fire. "I think I am going to like you very much."

"Did Little Wolf and Dreamer ask you to come here to talk with me?" he asked, smiling.

"No, they did not," she answered as she turned around to face him again. "They came to our camp and held the give-away for you. They told us of how you became part of the family. We met Pearlie, your sister, and spoke with her also. I like her very much. My granddaughter adopted your sister. It was a very beautiful story. It made our whole camp happy to hear it. After your family left I had the feeling that I would like to give you a gift. So now I am here to paint your eyes."

"I think that I am going to like you very much, too," he smiled.

"These grouse will taste better than your dried jerky tonight," she said without looking at him.

"That song you were singing was very beautiful," he said as he began breaking more limbs for the fire.

The following morning after Dancing Tree had returned from hunting rabbit, his favorite food, South Horse began her story.

"We will smoke this pipe together as I tell the story," she said as she began filling her pipe. "When the story is completed, I will burn the stem of this pipe in our common fire. The pipe bowl will be given to the first person I meet. That is the custom."

After lighting the pipe she tied four eagle plumes to the bowl.

"I will give these plumes to the mountain," she said gently. "The mountain is special for me.

"This land is very old," she began. "Its story and the story of the People who have lived here are as different and as many as there are beings who live here now. The stories are endless and powerful.

"The human being cannot live alone. Humans must have the company of other humans. Humans have tried living with each other in many different ways. Humans have attempted every devisable way possible to bring peace into their midst, and to find ways of living harmoniously with those things that surround them. But still, war between differing tribes and Peoples is common. Even more common is the strife that exists with human beings within their own camps. Many years ago when I spoke with my teachers concerning these things, I asked them a question. 'What is it that is common to all the laws that we human beings have created?' The teachers answered that it was order. Order, and the laws that follow order, are common to all peoples and are insisted upon by every human being. The law is symbolized by the four sacred arrows. It is this painting that I will place over your eyes. But before I begin the story I must question you. Are you ready?"

"Yes, I am," Dancing Tree answered.

"We are called the *Tsistsistasts*," she said. Her eyes were twinkling. "We are the People. Do all the *Tsistsistasts* live the same as everyone else who speaks our tongue?"

"I suppose so," Dancing Tree answered. "Yes, they do."

"If that is true, then what magical thing is it that makes such a thing possible?" she asked.

"Their way, their laws, I suppose," Dancing Tree answered.

"Then the secret, you believe, is the way and the laws?" she asked.

"That must be it," he smiled. "Yes!"

"What you are saying then is that your understanding of the way and of the laws is no different than Crazy Dog's perception of these things?" she asked without smiling.

"No, I do not believe that. No," he answered, frowning.

"You are ignorant of many things," she smiled. "What do you know of the way, the laws?"

"Not . . . not much," he stammered.

"Then obviously these things, the way and the laws, cannot be the magical power that makes all of us the same," she smiled.

"I suppose not," he answered.

"You also said to me, '*Their* way, *their* laws.' Do you remember?" she asked. "Who are the *they* you speak of? Why did you not say *our* way, *our* laws?"

"Because, ah—" he stammered, trying to think.

"Because you separated yourself from the *Tsistsistasts*," she laughed. "You do not have to be ashamed, because that is also common to all humans. If there was only one camp of humans in the entire world, it would be the same! People in that one camp would refer to the way and the laws exactly in that same manner, especially if those people had not created those laws and ways themselves. The Chiefs saw this paradox many years ago and tried to remedy it. That is why every four years the Sacred Arrows are burned and new ones created!"

"Why?" Dancing Tree asked. "What do you mean?"

"No matter how beautiful and no matter how perfectly the laws or the way may bring order into the lives of the People, those powers must be renewed; otherwise the People will become separated from their laws. They will no longer understand the power of their symbols, and it will not be long before the power they are following will destroy them. First the ritual will become important; then the law and ritual will demand that the People follow the law blindly. The People will become blind to their own law, and that power will devour them. The way and the law must be completely understood by the People and truly be a part of the People."

"Can you give me a hunter's example?" Dancing Tree asked.

"The first example came from your own lips," she smiled. "You asked for a hunter's example. You structure the way and the law into your world as a hunter. You do this because you want to understand what it is that is being spoken of. All people have their own language, their own way of perceiving. There is this, but there is more! The bow is the law, and the arrow is the way. They exist separately but they are together, one thing. Tell me, why is this?"

"I do not know," Dancing Tree answered.

"The bow sends the arrow," she answered. "We want to live, the

People say. The bow and arrow are a power that touches the buffalo. The buffalo falls down and becomes food for the People. But that same bow and that same arrow can also be turned against the People. There are many kinds of bows and many kinds of arrows.

"Within the Arrow-Renewal Lodge the bow represents the People, and the Arrow represents the Power. Every person is a governing body unto themselves, a tiny camp all to themselves. Together the People are a Medicine Wheel, a larger camp that must also be governed. The camp now becomes the bow and the People the Sacred Arrows. The first circle is now completed.

"The Arrows are renewed when the People have understanding amongst themselves. It is in this way that the bow is made stronger. Sweet Medicine taught of this way. Erect Horns brought the way into completion. One is female, the other male."

"There was a man who visited Crazy Dog," Dancing Tree broke in. "I was just learning to sign the language at the time. I could barely follow his talk, but he spoke of the laws. He told Crazy Dog that he was a man who carved signs in metal. He said that he was one of the People who was sent south to learn of the law. What did he mean?"

"Had he visited the Pyramid Builders?" she asked.

"Yes! That was it!" he said. "Where is that place?"

"There once was a powerful People who lived in the land called Steps Leading Up To The Sun," she answered. "The Round Knives On Their Heels Who Carry A Cross People traveled the great water many years ago, and destroyed those People. The war lasted three hundred years and now everything is destroyed. There are only a tiny few of their teachers left. Some of them hide here in this land. Rose Bush is one of those. There have been many who have gone into that place to learn, but now no one can do that anymore. There is nothing left.

"I am eighty-one autumns old. I have seen many things happen. Not very many things remain the same any more. Things have been given new names. Even Peoples have new names. The Way of the Shields began to die many years ago. It was only a fledgling eagle when it was at its greatest strength. We as a People needed time to build upon our new way. The Way of the Shields was powerful, and it healed the People. All of this is part of the same story; it is the story of the People of this land. It is the story of the law, the story I have been painting over your eyes."

"Will anything survive this terrible time?" Dancing Tree asked with sadness in his voice.

"The People will last," she laughed. "That I truly know. They will take many things with them from this time we live in, and from the time before us. The story is an arrow chain, a necklace that they will take. There are thousands of stories, thousands of teachings, but only a few will survive."

"What do you think will survive?" he asked.

"I do not know," she answered. "This, however, I can tell you. Those things that will survive will not be what they are now. They will have been changed. It is as I told you about ritual. The Sacred Arrows teaching may survive, or the Way of the Shields. Maybe even the Medicine Hat. I do not know. But one thing for very certain, they will not be the same. I have learned in these eighty-one years that ritual will take many of these things into the future, but little of it will be understood. It is a very old story," she laughed. "It has been happening that way for thousands of years. It is as I was trying to explain to you. People will hang onto these things and believe them to be holy, but of course, in themselves those things are not holy unless they are understood and made part of the People. The People may even begin to believe that the medicine bundle is holy by itself."

"You mean they would think that there was power in just having those sacred bundles?" Dancing Tree asked.

"You surprise me!" she smiled. "Surely you have believed that a hundred times yourself! I admit, it is a very complicated thing! The teachings are built around certain objects that are symbols, medicine signs for the People. Where is the separation between the spirit and the law? Where is the separation between the symbol object and the holiness? Will you try to answer me those questions?"

"Is there an answer?" he asked.

"The human mind is the answer," she replied. "I once saw an object that was a thousand winters old. I had no idea what the object was, nor its function. I took it to my teachers and asked them what it was for.

" 'It is very old,' they answered. 'One thousand winters old and it contains powerful medicine! Anybody who touches it will die!'

" 'Then I am going to die!' I remember crying.

" 'As dead as a cricket that has been ground up in the corn,' they answered.

" 'When will I die?' I cried. 'Can I do anything?'

"I was very young at the time, and I believed everything!

" 'You will die when you're a hundred and twenty autumns!' they laughed.

"It was a perfect time for them to explain to me about medicine objects, so-called holy things, and they did. They explained that the object was an ancient symbol of life and death. That it was a part of a whole teaching of a People who once lived in this land, a People who had changed. I was a great-granddaughter, down through the winters, one thousand times removed from those People. They explained that if we looked for them, we could find hundreds, even thousands of other objects: bundles, crosses, circles, and much more that at one time were thought holy and at one time were used as teaching devices for the People.

"They then spoke to me concerning the Sacred Arrows.

" 'It is taught,' they told me, 'that if any of the People should kill another human being, blood will spoil the eagle plumes on the Sacred Arrows. Those white, soft plumes will be soiled with blood. Is this not the teaching?'

"I answered that that was what I had been taught.

" 'Did you see blood on those feathers when they were brought out for renewal when Spotted Turtle killed Lance Man?' they asked.

" 'I don't know,' I answered. 'I think so.'

" 'If you saw blood, then it was in your mind,' they answered. 'There was no physical blood on those feathers. The Arrows are a teaching, a way of the People touching these understandings.'

" 'But they are powerful!' I stammered. 'They can blind the enemy!'

" 'Only the power of the law, and the order that prevails among us, can blind the enemy,' they answered. 'The enemy sees us as a whole People, a People together, a People devoted to the protection of one another; a People strong in the determination of love. This is what blinds the enemy! The Arrows themselves have no such power! The enemy sees us move together, orderly and as one body. That is what blinds them!'

"They also explained how it was that I began to believe such things. They explained that I had approached the Arrows in superstition and ignorance. They explained how at one time I could be helped because the Arrows were called holy, and how at another time I could become trapped. When we understand the symbols and the laws within the community they are holy. When we do not understand them they are an enemy. Misunderstood laws have to be fought and beaten. It is no different than if our dogs were to turn on our children and ourselves. The dogs would have to be fought. The laws are our camp dogs."

"Is this true of the way also?" Dancing Tree asked.

"The laws are *of* the People and the way is *from* the People," she laughed. "The People will always have a way, even when there is no way. But this is not so with the law. The law is only alive when it has the agreement of the People. It only takes one person to have a way, but there must be two or more people to have law."

"But they seem to have a place where they blur together." Dancing Tree frowned.

"Of course!" she laughed. "They blur together in the teaching lodge and within the community circle. The governed now make the law and follow it because of the way. The way teaches respect for the law, and around and around it goes."

"It makes me dizzy," Dancing Tree laughed.

"It will also kill you," she laughed.

"Kill me?" Dancing Tree said, trying to not giggle.

"As dead as a ground up cricket in the corn," she laughed.

Dancing Tree was going to speak but instead fell over backwards laughing.

"It is not funny!" she said, laughing so hard she held her sides.

"I know!" he bellowed with laughter.

The following afternoon, South Horse began again.

"Do you have any questions before we begin?" South Horse asked.

"I was wondering about other kinds of law," Dancing Tree said as he took a puff from the pipe. "You know, the everyday kind."

"While you hunt there is a conduct, a set of laws, that dictates success," she answered. "Some of these laws are imposed upon yourself for your own safety, others are in respect for the laws our Mother the Earth has given to the world we walk within. These laws must be learned. They are no different from other laws that exist. I have met women and men who walk a strong path while they are on the hunt, but when they are in the company of human beings they flounder and are afraid. When this happens they grasp convention and ritual. These persons are dangerous to themselves and to those around them. Of course the reverse of this exists also."

"Dangerous?" Dancing Tree said in surprise.

As quick as a thought, South Horse grabbed up a piece of wood and threw it hard at Dancing Tree's middle. Dancing Tree's reaction was instant, instinctive. The piece of wood had hardly left her hand when he had parried the blow.

"Dangerous because they have not learned how to care for themselves," she answered. "When we know the law we move smoothly. When we do not, we are hurt."

Dancing Tree sat there blinking.

She waited.

"I believe I understand," he answered.

"Do you want to make love to me?" she suddenly asked, leaning forward.

He fumbled in shock and surprise. "Ah . . ."

"You moved expertly the first time, and pitifully clumsily the second," she laughed. "There are men and women who, of course, would have been better prepared."

"There is a whole world of things to learn," he laughed.

"There is," she smiled. "There is a story about a People who lived in a land where no one believed the law nor understood it. They all winked at the law. They believed that it was a game, a human game that was to be played with. This was all right, of course, but for a few things," she laughed. "They were foolish because they did not see that they had devised laws that were as foolish as they were, and they foolishly kept the laws. They tried to live with them, even though those laws were destroying them. They were like a dried twig waiting to be broken by the first problem within their camp."

"Problem within their camp?" Dancing Tree frowned. "I would have thought—"

"That an outside enemy would be the force that would destroy them? Never! A People temporarily come together at times such as that. There is a second reality that faces such People, and it is this. When an outside enemy exerts tension against a People, then any anxiety or conflict within their camp will be reflected again and again within itself until it is many times more destructive."

"One way or the other, it is bound to explode," Dancing Tree said. "I see."

"The other problem with this kind of society is that its laws begin to separate the People," she went on. "It may take a hundred years, even a thousand, but eventually those people will destroy themselves. It is just this kind of People that Sweet Medicine had to face.

"Law is a strange phenomenon. It cannot be ignored. Law is as powerful as starvation or insanity. People are physically moved by such forces. They are moved to do many things. When the cold of the winter comes to the People they must act. They must keep warm, must have provisions, must slow down and do other physical things too numerous to mention. The reality is that they must act.

"Law also forces us to act. A People who understand their laws act in a completely different way than those who do not understand their laws. The laws that surround and encompass a People are very real, no matter if they understand the law or not. You are a hunter and you have used the seeing with fire method for hunting."

"I have used it more than once. Most of the time I have used it when I have been in a place that I had never been in before. I needed to know quickly just how many and what kind of beings lived in such a place," Dancing Tree said.

"The hunter lights one tiny fire," she smiled. "One tiny fire and that fire totally disrupts the circles of law that hide all the beings in the hunting ground. That one tiny fire is now a higher law, much higher than all the circles of law put together! First one being moves, then another, then another and another, until they have all been moved from their respective places. The hunter needs only to see the few to know the many!

"Ignorance of the law or understanding of the law is equal to that fire. First one human affects the other. Then the other and on and on until the entire society is affected. This has caused many things. Peoples have fallen in upon their own camps and have destroyed themselves. People have also moved in terrible wars against other peoples," she laughed. "What is always humorous about these things is this. No matter how foolishly a People may act, they are completely convinced they know what they are doing. These People could be acting in a completely insane manner, but question them and you will realize that they believe they know exactly what they are doing.

"There have been tribes of People who have put to death hundreds of other human beings, burned them and believed that they knew what they were doing! Look at the world around us!" She waved her arm in a sweeping gesture. "Look what must be confronted! It does no good whatsoever to plead or ask these new white-skinned People about why they must be so destructive! None! They will answer that it is their law! It is no different with our own People."

"It is frightening," Dancing Tree said with apprehension.

"The Sweet Medicine teachers left the land that is far to the south," she went on. "They left because they could not tolerate the law, and they could not change the law. They came here to this new land of Sweet Medicine. When they reached this place they wanted to build a new world. Here is the story.

"A baby was born. That baby's parents died when he was still an infant. That baby was the Sun Dance, the Sweet Medicine teachers. The baby's parents were the Teachers Who Look Into The Sky At Stars People, the shamans and shamanesses of that land far away in the south.

The boy was raised by four old women. He had only one buffalo robe to cover himself with. The four old women were four tribes of People who adopted and cared for the teachers from the south. As the boy grew older he became more powerful, and many of the People began to fear him. He became very handsome, but he was gentle. He could perform many wonderful things that astounded even the most powerful of chiefs. But those chiefs did not feel he would ever be a threat, because he was only one and they were many.

"As the Sun Dance way grew, so did the power of the Sweet Medicine chiefs. The most wonderful thing they performed was their ability to teach even the wild people. One day the child touched his arrows to a two-year-old buffalo bull. The robe of that bull was very beautiful. It was completely black.

"The symbol of that bull is a gift. Black Buffalo Robe was once the name of the People we now call the *Tsistsistasts*. They were a very powerful and beautiful People, but they were uncivilized.

"While he was caring for the buffalo, a great chief approached the young man and told him that he wanted the Black Robe for himself. Sweet Medicine refused to part with the Black Robe. They began to argue. The boy took the bone from the leg of Black Robe and touched the chief on his head. The blow was so severe that it killed the chief.

"What this story tells is that the chief of a very powerful People wanted the Black Buffalo Robe People as slaves. The symbol of the bone from the hind leg means 'walking structure.' Sweet Medicine took the law from the Black Buffalo Robe People and used it against the chief who wanted to destroy him and take the Black Buffalo Robe People as slaves. To touch the chief on the head means to take away his authority, his power.

"The combined strength of the tribe was brought together in war to kill Sweet Medicine. So Sweet Medicine hid away in the wild country. He appeared many times in the camp of those People who wanted to kill him. The first time they rushed to capture Sweet Medicine, he escaped in the form of a coyote. The first time they tried to capture Sweet Medicine, he became a coyote!" South Horse laughed so hard she had to rest.

"The coyote is the trickster. The People the Sweet Medicine teachers had to teach lived only within one law. That law was warfare. The strong captured slaves, and the slaves worked for them. Eyes Of Mirrors told me that he heard a very old story that said that some of the Sweet Medicine teachers let themselves be taken as slaves. They taught the slaves, organized them, and escaped with them.

"The second time Sweet Medicine escaped the military people, he escaped in the form of a magpie.

"The magpie, like the crow, is a bird that can talk. It can mimic human speech. Some of the Sweet Medicine People again came to the military Peoples, but this time they came as traders. As traders they could freely move among the military People. Once those People discovered this they put an end to it.

"Another time he escaped as a little medicine bird, the killdeer.

"Some of the Sweet Medicine People drew the military People into combat, but only as a ruse to lure them away from their camps. While they were gone, others of the Sweet Medicine people freed even more slaves.

"The fourth time the military People thought they had caught Sweet Medicine because they surrounded him, but Sweet Medicine had flown away as a blackbird.

"The blackbird is the bird trickster. They thought they had surrounded Sweet Medicine's camp, but it was the other way around because now many of the military chiefs were part of the Sweet Medicine camp.

"The fifth time he escaped as an owl.

"The owl is the symbol of fear. The Sweet Medicine People let fear break down the last lines of power of the military people.

"One day, after four years of struggle, the two camps finally became one camp. Sweet Medicine was seen by all the People standing apart from the main camp. He was dressed as a dog soldier. The military people chased Sweet Medicine, but they could not touch him.

"The next day when Sweet Medicine again showed himself to the People, he showed himself carrying a red shield. This is the symbol of the blood shields, the clans. It has to do with the teaching of the Names and the Vision Quest.

"Upon Sweet Medicine's third visit to the People he wore a robe with the elk sign. He carried the crooked lance, the lance that cannot be thrown, and he wore a headdress made of eagle feathers.

"The elk symbolizes the keeper of death and life. It is the sign of the peace chiefs. The crooked lance is the lance that cannot kill, the contrary lance. The headdress is the symbol of war. The headdress chiefs must speak for war, but they must always be balanced equally with the peace chiefs who can only speak for peace. The war chiefs and the peace chiefs must be equally balanced with women and men.

"On Sweet Medicine's fourth visit, he was dressed as a kit fox.

"This sign, the kit fox, symbolizes the family. The kit fox sign is the symbol used by the council. The council must contain an even number of people, half of whom are women and half of whom are men.

"On the fifth visit, Sweet Medicine wore an owl headdress and buffalo moccasins with the beard of the buffalo attached to his heels, and he carried a contrary lance.

"The contrary is vital to all Peoples! They are usually young, and may be either men or women. Contraries are the Backwards Teacher People. They make the laws of the camp pertinent to the People," South Horse explained. "The contraries dress themselves up in the laws, they act out the laws. It is humorous, and yet it is the most serious dance in the world! Nothing is sacred to the contrary! No tradition, no way, dance, or teaching. Contraries tease, cajole, laugh, and turn the law into mockery! They also examine the law, test the law, rebuild the law, and demand reason within the law.

"It is the contrary who turns the law inward upon the dog soldiers. The dog soldiers must be dedicated to the protection of the camp and its People, no matter what the circumstances. The dog soldier is the keeper of the law, but not its enforcer except in times of great peril. At these times the dog soldier must face all challenges, human or animal, or any teaching or tradition that might bring harm to the camp.

"If the law is the enemy, then the dog soldiers must attack and destroy the laws that threaten the People. The dog soldiers wear buffalo beards on the heels of their moccasins. This is the sign of their standing firm. These moccasins are called the Unable To Run Moccasins. The contrary lance is a sign of that circle of authority.

"On his sixth visit, Sweet Medicine carried a pipe and a bag full of tobacco. He moved around in circles like a Medicine Person, and he was dancing. The military tried and tried to catch Sweet Medicine but they could not.

"What you have heard is a circle. This circle is the sign of the healers and singers, the Medicine People. It is from this circle of authority that the laws are made.

"The People still persisted in not listening to Sweet Medicine because they feared the Sweet Medicine People would take away their authority. The tribe had to endure a very long period of starvation. They were a hungry People. They sent for Sweet Medicine, and he came back to the People. He returned from the south, from the land of the People Who Lived Under The Ground. He brought the buffalo with him as a gift for the People.

"The buffalo which Sweet Medicine brought to the People were many and powerful gifts."

"What were those gifts?" Dancing Tree asked.

"What would be gifts brought to a People torn by war and who were so violent?" she said.

"Peace, probably," he laughed.

Dancing Tree's flippancy unnerved South Horse, and she moved uncomfortably. Her face was cold.

"I will continue with the story," she said without feeling. "After Sweet Medicine returned, the People began to have a life that was more full. He shared many gifts with them. Sweet Medicine told the People where he had lived and how he had been harmed by the People Who Lived Under The Ground. He told them of how powerful those People were, and how cruel they were. He also told them of how beautiful their land was.

"The most powerful danced in a circle and celebrated. This chief's circle gave Sweet Medicine their daughter to be his wife, but Sweet Medicine could not marry her.

"The chief's circle was the law. The beautiful daughter was the camp, the circle of People. There was much to be done before the People could marry with the Sweet Medicine ways.

"The People packed. They harnessed their dogs to their travois, and Sweet Medicine and the young girl began their journey to the new land. The new land was called the Place Where Four Circles Meet With The Arrows.

"The dog is the symbol of philosophy. The travois is a sign for the teaching of the children.

"When they came to that new place, the new land, they entered a great Medicine Lodge within a mountain. The people in the powerful Lodge within the mountain instantly recognized their granddaughter, but the beautiful young girl did not recognize the *Miaheyyun*, the Powers. She stood behind Sweet Medicine because she was afraid. Sweet Medicine gave the young woman a sweet herb to eat, and she fell to sleep. While she slept she danced within the mountain with Sweet Medicine.

"The Sweet Medicine teachers did have the People physically move to a new land. They also symbolically moved the People into an entirely new way of mind. The symbol of the mountain is the sign of the new way. The reason the young circle of People did not recognize the *Miaheyyun* was because the young circle of People was ignorant. The Sweet Medicine teachers taught the People through the method of dreaming.

"The powerful *Miaheyyun* within the mountain were overjoyed to see their grandson, Sweet Medicine. 'Welcome, grandson!' they said. Come into this great lodge and take a seat in the back of the lodge.' Those people, the *Miaheyyun*, were all the wonderful and beautiful things of our Mother the Earth. They were the buffalo, the antelope, all the other animals, the fishes, the birds, the rocks, the trees, the winds, the berry bushes, the grasses. They were all the beings that exist upon this our Mother, the Earth.

"There are twelve great mirrors. These mirrors reflect all things. They are called the *Miaheyyun*. To take a seat in the back of the lodge means to take the place of authority. The west is the symbol of looking within the heart. That seat in the back of the lodge is also the place of gathering and giving away.

"Many people of many colors were sitting in the lodge. They had many voices. These were the *Miaheyyun*. Four of these powers were the principal powers, the principal people. A black man sat to the right of the door to the lodge. To the left of the lodge door sat a red man. To the back of the lodge, sitting at Sweet Medicine's right, was a white man. Sitting to Sweet Medicine's left was a man who was all gold. All of them were beautiful.

"White is the symbol of wisdom. Black is the symbol of introspection. Red is the symbol of trust and innocence, and Gold is the symbol of illumination. These are the symbols of the four great directions: the North, the West, the South, and the East.

"Sweet Medicine sat within this circle for four days and four nights. Then the principal people spoke, saying, 'You must now choose one of us from which to learn. Which one of us do you want to choose?' Sweet Medicine told the principal people that he wished to resemble the man who was red. Suddenly all the men disappeared and in their places were medicine signs, things that resembled powers that were upon the earth. To the south was a reed, an arrow reed. To the west was a black stone that mirrored the stars. To the north was a white shield with feathers, and to the east was gold tobacco.

"Then a man colored like flame stood up. Sweet Medicine had not seen that man because he had mistaken him for the center fire. 'Follow that person,' the voices of the principal people said to Sweet Medicine.

"This center man, or way, brought the chiefs and the Sweet Medicine people together in a circle. It was decided within that circle what the laws of the nation would be.

"Center Man Of The Fire made four Sacred Arrows from the river reeds. 'I tip this first Arrow with the white stone,' Center Man told

Sweet Medicine. 'I tip the second Arrow with red stone. I tip the third Arrow with a black stone and the fourth Arrow, I tip with gold stone.'

"These are the laws of the four directions.

"Center Man asked Sweet Medicine if he wished to make a gift to the Arrows. Sweet Medicine said that he wanted the circle of chiefs to balance the Arrows with gifts of white eagle plumes. The chiefs brought the plumes forward and placed them upon the Arrow shafts.

"The chiefs had combined the laws of their camp circles with the law of Sweet Medicine.

"Sweet Medicine then wrapped the Arrows in a coyote hide and placed the Arrow Bundle upon the back of a beautiful young woman.

"The woman here represents the entire tribe. The Sweet Medicine chiefs wanted all the people of the tribe to participate in the law.

"The hunters, the young men, and the Medicine Men were out hunting buffalo when all this happened, and they did not know what had taken place. They saw Sweet Medicine coming to the camp singing, and they saw the Arrow Bundle on the back of the young woman. The Medicine Men became afraid and ran to the hunters and young men, telling them that a dead woman was carrying the Arrows. But they knew that she was not dead. They knew that she was asleep. They lied in order to gain power for themselves.

"The hunting societies and the other societies were scattered out. The Medicine Men, the priests of the old laws, wanted to control the People.

"The Sweet Medicine Teachers, the new law keepers, wanted to marry the People. They wanted the People to carry the new law and to be the ones who would give birth within the marriage, to be the mother of the law.

"Heaps Up Stones, or Temple Builder, a chief, saw that he could grab the young woman while she was asleep and possess the Arrows. While Sweet Medicine spoke with the hunters, Heaps Up Stones grabbed the young woman and raped her. Then he hid the Arrows in his lodge.

"Heaps Up Stones, a powerful young chief of the Mound Builders, the trading people, now had complete control of the People.

"Now Heaps Up Stones sent one hundred dogs, fierce dogs, to the camps of Sweet Medicine and killed him.

"Those dogs were dog soldiers. They were an army.

"Center Man had a son who was a Medicine Person. He told his son to wait for him at the place called Listening Mirrors.

"Listening Mirrors was the place where Center Man had been born.

"Center Man knew that Heaps Up Stones was going to send two hundred fierce dogs against him, so Center Man sent a coyote to Heaps Up Stones' camp. While the dogs attacked Center Man, the coyote stole the younger sister of Heaps Up Stones' wife, and hid her in the place called Listening Mirrors.

"Center Man was killed, but before he died his Medicine Men, the Kachina People, had tricked the war chief and had stolen away a portion of his camp. They stole the young people, represented by the young woman.

"Heaps Up Stones was very angry. He called Wild Enemy Child and promised him that if he found and destroyed his wife's younger sister, then he would give him two of the Sacred Arrows.

"Wild Enemy Child symbolizes the tribes of the north. The war chief promised the Wild Enemy Child People equal power if they were to destroy the people who had fled his camp.

"The Wild Enemy Child sang a war song. Splitting into two parts, he became two people, each more terrible than the other. While Heaps Up Stones slept one attacked his camp and killed him, but he did not get the Arrows. The other twin attacked the People who lived in the place called Listening Mirrors and drove them onto the prairie. Disappointed that he had not killed the People of Listening Mirrors, the other twin fell upon his brother and they murdered each other. Each one believed the other had stolen the Arrows.

"The Wild Enemy Child People, the tribes of the north, formed into two confederations. One attacked the Mound Builders and destroyed them, but they did not gain control of the law because they did not know how. The other attacked the stone cities of the south, driving the People west. Then the two confederacies attacked each other.

"The People who now called themselves the Listening Mirrors People found themselves in a strange and desolate land. The People faced starvation as they wandered in search of food. They ate their dogs to stay alive, because that was all there was for nourishment."

"I will start the fire for our meal," Dancing Tree smiled as he stood up. "All that talk about starvation is making me hungry."

"After we eat," South Horse said as she began to prepare the food, "I will begin the story again. If you have any questions or do not understand the symbols, ask me. I will answer and continue the story."

Dancing Tree walked to the nearest spring and filled both water skins. As he stood there he suddenly felt an impulse to sleep. He sat down to keep his balance and shook his head, trying to throw off the feeling.

"I have asked you to listen to the grandfather of the prairie," a voice said from within his head.

Dancing Tree shook his head again and blinked his eyes.

He heard the voice again, but this time it seemed to come from nowhere and everywhere at once.

"Do not be afraid," the voice said, clearly and gently. "Rose Bush has given you this song in order that you might speak with the grandfather of the prairie. Be quiet within yourself and mindful. Be at ease and bless yourself."

Dancing Tree splashed his face with water from the spring and sat down again. He waited.

Another voice, a voice with the sound of a thousand hoof beats of running horses, engulfed Dancing Tree. He became dizzy with the sound of it.

"I am the grandfather," the voice said. "Do you have a question, my son?"

"Am I going mad?" Dancing Tree grimaced. "What is the matter with me?" He was frightened.

"You are not going mad, my son," the voice said as it began to fade. "There is nothing the matter with you."

"Wait!" Dancing Tree shouted, jumping to his feet. "Wait!"

He looked around, his eyes full with hope, but all he heard was the wind playing through the grass.

A rage of disappointment flooded into his stomach.

"Where was my mind?" he asked himself. He bit his lip. "Why wasn't I awake?"

He turned to leave and almost collided with South Horse. Dancing Tree had forgotten about the old woman.

"Are you hurt? Is there something wrong?" she puffed, out of breath. As she spoke, she was stuffing his bow, quiver, lance, and shield into his arms. But everything just tumbled through his hands and piled around his feet.

"I am a fool!" he said under his breath to the old woman.

He stepped over his bow and quiver and walked to the fire, fuming with anger.

"What happened?" the old woman asked as she sat down across the fire from him.

"Did you hear anything?" he asked as he poked at the fire.

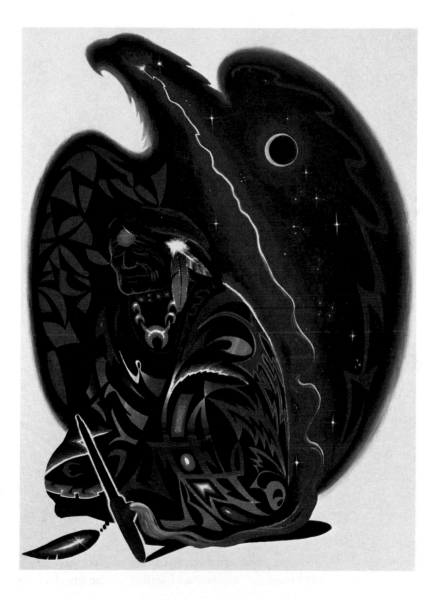

"I heard you yell something," she said. She was watching him carefully, scrutinizing his every movement.

"Besides that," he grumbled as he threw the stick he had been holding down the hill.

"What happened?" she asked, slitting her eyes.

"Tell me exactly what you heard," he commanded her.

She shrugged her shoulders.

"I heard thunder, way over there," she said, pointing to the west.

"What kind of thunder?" he asked, grabbing at a twig that had rolled from the fire.

"Ordinary, everyday thunder. Why?" she asked as she turned two rabbits on the spit.

He sat there nervously poking the twig at the fire.

"I brought the water," she said quietly. "Have a drink and tell me what happened."

"I was hearing voices," he answered, letting out his breath. "I know it had something to do with Rose Bush, that rascal!" He looked into her eyes. "I am very disappointed! Terribly disappointed." He looked down at the fire again. "I missed the trail of something important. I know it! I feel it!"

"Tell me what happened," she urged again as she put more wood on the fire.

Dancing Tree quickly explained what had happened. After he finished he waited. The old woman sat for a long time saying nothing. Finally she spoke. As she spoke, Dancing Tree noticed that her whole manner had changed, even the sound of her voice.

"You will have to talk with Little Wolf and Dreamer about that experience," she said. Her voice was kind but carried a note of cold finality.

"I will speak with Crazy Dog," he said matter-of-factly.

"Crazy Dog?" she smiled. "Which Crazy Dog?"

"Crazy Dog is the uncle of Little Wolf and Dreamer," he answered, looking at her with puzzlement on his face.

"Then speak to that Crazy Dog," she laughed as she handed him a roasted rabbit to eat.

After they had eaten, Dancing Tree watered his horse and the woman's little donkey. Then the old woman began her story again, but Dancing Tree had a hard time listening. His mind kept wandering into dreams.

"These stories are the ancient face of the law," South Horse said, watching him. "You must remember that." And she began again.

"At evening those ancient People made Camp by a beautiful stream called White River. The leaders stepped to one side and sat down in a circle like the half moon; it was a half circle. They called to the People as they passed by them to make the other half of the circle, but the People would not listen to them. As they sat there watching the People pass by them, a very old woman chief who was called Little Medicine Bird, or Morning Star, told the young chiefs to go to the young women and to beg food from them. 'Go to the young women two at a time,' she told the chiefs, 'And ask them if they will be your wives.'"

South Horse waited a moment for a question, but none came.

"The women in the camp owned all the dogs, and the dogs carried everything of the People. One of the young chiefs who begged to be fed was the son of Center Man. He went up to a very beautiful young woman and spoke to her. She was the daughter of Little Medicine Bird. She fed the young Medicine Chief.

"'What kind of food was that?' the Medicine Son asked after he had eaten.

"'That was my dog,' she answered. 'Now I must carry my own burden, because you have eaten my dog.'"

"What does that mean?" Dancing Tree asked without looking up. He was poking at the fire again.

"The People responded," she answered. "The dog is the symbol of philosophy. The People shared their philosophy with the young Medicine Chiefs."

She waited, then began again.

"The young Medicine Son explained to the young woman that he wanted her to accompany him to the north. He told the young woman to gather up all the dogs from the People, even the puppies. 'Gather up even the lame dogs, the blind and the old ones,' he said to her. 'Gather up even the suckling pups that have not opened their eyes. Gather up the mean dogs and the half-wild ones. Gather up the pets and the dogs that have been trained to do tricks or to attack on command. Even gather up the dogs that the People coddle and think are humanlike. Gather up the dogs that are an ancient breed and the ones the People believe hold special powers. Gather up the hunting dogs, the watch dogs, the children's dogs, war dogs, spirit dogs. Gather up the dogs that carry their burdens faithfully, and the ones that bite and tear at their harness. Gather them all and they will carry our burdens north.'"

She waited again, but Dancing Tree had no questions.

" 'We will be on the walk north for forty-five days,' the Medicine Son told the young woman. The young woman consented and did all that she was asked. They traveled north together. They found five special dogs to carry their lodges. One of the dogs was colored black and white, one was gold and red, one was gold and blue, one was blue and black, and the last dog was many colored.

"On their second night, the woman taught the young Medicine Son how to set up the dwelling lodge. He in his turn showed her how to make two sleeping beds from sweet sage, the sweet sage of the buffalo.

" 'My Father, Center Man, told me to take you to the ancient people's mountain,' he told his wife. 'I am to take you into the great Medicine Lodge. It is the ancient symbol of the Medicine Wheel. My father promised that we would be given a ceremony that would heal us and make us a strong People. Everything will be renewed, and the gifts of the law will return with all living things, even the grasses and flowers.'

"The Moon had been crescent and now it had grown to half. The Medicine Son asked his wife to stop at the river called Breaking Apart The New And The Old.

" 'You have taken me as your wife,' the young woman said to the Medicine Son. 'But we have not yet touched in the Human Dance. In order that there might be a birth, we must dance.'

" 'The power of the healing medicine sings within our lodges,' the Medicine Son answered. 'We are entering into a new place, and we have seen that a wonderful new dance will be shown to us. That dance is from the ancient people. We must be patient. When we return to the prairie we will touch. First we must enter the great mountain.'

"They journeyed until they came to the place called Forest That Touches The Sky. In the midst of that forest was a mountain that gleamed pure black like glass-earth arrowheads. Four lakes lay at the foot of the mountain in a circle. One lay to the east, one to the west, one to the south, and the last lake was to the north.

"The moon was full again, and below it shone the morning star. It was a beautiful new morning. The Medicine Son and his wife rolled a large stone away from the mountainside and saw a passageway. It was the door into the world of the Sun Dance. When they were inside, the rock closed behind them to protect them. This was their first sign, a symbol of marriage with their Mother, the Earth, and with each other.

"They saw a great and powerful lodge within the mountain.

Twelve painted and carved poles were joined together at a flowering tree in their center, like many spokes of a wheel. Each painted and carved pole rested at its outside end upon an equally beautiful forked pole. The flowering tree was forked, just like the outside poles, but its forks were like two living arms cradling the thunderbird nest. In its branches were many leaves, like mirrors."

"Tell me," Dancing Tree said, sitting back on his heels. "What does this mean?"

"The original Sun Dance lodges of the Four Mirrors were very beautiful to see," she smiled, remembering. "My great-grandmother spoke of these lodges. She said that the first lodges were constructed in this way. The twelve forked poles of the lodge were carved and painted in many colors. The rafters were also carved and painted," she smiled. "It must have been very powerful. The center tree was the most beautiful of all! Do you know of the great canoe people of the north?"

"I have never heard of them," Dancing Tree answered.

"The carved trees of the canoe people are different now, but in many ways they still resemble the center tree of the ancient Sun Dance Lodge. The Sun Dance Lodges of today are less beautifully made than they once were."

Dancing Tree had no comment.

South Horse continued her story.

"These things were of the earth, the sun, the moon, and the stars. They were a sign for the People to bring all things together and to seek harmony. Standing in a circle around the center tree were twelve painted powers. These powers were in pairs, and each pair were twins.

"Each pair consisted of a man and a woman. One pair was the white buffalo teachers. The second pair was the golden eagle teachers. The third pair was the red antelope teachers, and the fourth pair was the black crow teachers. Standing northeast was a little boy who wore a magpie as his headdress. Standing to the southwest was a little girl with the headdress of the meadowlark. Standing to the northwest was a very old man. He wore a headdress of flowers. Standing to the southeast was a very old woman, and her headdress was sweetgrass.

"The Power of the Universe spoke with the Medicine Son and his wife, saying, 'This thunderbird nest you see before you is empty because the human beings are all orphaned. Adopt one another, and care for one another. Remember that all people are alone in their lodges, their earth lodges, their bodies. I have given each human a council fire and twelve speakers as guides. Recognize these speakers and care for them. They are more fragile than darkness and light, more gentle than the dreams that flow in the rivers of your remembrance. You will have a new name when you enter into your earth lodge. You, Medicine Son, will be called Erect Horns Dancing because you will be the keeper of the buffalo. And you, my daughter, will be called Medicine Buffalo Woman. You will take this teaching of the Sun Dance Way and bring its reflection into the world just like a birth. You are the People. Everything must approach you in caring and love. All things must touch you in marriage in order that there can be a birth within the world. You are the Sun Dance, you are the Way, you are the People, and you are the Sacred Lodge. When you leave this sacred mountain and journey into the world, you will teach the People of the Sun Dance Ways. Teach the children to be a mirror to themselves and a mirror of these Medicine Persons you now dance with.'

"When Erect Horns Dancing and his wife, Medicine Buffalo Woman, left the lodge of the Sacred Mountain, all things moved with them. The stars danced with them, and the day and the night and the sun.

"All the beings of the earth followed the Two Medicine Children."

The old woman stopped again and waited, but Dancing Tree had no questions.

"The People moved back onto the prairie, and they were strong," she went on. "The People came to the river called Lightning Runs Down Fast, and they made camp. That very same night they were attacked by the People who called themselves Lame Arrows. The People joined together and protected each other. They began to sing together the song they had all learned in the Sun Dance. The Lame Arrows were confused and became frightened. Suddenly one of them called out in the night that she was alone and afraid. The People heard her voice, and they were surprised that she spoke their language.

" 'We will light council fires!' Medicine Buffalo Woman called out so everyone could hear her. 'These People are our relatives. They speak our language.'

"Many council fires were lit, and all the People could see each other. Medicine Buffalo Woman went to the frightened woman and put her arms around her. 'This is my sister,' she said to all the People.

"The People brought their relatives into the Sun Dance and they became one People. This dance took twelve moons. Erect Horns Dancing painted a lodge and placed the Four Arrows within it. Those Arrows were spotted with blood and were broken. He called all the People who called themselves Lame Arrows together. The young woman who had cried out in the night burned the Arrows. Then she told her People to make new ones. This was the first Arrow Renewal.

"Soon after this, the great camp divided into twelve camps and scattered out onto the prairie. But every four years they still came together for the renewal."

Dancing Tree stood up, yawned, and stretched.

"That was a beautiful story," he said as he reached for the water.

"It took about fifty years of observation," the old woman laughed. "But I did finally learn to read the signs of people. You are anxious to leave, to go to your family."

"No! No!" he said, turning around to face her. "Take all the time you need."

"Take all the time I need for what?" she said in an even voice.

"You know," he said, trying to laugh. "To teach me."

"I will also leave," she said as she began to arrange her traveling gear.

"Wait!" he said, putting down the skin of water and walking to her side. "I did not mean to offend you. You are right, I am anxious to leave. Look, it is true." He squatted down beside her. "I am very grateful to you. You gave me a tremendous gift. You came a great distance to give me that gift. I am sorry, truly sorry. I do not know what was the matter with me. Come, let us talk."

"You know, it is a very strange thing," the old woman said as she began to relax again. She laughed musically. "I am a very old woman. I have learned the teaching over and over a hundred times within the four seasons, and every time I am surprised." She laughed again. "Do you suppose I will ever learn?"

"Learn what?" he asked, trying to smile. "I am sorry . . . I—"

"It is all right," she said, waving her hand in the sign of quiet. "Do not be troubled. If I were young and beautiful, you would be snorting and pawing the dirt." She laughed. "Then I would have a different kind of problem. The problem here, my son, is that I came to you instead of you coming to see me."

He began to speak, but she made the sign of respect and silence.

"Your actions and feelings are human," she smiled gently. "I am just as complicated within my humanity as you. I should have sent word, or told your sister and brother that I would see you. The story Dreamer told of you, and Little Wolf's description of you, caused my heart to fly away just like it used to when I was a girl. I saw you not as you are, a young man, an anxious and energy-filled young man, but as something else. I have never seen or met a person from the tribe of People you came from. Never. You were unusual, different, even frightening, and that caused me great excitement.

"Now look at you. You are embarrassed," she laughed. "It was very exciting for me to come here! I suppose, for the briefest movement of time, I even forgot how old I am. I live in a world so different from yours that you would be confounded by the experience of it. Just being a woman and understanding what that means would demand tremendous energy of mind from you. That difference alone, if you learned of its wonder, would transform you! You are learning our customs and ways. Those things are a mountain of learning for you. You are learning about yourself. You are a land so vast and powerful . . ." She stopped and looked up into his eyes. "Do you see that prairie?" She pointed. "Can you imagine what there is to see and discover on that prairie?"

"On the prairie?" he asked, raising his eyebrows. "There is only prairie on the prairie. Maybe a few people and the beings we hunt."

The old woman shrieked with laughter and threw her hands into the air.

"You are making a fool of me," Dancing Tree said angrily. "I know of many things other than just the prairie. There are magnificent and very large—" He sought for a word that would describe cities, the cities he had heard about as a child—"lodges that are made of stone that reach to the sky! Those are not on the prairie!"

The old woman shrieked with laughter again.

"You make me laugh!" he said, raising his voice to emphasize his words. "Your understanding of what exists in this world is so small. You people have no idea of what truly exists!"

"What truly exists?" she asked, sobering.

"Nothing," he said, looking away. "Nothing."

"I was laughing with you, not at you," she said with kindness. "I have heard of those places that are made of stone and reach to the sky. Those places have existed south of here for thousands of years. I know that the white man lives in stone and wood lodges that tower up to the sky. I also know that thousands of thousands of people live in just one of those places. Those places, my son, are on the prairie just as the mountains are on the prairie. The prairie is the great floor, the foundation for all.

"Dancing Tree, your mind is as wonderful and as great as all the prairies! What you can discover about yourself is as breathtaking as all the things, all the people, all the places, and all the marvels of the whole world! But what we humans build upon our world is nothing compared to what is already contained in even the smallest particle of this world. We build with metal, stone, hide, and wood, but the world builds with life. The universe that surrounds this world also surrounds other worlds and suns and countless stars. The universe builds life. This one world that the universe has created is alive, differently than either you or I are alive, but it is alive."

"May I ask you a question, grandmother?" Dancing Tree asked, looking up into the old woman's eyes. "May I?"

"What is the question?" she asked gently.

"I have never asked this of anyone," he said, leaning closer. "And please do not laugh. But you know, I have no idea what all this talk is for. I mean, what can you do with it? It is beautiful and makes me feel beautiful, but what is it for? If it made me a better hunter or warrior, it would be different. But it is like eating air. Do you understand what I mean?"

"Of course!" she smiled. "Of course I do! But let me give you an example of how this air-eating can help you. Let us suppose that you are thirsty. It is natural to drink water, is it not?"

"We have to have water," he answered.

"But we humans have done a very strange thing," she explained. "We have made laws about drinking water. We have made laws, and our ignorance has made laws. What would you think about a law that said that you could only drink water when it rained. You opened your mouth when it rained, tipped your head back, and drank. To drink water at any other time would be forbidden. What would you say about that kind of law?"

"I would break that law," he laughed.

"You probably would," she laughed. "But there are people who would not. What if there were many 'would not' people, and what if you never thought about drinking water from a stream?"

"I naturally would experiment," he smiled. "Of course!"

"What if you saw your brother experiment and saw him drown?" she smiled. "And what if you were one of the people in the council who decided that for the good of the camp no one else should do such a thing?"

"I think I am beginning to see what you mean," he said.

"I once lived in a camp of slaves," she said as she handed him a bowl of buffalo berries. "I was a slave for twelve years."

"How did you escape?" he asked, intrigued.

"I escaped as soon as my daughter was twelve years old," she answered. "My slave master was also a slave. In fact everyone in the whole camp was a slave and did not know it."

"If everyone was a slave, who or what was it that kept you captive?" he asked. "Are you serious?"

"I am very serious," she smiled. "The law, our custom, was our master. I lived alone with a man and one child. He was from the People called the Black Lodge People. Each family lived alone, each to their own lodge. The women of the camp never helped each other, and each woman raised her own children. The men of the camp did all the hunting and farming. Each of us had our own corn garden. No one ever helped anyone else. The men worked together during the hunt, but after the hunt was over, each man farmed alone. It was terrible.

"I was completely cared for. My husband loved me and tried in every way to please me, yet those twelve years were the most horrible years of my life."

"Surely you are teasing me!" He laughed heartily.

"It was no joke, living that way." She frowned, remembering. "I was terrified. As a woman, I lived in and controlled my own tiny world, my lodge. But outside of that lodge I was helpless. The strangest paradox of all was that even though the men made the laws and governed the camp, they too were helpless."

"You are confusing me," Dancing Tree smiled. "Are you intending that I be confused? You lived no differently than anyone else I have known."

"Little Wolf and Dreamer do not live in that manner," she said, taking a bite of berries. "If a woman's husband died she was left alone until she found another husband. She lost everything. Her lodge, everything. The husband's fathers and grandfathers would be given the lodge and the garden."

"That is completely silly!" Dancing Tree laughed. "There is land enough for everyone. There is land ten thousand steps wide from the middle of every camp," he laughed again.

"Not in that camp," she frowned. "It was strictly forbidden to start another garden by yourself. The men in the camp had the land divided and parceled out around the camp as far as you could see. To break the law in that camp meant banishment or death.

"I saw nothing wrong with that arrangement for years—nothing. It still amazes me when I think about it! I never saw the loneliness or the insanity of our way of life until my daughter was seven winters old.

"I will always remember just how my awakening began. I was hoeing the garden when my sister came running. I could see that she was crying. I asked her what had happened, and she told me that her husband had divorced her, thrown her out for another woman. We had no other family in the camp because we were newcomers. We had no uncles, aunts, nothing.

"My sister was seven years younger than I, and she was very pretty. Her husband had discarded her because he said that she was barren. It was the beginning of the hunting time, and all the men had just left. My sister came into my lodge, and we discussed what we should do. The only unmarried man in the camp was a wizened, terrible old man who had much land and even more power. Because of the law, she would be forced to marry that man. It was a terrible problem.

"We went to seek advice of a woman in the camp who was called Oldest Mother. She was not older, as you might think, but was rich. She had parents and many sons. We spoke to her about my sister. Her only advice was that my sister needed to do something useful. I asked her what she meant by useful, and she said that if my sister could do something that the men could not do, she might still have a place in the community. Otherwise, she would have to marry the only man there was left.

"My sister and I waited and waited for my husband to return. We needed help desperately, and he was the only one we could turn to. When he finally returned we explained the problem. I will never forget that day. My husband's response left me numb. I was so paralyzed with fear and disgust that I just stood there trembling."

"What could he have said that would have been so terrible?" Dancing Tree smiled.

"He said that my sister had only two choices," she said, looking into the eyes of Dancing Tree. "Just two. One was to marry the terrible old man. The other was to buy a husband from another camp. In those days there were no horses. The nearest camp was a twelve-day walk. It was a dangerous trip. And I knew what he meant when he said 'buy a husband'! He really meant selling my sister, just as she and I had originally been sold by my parents. I even knew the cost. The trip alone would cost twenty quilled belts and twenty blankets. That was the price for the escort that would be required.

"We both begged my husband to let my sister remain with us until the following spring. We were hoping, of course, that something would change. After much pleading and crying he finally consented to ask the council for permission. He was not a man who would stand up to authority. He was frightened of the council.

"We held our breath. He was gone all day. We harvested the garden and kept looking over our shoulders to see if he was returning. Late at night he finally came to the lodge. I asked him where he had been and why he had been away so long. He answered that he had been gambling.

" 'Tell us quickly,' I said, 'What did the council say?' He yawned and told me that the council had said my sister could stay. We wept for joy! But by the time of the first snow, when the winter dance began, my joy became tears. I was returning from the river when I heard sounds near where we stored our corn under the ground. I looked around and discovered that the sounds were coming from our corn kiva. I looked in because I was afraid that there might be trouble. I saw that my sister had gone to get corn. My husband had followed, and he was trying to rape her.

"I just stood there like a stalk of dry grass. Something inside me snapped, like when a bowstring breaks. I did not care if my husband wanted to make love to my sister. That was not what bothered me! I began to cry because I now felt what so many other women before me had felt. I had walked around in terror, knowing that I might one day be the woman who would be left out, but I had never allowed myself to think about it! In fact, as time passed I had become smug about it, believing that it could never happen to me. I had dreamed of the day when I would have riches and grandchildren. Now I realized that if my husband left me, I would have nothing, could do nothing, and that he, my husband, gave me my only identity within the camp. I was—there and then—completely illuminated to my slavery.

"That night, as I lay by my husband, I stayed awake thinking. I thought of the other women around me. I thought of my daughter. I thought of the social dances and the council. I saw everything for what it was. Nothing! It was as if I were standing on a mountain and watching the people in my camp. I watched the children. I watched them play. They were alone, as alone as the mothers who waited on them. I saw the mothers raising their children completely alone. I watched the children grow and I saw them become just like me and the other men and other women. I watched as the daughters were married into other lodges, where they would live alone. I watched, and I cried for them.

"The following morning I asked my sister if my husband had raped her. She answered that he would have if I had not come along.

"By the time of the Getting Ready For The Spring Dances I had been completely pushed aside. My husband did not even bother to sleep with me any more. He slept with my sister, who was afraid to stop him. She and I spoke about it many times, and tried to think of an escape. I shared all my thoughts with her, and she with me. By the time the End Of Planting Dance came we both knew that we had to run away. We packed food and blankets and hid them down by the river.

Late that night, we took our two dogs and two more that we stole from the Rains Helping family, and we quietly slipped out of the camp.

"We traveled for sixty days. We were tired, ragged, and very near starvation when we met Two Horns Singing. He was a young man from the tribe that calls itself the People. He was upon his Vision Quest and was very surprised when we stumbled into his fasting circle. He took us to his village, where we were fed and clothed. We both married into that People, and I have never left them."

"Somehow I am not understanding your story," Dancing Tree frowned. "In what way were you treated differently in the second camp?"

"I was treated like a human being," she smiled. "A real human being. My child was a child among children. All the children belonged to the People. All the children were brothers and sisters. There was equality, joy, and laughter among the People. The council was equal. Half the council members were women and half were men. The Medicine Women and the Medicine Men were equal. No one owned the land! No one owned another human being. Everyone had a say in the law. If the People were unhappy with the law, they changed it. All the People worked together. We all shared the work. Each lodge was separate and a power unto itself, but every lodge was part of the mother circle, the camp. No woman was slave to her husband in that camp. There was no competition between women for wealth or food, and never for a husband! If a woman's husband died, she was cared for by the circle of People. If a woman died, the man was cared for by that same circle of People. It was a beautiful place for my daughter to grow!"

"You never mentioned taking your daughter," Dancing Tree said as he stood up and stretched. "I thought you had left her back with your first husband."

"Sometimes I cannot understand what kind of ears you have," the old woman said, getting to her feet.

"Is our meeting completed?" Dancing Tree asked when he saw that the old woman was beginning to pack.

"Our meeting ended this morning, but I refused to see it," she answered.

"I will catch your donkey for you," Dancing Tree said as he reached for his moccasins.

"I will catch him myself," she said, turning to him. "Do not apologize to me because it will force you to lie. Your actions and feelings are clear, as clear as your boredom. I know that you are anxious to be with your family. I am grateful to have had a chance to talk to you, my son. I know that you are equally grateful for what you have received. I admire you for showing me your feelings, instead of trying to hide them. That is an attribute. But courtesy is another thing that you must learn."

Dancing Tree opened his mouth to speak, but she made the sign for quiet and respect. To speak now would be to dishonor her request, so he sat there in silence.

He watched her mount her little donkey and marveled at her agility. As she rode away he noticed that she appeared to be a little girl or boy again. At a distance it was really hard to tell.

He sat there long after she had disappeared, trying to understand why he had been so rude, so unfeeling. Finally he caught up his horse and leaped to her back. As he rode to his camp, Dancing Tree fought the disappointment and anger that tore at his heart.

"Why?" he asked out loud to himself. "Why couldn't I like her?"

The following day as Dancing Tree neared his camp, he noticed a figure squatting on a rock farther up the trail. The figure stood up and motioned him forward. He forgot the turmoil that had punished him all morning and felt a wave of relief lighten his body. As he rode slowly forward, he noticed that the figure had squatted again. It had lit up a pipe and was smoking. He was nearly abreast of the rock before he recognized that it was Crazy Dog.

"For awhile there, I thought you were a rabbit," Crazy Dog grinned. "The wind has blown your eagle feathers up, and they look like great big ears."

"Is that right?" replied Dancing Tree, smiling up at Crazy Dog. "I was certain I saw a gigantic mouse sitting on a rock, smoking a pipe."

After the two men had exchanged greetings they both sat down at Crazy Dog's fire and began to talk.

"How much longer will Little Wolf and Dreamer be out gathering herbs and berries?" Dancing Tree asked as he began to eat the food that Crazy Dog had prepared for him.

"Probably another ten days or more," Crazy Dog said. "Tell me. How was your journey back from the camp of Rose Bush and Silver Comb?"

"Don't you want to hear what happened to me at the medicine camp?" Dancing Tree asked, looking up.

"There will be many nights when we can speak of it," Crazy Dog smiled, "so let us wait. I wish for Little Wolf and Dreamer to hear of it also. Telling the story the second time is not like the first."

Dancing Tree grinned, then frowned. "Well, besides becoming lost once, I insulted South Horse, the Medicine Woman."

Crazy Dog's eyebrows went up.

"I had no idea why an old woman would want to talk to me," Dancing Tree frowned. "Not at the time, anyway."

He moved nervously and tried to make himself comfortable.

"Is it customary for old women to seek you out in the middle of the prairie?" Crazy Dog laughed. His eyes were twinkling.

"Not usually," Dancing Tree smiled. "But worse than that, I insulted myself and the grandfather of the prairie. Rose Bush had put his voice in my head, somehow, and had commanded that I speak with the grandfather. The grandfather told me he would answer any question. Any question, can you imagine that? Any question at all. But in my confusion, the question I asked was foolish and meaningless."

Crazy Dog sat quietly, listening, giving Dancing Tree the comfort of a friend who cared.

Dancing Tree scowled. "I met two war chiefs from the camp of Standing Up Man," he said. "They were of the Brother People. They were on their way to talk to the very person I had left, South Horse. They told me that South Horse was one of the most powerful Medicine Chiefs left in the world. They said she was more skilled in the law than anybody alive. They were going to see her. They had dreamed of talking with her for twenty years, they said. Twenty years! I had been sitting right there with her, acting like a stupid and angry child!"

"That was a very important part of your Vision Quest!" Crazy Dog whooped with joy. "Be happy, my son! Celebrate all that happened to you, everything! Even your getting lost was part of that Quest! That powerful woman knew all along that you were a stupid pup," he laughed. "She loved you despite everything! Tell me the story with smiles, not frowns. You were what you were and are what you are. Celebrate that, learn from it. How many have ever experienced the wonderful circle that you have held in your hands! Awaken and dance. You are now back with your family! Throw your scowls into the brush where you last relieved yourself and enjoy yourself!"

"I did have a powerful adventure," Dancing Tree smiled. "But I can't help but hope that old woman is not too angry with me. The grandfather is probably also angry at me. It breaks the harmony of what I experienced. Do you understand what I mean?"

"You are trying to throw responsibility away from yourself," Crazy Dog laughed. "That is all. Answer me, did you care if South Horse liked you or was mad at you before you met her?"

"How could I?" he laughed. "I had never known her."

"Are you telling me you know her now?" Crazy Dog smiled. "Or is it just that your vanity is a bit tangled? Are you afraid she will tell everybody she meets for years and years that you have the sour disposition of a porcupine?"

Confusion raced across Dancing Tree's face. He could only blink.

"Your first camp taught you a law when you were still a child," Crazy Dog grinned in good humor. "We call those laws, Law Born In Ignorance laws. Surely the Medicine Woman taught you about those things, didn't she?"

"I never gave her a chance," Dancing Tree said without looking up.

"There, sitting on your head like an owl, is another law," Crazy Dog laughed. "It is the old Feel Sorry For Yourself law. Children use that law to get their way with their mothers. I am not your mother."

"My stupidity sometimes amazes me," Dancing Tree said with a scowl.

"The next law!" Crazy Dog said, whooping with laughter. "You are covered with them! Now it is the old I Will Beat Myself law. Go ahead, beat yourself to death. Why not tear one of your eyes out of your head? That will teach you!" He shrieked with laughter.

"Wait!" Dancing Tree exclaimed. "I am not eating air!" He began to smile. "It is just like hunting. I had to begin all over when I learned to hunt. I did not forget what I had already learned, but I had to begin to understand In a new way."

"It is something like that," Crazy Dog said. "It is a renewal," he smiled. "What is this about eating air?"

"I told the Medicine Woman that the teachings were like eating air, that they did not help me," he grinned.

Crazy Dog clapped his hands together in delight.

"I can just see her," Crazy Dog giggled. "I will gamble that she was jolted right down to her moccasins! Right now she is probably laughing and telling everybody about you!" He threw his head back and bellowed with laughter. "Now she is not only convinced that you are one of the most sour individuals in the whole world, but also that your brain is no larger than that of a mouse! She must have been completely convinced that you were not only insulting, but even stupid!"

Dancing Tree rose to his feet, shaking with anger.

"And violent," Crazy Dog said as he slowly got to his feet. "Ridiculous and violent. Without any brains at all. I can hardly wait to tell Little Wolf! Dreamer will laugh so hard she will fall to the ground. I knew you would fail. How could you not fail? Everyone will be laughing!"

Blinded with anger, Dancing Tree dove headlong toward Crazy Dog. But Crazy Dog expertly grabbed the younger man's hair and pushed his face into the dirt. Bellowing with rage, Dancing Tree jumped to his feet and spun to attack Crazy Dog. He was so startled at what he saw when he completed his turn, he nearly fell down. Crazy Dog was rolling on the ground laughing as if he were insane.

Dancing Tree had fallen to his knees with the momentum of his charge. The look of shock on his face forced Crazy Dog to laugh even harder.

"It is easy to manipulate you," Crazy Dog said with a stern voice. "Too easy!"

Dancing Tree could only blink.

"You must learn to use your mind," Crazy Dog said. "Get up from the ground and be an adult! Your anger is a law that binds you hand and foot. Does it matter if that Medicine Woman should think you stupid? What does it matter if she found you sour?"

Crazy Dog lifted Dancing Tree from the ground with one strong jerk of his arm, standing him on his feet.

"Vanity and anger are laws more terrible than any others yet devised," Crazy Dog explained in a clear but stern voice. "Live with them and after awhile you will no longer have the power of decision. Even the clothes you wore could only be those kinds of clothes that everyone else wore. Your hair would have to be exactly like everybody else's. You would make no decisions of your own. I have seen tribes, including the white men, in which each person dresses alike in every detail. Think!" Crazy Dog roared to emphasize his words. "Think! Children mimic each other and their parents. They structure their world in that way. Children are desperately afraid to be different. They strive to be exactly like the models they see around themselves. But you, Dancing Tree, are no child!"

Crazy Dog dug down in his medicine bag and brought out a woman's whalebone corset.

"I have been saving this strange thing for you," Crazy Dog grinned. "I want you to have it." He threw the corset into Dancing Tree's lap. "That thing was worn by a woman, a woman from the world in which you were raised. That thing was contrived to hold the woman's belly flat. The woman who wore it no doubt thought that it made her pretty. No one forced her to wear that thing. Or at least, no *person* did so. It was her own law of ignorance that forced her to wear it.

"You, my son, wear similar devices that hold you in. You gave me only two choices when you came at me to do combat. I could have knocked you on your thick head, or I could simply have startled you in the manner that I chose. I knew that the second way would be more gentle and a better way of teaching."

THE WHITE LODGE

THERE WAS A GUARD standing at the gate, but the gate had rusted years ago, and only parts of it remained. The wall, too, had fallen from neglect. There were great gaps where it had crumbled. But the strangest thing about the wall and the gate were the places that were shiny new and seemed to be built from gleaming metal. The guard was young, but her clothes were old and ragged. She carried an assortment of weapons, most of which were broken and useless.

"What is your name?" the guard asked in a tired monotone.

"Estchimah," she answered.

"In this city you are No Name," the guard replied in her monotone. "Enter."

No Name took four steps into the city and became totally lost. She wandered up one street, down another, around and around. The city seemed to be a maze. No Name sat down, confused. After a while she looked up and asked a passerby which way led out of the city.

"Why do you want to leave the city?" the passerby asked.

"The streets twist and turn and confuse me," she replied.

"Go to the Temple known as Earths of Foxes," a woman offered, pointing the way.

A man and a woman guarded the temple door. They were twins and very old. No Name walked up to the door. Before she could ask permission to enter, the twins opened the way. Despite their great size, the doors opened smoothly, without the faintest sound.

"Enter," the twins commanded.

No Name entered.

"Sign your name," a plainly dressed woman said quietly.

"I cannot see!" No Name said, trying to shade her eyes. The foyer she now stood in shone brighter than even the brightest day. Those who had built the temple had used cut glass, mirrors, and crystal to reflect the light from every direction into the foyer. Dazzling rainbows glistened through the millions of crystals and were magnified a thousand times by the mirrors covering the walls, ceiling, and floor. In the middle of the room was a statue of clear polished glass. The image was of a very beautiful nude young woman.

"This light is unbearable!" No Name screamed. "What could the builders of such a place possibly have had in mind, to make it so beautiful and yet so painful?"

"This is the Moon Room," the plainly dressed woman answered. "This room reflects the light from the moon and the stars. It is very beautiful to see."

No Name noticed that the plainly dressed woman did not blink from the unbearable light, and she thought that the woman must be blind.

"Wouldn't it be better if your guests arrived at night?" No Name asked.

"No," the plainly dressed woman answered. "No one enters after dark."

"I have come here to ask for directions out of the city," No Name said.

"Go to the room called Boundary of Blood. It is through that passageway

and down the hall. It is the first door on your right," she said, bowing low.

The darkness of the hall soothed No Name's eyes. As she wandered, she noticed the walls were covered from floor to ceiling with delicately carved inscriptions. Each was written in a separate language. Every language ever spoken upon the earth was represented, and each told the same story. Small statues also lined the hall, each one the same size. These had been carved or molded from every material imaginable, from the most common things to precious stones and gleaming gold and silver, including substances of a future time, still to be discovered.

No Name thought many of the statues pretty. She touched a few of them, marveling at their beauty, but she had no true understanding of their exquisite artistry. She avoided many of the more perfect art forms either because she didn't understand them or because she found them repulsive. She stopped when she came to four long rows of soldiers, each one different in its armor and weaponry, each from a different age. She smiled. Their machines and uniforms held her in fascination for a long while. However, the longer she admired these forms, the more aware she became that something was wrong about them. She looked more closely and slowly a horror crept over her. Their faces were all the same! She picked up one of the statues and studied it closely, trying to see what it was that frightened her. There it was! Just below the skin was the grinning face of indescribable terror! Shaking, she dropped the statue to the floor and ran.

Finally she stopped and leaned against the wall, trying to catch her breath. Then she noticed the door inscribed "Boundary of Blood," the door the blind woman had told her to enter. She opened the door and stepped inside.

The room seemed to explode in her face. It appeared to have no end. It was a composite of geometrical lines, colors, and shapes alive within their own force of millions of intersecting points. An old grandmother

suddenly emerged and walked toward No Name. Her clothes made her nearly invisible within the color and lines that flowed around her.

"Welcome, my child," the old grandmother said, bowing low. "My name is Dance Hammer. The lance and bow are at your feet. Herbal sweet grass has been placed upon the fire, and the moon and stars are reflected in the dark pool of your remembrance.

"You have brought yourself into the Maze. Four sleeping lions have been awakened. These lions are each of a different color. The black lion hunts in the Sacred Mountains and has been married to the Medicine Deer. The white lion hunts in the forests of everything taught and is married to Erect Horns, the antelope. The golden lion hunts along the great river and is married to the thunderbird. The red lion hunts upon the prairies and has married with Sweet Medicine.

"There is a new language spoken here. It is the language of questions. My name is Upside Down, and I am the keeper of this lodge. I am holding the bowl of worry. It is a bowl carved from the wood of the Sacred Tree. The humans have placed this bowl in my hands. The humans carved it from the roots of the Sacred Tree.

"Many have visited my lodge and have asked for the carved bowls because they feared the lions. The lions are four voices when you take them from this lodge. One carved bowl is pure gold when you take it from this lodge. It will make you rich, and the other will make you poor.

"My robe is yours for the asking.

"Do you have a question, little sister?" the old grandmother said.

"I am seeking directions," No Name answered.

"Go then to the room upon your left. It is across the hall. Bless you, my child," Dance Hammer said, bowing low.

No Name entered the second room. Its name was written above the door. Its name was Painted With Colors Having Eyes. The room seemed to be painted in moving water.

"Welcome to the Lodge of Shadows, my child. My name is White Buffalo Robe," the old grandmother said, bowing low.

"I need directions out of the city," No Name said.

"I know," White Buffalo Robe said as she sat down. "But first I will tell you a story. There was a large camp of People and they were confounded by the many thousands of mice that were among them. They sat together in a circle to discuss their problem, and they decided to call an owl amongst them to eat the mice. And the chief sat the owl upon his own head. But the mice did not diminish, and a second owl was called, and a third, then hundreds. After a while everyone had an owl upon their head. And still the mice did not diminish. A little child saw these things and asked the grandfathers why everyone had owls upon their heads, but they would not answer because they were ashamed.

"If you wish to be rid of the mice, the little child said, then bring a cat into the camp. And the people listened, and the owls, all but a few, flew away, and balance was brought to the camp."

"My problem is not owls," No Name laughed. "It is directions that I need."

"Then here you are," White Buffalo Robe said, bowing low. "Go to the room that is upon your right, down the hall. Peace, my child, peace."

No Name found the third room and entered. Its name was Burning Of Waters.

"Welcome, my child. My name is Dream Ring," another old grandmother said, bowing low.

"Why is this room so plain?" No Name asked.

"Drink this," Dream Ring said. "It is from the green fruit of the Sacred Tree."

No Name drank, and suddenly saw and felt the fire.

"Why doesn't the fire burn me?" No Name asked.

"Because you trusted me," Dream Ring answered.

"I think that I am lost," No Name said. "Can you help me?"

"Yes," Dream Ring said, as she sat down by the young woman. "Here is a story. These are Four Arrows. The white one will become red when you give it to your teacher. The green one will become blue when you give it to your teacher. The black one will become like lightning with its colors when you give it to your teacher. And the gold one will become like the sunset when you give it to your teacher. Go to the room known as Belonging To The Sun, and give these Medicine Arrows to your teacher."

"Thank you," No Name said, bowing low.

"Thank you, my child," Dream Ring said, bowing low.

No Name went as she was instructed to the room that was named Belonging To The Sun. She was greeted there by the woman who was dressed in plain clothes.

"You are the grandmother who was blind! But now you can see!" No Name said in surprise.

"Yes, I am. I can see, little sister. My name is Keeper Of The Medicines Of The Moon," she said, bowing low.

"Here are the Arrows that were given to me," No Name said, bowing low.

"I will bind these Arrows within the song of changing that is your medicine," Keeper Of The Medicines Of The Moon smiled.

"My medicine?" No Name exclaimed in surprise.

"Lonely Person is sitting at the stream that has been given the name of the clouds. Lonely Person has discovered a quill pen from magpie's tail, and she draws signs of the mountains upon birch. She writes in painting from her own blood. She writes the fawn's dream."

No Name listened intently as Keeper Of The Medicines Of The Moon continued.

"Lonely Person could not know that she would marry Heyoehkah. Grandmother Deaf Woman had given Lonely Person moccasins for her dance that were as beautiful as our Sacred Lodge could offer, but they weren't enough. She had hidden them away. She was ashamed because they were not new.

"The turtle had been turned upon its back at that place. The signs of the painters were washed with the rains that touched the earth, the rains that could run under the back of that ancient shell. The water was cool upon the belly of the old turtle, but her dread of the sun grew with each passing cloud. Would she be left alone upon her back to the summer heat?

"She cried out silently to Lonely Person. Lonely Person heard a reflection deep within her heart that spoke to her of the ancient turtle and her painting, but she was so sad she did not understand the cry of the turtle. And this is what Lonely Person did as she sat at the stream of the clouds.

"Lonely Person wept in her heart because she believed she was not beautiful. She believed she could not give fully of herself and of the things that sang in her being. She longed to become herself. She longed to dance within the circle of fire that reflected a million eyes of the stars into the camp circle. She translated the turtle's cry into a bitter painting of sorrow.

"Heyoehkah had been driven from the camp because he was mad. Heyoehkah was alone upon the prairie. He heard Lonely Person's thoughts and ran toward the mountains with the feelings of spring in his heart. He heard the singing of the earth. The Medicine Leaf falls quietly to the ground from the tree struck with lightning and fire. The Medicine Leaf has been painted upon the face of the mountain by Sweet Medicine. Turtle had stolen the Medicine Leaf from the mountain, thinking it was the power of Lonely Person. Everything was the song in Heyoehkah's heart, everything was in his mind.

"When Heyoehkah came to the mountains he saw Lonely Person, but he could not approach her because he had been driven from the circle. He made medicine, and the mountains heard his talk. They made seven rainbows and they listened to Heyoehkah's song.

> *I walk upon foolish words.*
> *I run around many waters.*
> *I am you within wonder.*
> *Hear what we do not say.*
> *Open the lodge door.*
> *No poorer than stone,*
> *More rich than weeping,*
> *Introduce me!*
> *I am Crazy Dog!*

"The six grandmothers were awakened by the laughter of a little boy. It was the laughter of Seven Arrows, and they saw far beyond Heyoehkah's prayers. They began to sing to the center of the earth where Lonely Person had dreamed.

"Stars dance with fireflies upon the earth, for night's meeting with Dreamer. And so the grandmothers spoke to the fireflies, saying:

> *Where are the shadows?*
> *Where is the transformation?*
> *Where does everyone walk?*
> *Can they touch fantasies?*
> *Does night remember?*
> *Introduce us!*

"Dreamer heard these things, and she thought she would trick

Heyoehkah. She would enter the young man's body so that she could marry Lonely Person.

Come Heyoehkah!
Fall asleep.
Walk with me.
Open your eyes!

"But when Heyoehkah fell asleep, Dreamer saw the night. It was Lonely Person changed.

Lonely Person danced,
Turning the turtle over.
Red Leaf lit up the night;
Like a bright fire he sang!

"And Heyoehkah awoke to dance with the young woman who had been given the name South Horse," Keeper Of The Medicines Of The Moon concluded.

"She was the camp. She was the People. And Heyoehkah? Heyoehkah is everyone who hears this song. A Crazy Dog's song!"

ESTCHIMAH HAD no more stepped from the circle of the city to the prairie when she was stopped by a very old woman.

"Please, my child," the old woman begged, "will you help an old mother?"

"What is it, grandmother?" Estchimah asked.

"My little donkey is old and becoming blind," the old woman answered. "Will you lead her for me?"

"I am going to the mountains," Estchimah said. "The journey will be much more enjoyable with a companion."

Estchimah walked along the dusty path for hours, stopping only now and again to rest, drink, or eat, but the old woman never moved from her perch on the donkey. She never drank, ate, or rested. She never spoke a word. Estchimah tried many times to converse with her, but for all her efforts she might have been addressing stone.

"Don't you ever speak?" Estchimah asked for the hundredth time, hoping she would say something. The old woman's silence was making her uneasy.

They were crossing a small stream, and Estchimah was mumbling half to herself about the mud, when suddenly with a very loud and booming voice, the old woman spoke.

"Hail Burning Of Waters!" she thundered. She paused briefly and then began chanting in a loud voice.

"Smoke from the campfires twisted together and flowed along the ground like a dragon. The air hissed as the wet wood burned, turning the morning sun blood red. Hard gray silhouettes of people spoke together sleepily about dangerous dreams, and were cursing the mud. The ribs of their slate-colored tent stood out crookedly like arrows driven into the ground. The taut skin of their tent was shaped like a dog that had lain down to starve to death. The priests and the priestesses were awake.

"Plans for the ceremony had been ruined by the rain. Now each of the visitors sat sullenly, wondering what to do. One by one each gray figure stood up, stretched, and began to walk away in boredom. All went their own way.

"Soon the camp was deserted; not even the chief priest and priestess remained. The morning breathed quietly, changing its face into a most wondrous day and shining as brightly as music. The abandoned tent fell down in a soft bundle to rest. Magically, within that same instant, the wood on the seven drenched campfires dried and flared into life, becoming seven bright signs.

"Each priest and priestess had wandered to the same lake, but because

of the great size of that powerful place, all had thought themselves alone. They saw their own fear and were surprised. Then everyone saw their new reflection and began to dream.

"A serpent, so fearsome and powerful it dwarfed even itself, seemed to rise out of the reflection, determined to destroy. But just as smoothly as it had appeared it turned into a delicate flower.

"The priests and priestesses returned to their camp. Now their fires were burning, and their lodge tent had been made beautiful. It was now like a great wheel with mirrors to remember the dream."

After the old woman had spoken she became silent again. She would not talk, nor would she answer Estchimah's inquiries about her sudden story at the stream. Estchimah decided to watch her more closely. They plodded on, Estchimah walking and the old woman riding the little donkey.

It was almost noon, and it was getting hot. Estchimah had stopped for a drink from her waterskin when she noticed a powerful young eagle that had just landed in the tree over her head. She was about to point out the eagle to the old woman, when she heard her speak again. But this time her voice was like the pure sound of water.

"Hail Painted With Color Having Eyes," she sang. Then she continued.

"It is now as it was when you held the river reeds in your hands. The fragrance of what you hold within your hands speaks to you of the very essence of growing. As you hold the bundle you wonder, and you try to understand what you have gathered at the river. You see the grass and the trees, and you enjoy the flowers. You blink, trying to remember this place, but quickly you put aside your remembering and forget as you turn to begin your walk back to the circle of lodges.

"The quiet joy of a mysterious song is part of you when you sit down by your lodge fire. But uneasiness buzzes around your head like an angry bee. You don't want the dream to leave you. You don't want to be angry. But you feel your eyes opening wider in anger, and suddenly you

begin to hate. You want to kill your enemy, the bee, but before you can do so it flies away. Now you feel defeated, even embarrassed. You look to see if anyone has seen the transformation of your mind.

"Transformation? Is that what you thought? How strange. It must be because it is so early in the morning. You rub your eyes as you begin the task of stripping the willow reeds. What was it you were going to make? Oh yes, it was a carrying basket your mother asked you to build for her work.

"The world seems to turn under your hands as you fit the willow reeds together into the first circle. You realize suddenly that this would be a good drum if you could find that fragment of hide that had been cut and put away. You begin to look within your lodge and discover that it is still there, where you had carelessly thrown it away among the rest of your childhood things.

"Much of the mystery disappears when you touch the tiny child's shield. The shield was the drum, and it was the willow basket, and it was the river and the bundle. And now you remember . . . or have you forgotten?"

"Are these your prayers?" Estchimah asked, totally bewildered.

But the old woman said nothing.

While they walked, Estchimah again watched for any sign that might cause another song from the old woman. She didn't see anything, but suddenly the old woman spoke again. This time her voice sounded like all the winds of the earth together. Estchimah spun on her heel to see who the old woman was greeting. She saw that it was an old and very beautiful tree.

"Hail, Boundary of Blood!" the old woman cried. "An adventure upon the paths within changing walls, where the temple builder lives. A dark river where the eye blinks with every stroke of his ruby hammer, carving the dress of Sweet Medicine, carving the dress away until she stands naked, the sun upon her face, within that dark place where the eye

blinks. It is frightening when it is within a dream, because you are prisoner of the mind; without form you drift onto the anvil beneath the hammer.

"There, you watch the geometry explode around your head as your feet carve the dress of Sweet Medicine, carving it away until there is nakedness. The paths and walls shimmer like the aurora, illuminating the dark river. There is unspeakable terror because the river is the Power of the Universe.

"Lightning runs in patterns from the ruby hammer along the arm of the temple builder and glows like burnished suns in his eyes. His eyes are like the eyes of a cat, only four hundred million times as large. They become diamonds for the necklace Sweet Medicine will wear when she stands naked.

"The image of Sweet Medicine reflects upon the turning path. Your heart weeps and laughs as you touch Sweet Medicine's belt, jolting your soul into mystery. Even though your tears flow like the joy of fresh mountain streams, you struggle. Because you are afraid, you struggle. You want to love her and do not want the spell broken. That is why you struggle. That is why."

Estchimah walked along, again determined not to miss anything. She watched every flower, tree, bird; anything that might be the next sign, but her guess was wrong every time.

Suddenly the song began again. Estchimah turned quickly, but the evening sun blinded her and she was unable to see the old woman.

"Hail, Lodge of the Sun!" the old woman called. Then she went on in a strong voice.

"Following behind the old woman, waiting for the water to leave the ground, the apprentice sees the old woman mix ashes from the sacrifices for holy offering. In the great desert where the old woman lives, is the valley of sand.

"An ancient spinning wheel is set up beside a new loom constructed of animals' bones. The task begins. The offerings are spun together, then are woven upon the loom. Suddenly the hair of the apprentice is caught in the loom of the old woman's work. A tiny sound of the thunderbird is heard. It is the quiet sobbing of the apprentice.

"The old woman appears as an evil witch, bending over her work, laughing as she spins and weaves. The little girl tries frantically to free her hair from the loom but finds she is creating braids in the weave. Flecks of blood appear along the strands, tracing rivers of design. She cries more loudly and claws at the old woman, asking the ancient mother to listen. The spinning stops. The shuttle ends its movement. The sun becomes the moon cradled between the horns of Sweet Medicine. Sweet Medicine listens to the nakedness of the apprentice and transforms the weaving into a robe of flowers for the girl-woman to wear.

"In the valley of sand within the great desert the garden is growing and the earth is renewed. There is rejoicing. The Vision Quest has begun."

The old woman suddenly vanished, her little donkey with her. Estchimah looked down at the cord she had been leading the tiny donkey with, and saw the embroidered scarf Twin Chiefs had given her.

THE FOLLOWING AUTUMN Little Wolf decided it would be better if their camp were to move into the shelter of the mountains for the winter. A group of white men, either soldiers or travelers—he never knew which—had attacked him on his return from scouting out the only herd of buffalo left upon their hunting ground. He did not wish to chance meeting them again, or for them to find the camp.

The incident had nagged at Dancing Tree while they traveled, ruining his sleep.

"I am miserable," Dancing Tree grumbled one evening. "I can hardly eat."

"Why?" Little Wolf asked in surprise. "Our trip has been beautiful."

"I would rather not speak of it," Dancing Tree said, forcing a smile. "It will soon pass."

"You have my curiosity standing out as straight as your whiskers," Crazy Dog laughed. "Come. Tell us of what is bothering you."

"I have grumbled about it before," Dancing Tree replied angrily. "It makes no sense to me at all that my other brothers should insist upon killing every one of the People they can find."

Little Wolf shook his head.

"I really do not know why they are like that," Crazy Dog said, putting down his bowl of food. "But it is becoming more dangerous for the People every year."

"I met two men years ago who were upon a peace mission. They told of the same problem," Dancing Tree said.

"You have not spoken of this thing with us," Little Wolf said, becoming interested.

"I know," Dancing Tree answered. "Because I have been wrestling with the problem of it for years."

"Pearlie once said you had met two men just before she moved to the camp of Thunder Chief," Dreamer said. "Wasn't it before you became a People?"

"Yes," Dancing Tree explained. "We were somewhere out upon the prairie. Only the Great Spirit knows where, because we were so lost. Then we stumbled by chance upon a pony-fort lodge that had never been lived in. That is where we met these two people. They told us they were on a peace mission. They were whitemen who lived among the People, and were angry because their relatives were being killed."

"Let me understand," Crazy Dog interrupted. "Were these two whitemen you met, or two of the People?"

"They were whitemen, as I am," Dancing Tree explained. "And they lived among the People, as I do."

"I see," Crazy Dog frowned, thinking. "I can see why you have been wrestling with yourself. You somehow believe that if you too were to make a peace mission, you might save our lives."

"Yes," Dancing Tree said, letting out his breath.

"Crazy Dog at one time believed as you do," Little Wolf said without looking up. "He tried to bring peace, but everyone was murdered in the camps both of Dreamer and of my mother."

Crazy Dog looked down at his hands.

"But I am a whiteman," Dancing Tree said with concern. "Perhaps it would make a difference."

Nobody spoke. The only sound was the crackling of their fire.

"I do not think so," Crazy Dog said at last. He spoke with emotion. "I think they would kill you."

"Can you even remember the whiteman's tongue?" Dreamer asked. She seemed to be pleading with her eyes as she spoke. "Could you even make yourself understood?"

"Not enough, I'm sure," Dancing Tree answered. "I have tried at times to put my new understandings into my former tongue, but I cannot. I really do not comprehend it."

"I understand what you mean," Crazy Dog said, setting down his bowl of buffalo berries. "It is a tremendous task. I realized this when I began to learn my first new tongue. It was among the Desert People. But it taught me much concerning understanding between Peoples. When I visited them I was instructed never to use the sign language. My teacher had given me this problem," he laughed. "Problems upon problems arose with my very first encounter with the Desert People."

He was laughing so hard he had to stop.

"I walked up to that small camp of corn growers and I sat down. I wanted them to know that I meant only peace; that I had not come to harm them." He began to giggle. "Two of the older men approached me and asked me in signs if I were lost. I wanted to answer them, but my instructions were not to use the sign language. So there I sat, looking stupid and suspicious. But even more complicated than this, I realized I was failing at my task because I could read the signs of my brothers who were trying to communicate with me." He laughed again.

"Your teacher sent you upon a good trail," Little Wolf laughed. "Then what happened?"

"Well," Crazy Dog went on, "I sat there and sat there, trying to figure out what I should do. Should I sign to them that I could not use the sign language because my chief had said not to? Or should I just make believe I could not read the sign language? I decided the second possibility would not work, simply because I could really understand the signs."

"How did you solve the problem?" Dreamer asked. "You must have been very clever!"

"No, I was not," Crazy Dog laughed, slapping his leg. "I was as dumb as a newborn owl. I just could not figure it out no matter how hard I tried. So I simply approached one of the old men who had signed with me before, and explained everything to him in signs. And then, of course, I had to sit tight until the old man stopped laughing.

" 'Let that be your first teacher,' he signed. 'Because there are always the signs between Peoples, even if those Peoples do not know the common sign language of the hands.'

" 'How is that?' I asked, wondering.

" 'Consider this,' he signed. 'Is not the earth a sign? The air? The birds? Children? Dogs? Water? Fire? . . .' He went on and on until I thought he had named almost everything in the entire world. Then suddenly he stopped. I sat there wondering what to say or do. I mumbled.

" 'I do not understand your tongue,' he signed, 'So mumble, if you will, within the signs.'

" 'How did you know that I was mumbling?' I signed.

" 'Your head must be more thick than even a bear's,' he signed and laughed.

"I sat there thinking.

" 'Come,' he signed. 'I have named almost everything within the entire world that is a mutual sign among Peoples. What were those which I did not mention?'

" 'Mumble,' I said in signs. I thought he would explode laughing.

" 'Would you understand if a thirsty person made the sign for drink?' he asked in signs. 'Or a person who was crying touched the heart?' And he went on and on until he had named the other half of the signs that are understood between Peoples. Then he stopped again and looked at me.

"To save time I signed, 'Mumble,' again.

"He shook his head. 'What about the signs between animals?' he asked in signs.

" 'What do you mean?' I signed.

"He fell down on his back, laughing. I had to wait until his fit of laughter passed before we could talk again.

" 'What if a buffalo bull put his horns to the ground and began to chase you?' he signed, shrieking with laughter.

"I grinned at the time, but I felt like an egg that had just been stepped on."

After the laughter around the fire subsided, Crazy Dog went on.

" 'Your teacher has given you a good trail,' the old man signed, suddenly growing very stern. 'I will tell the entire camp not to sign with you, and you must not sign with them.'

" 'I will not,' I signed.

"He began to laugh again. 'You are as hardheaded as an elk's horn,' he signed. 'Look. I mean you cannot make even the slightest sign. Not pointing, not touching. Nothing. Do you understand?'

" 'Yes,' I gulped and signed.

" 'After one summer, then come to me and speak to me in my tongue,' he signed."

"You learned then, didn't you?" Little Wolf laughed.

"I did not," Crazy Dog answered. "Yes. I learned to speak many words, but it was difficult. When I began to try to make myself clear to the old man later, I could not. But he did not laugh. I realized that the tongues could build a bitter wall between Peoples. I could ask for a drink or for food but not much more. When it came to expressing my mind or my heart, I failed miserably."

"Our world can be a tangle," Little Wolf said.

"Surely," Crazy Dog replied with sadness. "It surely can. And the problem I spoke of concerning the wall can be even more troublesome if there is a difference in symbolic understandings between Peoples. Dancing Tree will agree with that. Will you not, Dancing Tree?"

"I will," Dancing Tree agreed. "It was more difficult for me than you can imagine when I first began to learn the symbols."

Talk ended with Crazy Dog's story concerning his stay among the Desert People, because the camp needed to prepare for the winter. There were no buffalo to be had and almost no elk, so Little Wolf and Dancing Tree relied upon hunting for deer. The search for food was very difficult. Everyone toiled from daylight until dark for many days.

Like a song we awaken within the path of our discovery and marvel at our reflection upon the holy mountains. And like the tiniest stream of water within those mountains, we search for the flowers that will nourish our dream. It is the Medicine Way of touching everything that is sacred in the dance of promise. This is the gift of the rainbow, our fantasy.

"A FEW MORE DAYS and we can all take a good sweat bath," Crazy Dog said one night while they ate. "We will . . ." he stopped talking and looked up in surprise.

Everyone turned to see what was wrong.

"I hear a woman," Little Wolf said, leaping to his feet, "and she is hurt, I think."

Dancing Tree scooped up his lance, bow, and quiver and raced out to the place he and Little Wolf had already chosen as best for the defense of their camp. Little Wolf doused the fire with the buffalo-skin bucket kept beside it for just that purpose and found his own place of defense. Crazy Dog and Dreamer plunged into the darkness to their emergency store and their horses.

"Please do not run," a woman's voice cried. "It is I—Rainbow."

"Rainbow?" Little Wolf asked out loud.

"There may be someone following her," Dancing Tree called to Little Wolf. "It is too late to believe the camp is hidden. Should we run?"

"No," Rainbow called into the night. "There is no one following! Everyone in the camp has been killed. Thunder Chief, Pearlie, Painted Cloud—everyone," she sobbed.

Dreamer found Rainbow in the darkness and began to console her.

Little Wolf and Dancing Tree took turns watching over the camp through the night. The night was cold, and Dancing Tree pulled his robe tighter around his shoulders.

"Pearlie is gone," Dancing Tree thought, biting his lip. "I never cried, never said anything."

He tried to get himself more comfortable in the cold. It was quiet. No one was following, just as Rainbow had predicted.

"Strange," he thought. "I did not feel anything. I wonder why? What was the matter?" Then he began to remember another time.

"IT'S MORE THAN a good jump down to ol' Moot's place, sure," Pearlie had said, pulling on her large, floppy hat.

"I still says we up an' planted the wrong eatin' stuff. Moot ain't comin' 'cross with no tradin' hosses for punkins, I'm thinkin'," Calvin said, frowning.

"You're always kickin' up dirt 'bout business," Pearlie grinned. "You ain't pokin' no holes in this idea, no way. Last year corn or wheat were worth nuthin'. Every plowhaid hereabouts jabbed it in the groun', an' so did we. This year is mighty differnt. We got tradin' punkins!"

"We should o' made the trip up aways and poked aroun', sure!" Calvin said as he walked out the cabin door. "We should o' looked, I'm thinkin'."

"Why?" Pearlie asked, running after him. "You would o' poked an' seen what was planted, sure. But some butthaid would o' asked what you was plannin' to dig for, an you would o' told!"

"Dammit, Pearlie!" Calvin said as he climbed into the wagon box. "Jes' take a look-see! Did you ever see so damn many punkins? A whole wagon load o' punkins! We should o' come aroun' with corn or wheat, sure!"

"Wheat an' corn were worthless last year!" Pearlie laughed as she climbed up and sat beside him. "This year we're rich, sure! Who would o' thought 'bout punkins? Best chance we ever took!"

"Mules," Calvin grumbled, clicking his tongue for the animals to move. They just stood, not pulling. "Git!" he bellowed and slapped with the reins. Finally the two old mules tossed their heads and slowly began to pull.

"Looky them thar idiots!" Calvin scowled. "Actin' like they was suprised. Lordy! Gawddamnit all, anyway!"

"Mules're all right!" Pearlie smiled. "You jes' got to get used to 'em."

"Used to 'em!" Calvin cursed. "All my damned life I've been slappin' their butts! They jes' ain't purty, nohow. Look at 'em, hot jingo, what I'd give to see two shiny-assed Morgans, lordy gawd, sure!"

"With these punkins we got here we's gonna come up with good tradin' stuff, I'm bankin' on it!" Pearlie smiled as she sat back to dream.

They rode in silence as the wagon bumped along the rutted road toward Moot's trading store. It was no use fighting the time. They both knew it would be a very long ride, so they dreamed quietly as they rode.

"Take the reins," Calvin said as they passed a small creek. "Soon's the water clears I'm dippin' my tongue. I'm thirstier'n a duck."

"No use me holdin' the reins," Pearlie frowned. "Why for you want me to handle the reins? I'm goin' to dunk with you. The dust is coverin' my tongue same's yours. These ol' rathaids know the road. I'm comin'."

"You's the mos' stumblin'-into-messes human what ever, you know that, Pearlie!" Calvin scolded. "You ever thought maybe I'd care to up an crap?"

"You sat an hour in the half shed already. I saw that all right. What you up to?" Pearl frowned. "Common, throw it out!"

"So I did!" Calvin pouted, showing his lip. "Maybe I'm wantin' a walk or somethin', ever think o' that?"

"What you plannin'?" Pearlie asked as she studied his face. "What you thinkin' o' doin'?"

"Gawds a mighty, nothin'!" Calvin bawled. "Christ!"

"An' you's gettin' mad, sure!" Pearlie said, still studying, now even more closely. "An' why's you gettin' so red 'bout the neck?"

"I ain't red!" he almost shouted. "What's in your haid, anyway? I ain't red 'tall."

"You's bigger'n a horse kick!" Pearlie laughed, still scrutinizing his face. "You's even 'barrassed, sure!"

"I ain't 'barrassed, nohow!" Calvin howled. "An' you jump on that quick! All I wants is to lap up some crick."

"I would o' caught you, you know," Pearlie laughed.

"You would never o' caught nothin'!" Calvin blushed. "Girls ain't s'posed to flap their jaws in that kind o' lingo. Ma's thumped your haid already for that more'n once. It's 'barrassin' to hear it!"

"Thumped, sure!" Pearlie laughed, now even harder. "But what's sayin' I said a wrong thought, huh? You's the one what got his haid in a scrap heap, not me."

"You said *catch* me!" Calvin mocked. "So what's that? Thinkin' 'bout shuckin' corn or somethin'? An' stop that damned laughin'! I'm plumb fed up, sure!"

"I was jes' teasin'!" Pearlie snickered. "Jes' havin' fun! Lope over an' wet your whistle. I'll wait."

"I ain't," Calvin pouted. "Not with you thinkin' thataway, no siree!"

"Go on!" Pearlie coaxed. "I'll drive these mules which ain't needin' no handlin'."

"So you caught a thought!" Calvin bellowed, "So does that make me a no-account? Thar ain't nothin' wrong 'bout dreamin' a bit, is thar? Is you so holy? I mean, doesn't you fall into devil traps, too?"

" 'Course," Pearlie said, sobering. "I meant no harm, sure. I was jes' kiddin'. I mean, I really didn't know you was 'bout to dream a little. I'm sorry. I really am, sure."

"Gawd!" Calvin cussed. "This is the mos' 'barrassin' talk I ever been tangled into. Fires o' hell! Now I is 'barrassed, an' with my own sister! Won't my misery ever end?"

"Forget it!" Pearlie said. "Looky, ain't that ol' Dan?" she pointed down the road.

"It is!" Calvin said, looking up. "An' he's loaded down heavier'n a lead-shot duck!"

"Wheat!" Pearlie laughed with excitement. "A whole stompin' load o' wheat!"

"I'm arunnin' up an' scoutin' out his story," Calvin grinned as he jumped from the wagon."

"Me too," Pearlie giggled with excitement, as she jumped down.

They both ran until they caught up with Dan's wagon.

"Howdy!" Calvin called out cheerfully as he ran up alongside the driver.

"Howdy, Miss Pearl," Dan said, tipping his hat to Pearlie. "I see you's still livin' with your egghaid brother. I thought you would o' sold him to the gov'ment by now, for rifle shot. You know, bein' that he's got a haid made o' brass." He roared with laughter at his own joke.

"Brasshaid, huh?" Calvin grinned. "Looky thar, he's up an' tradin' off his livestock feed! Come winter the frumphaid won't have no feed for his cattle! Looky that, Pearlie. It's his oats!"

"Laugh on!" Dan sniggered. "I've kept my winter oats. This is my tradin' stuff! Now what do you think 'bout that?"

"Lordy gawd!" Calvin whooped with laughter. "You poked the wrong thing this time, you ol' polecat! It won't hardly bring a crate o' hens! Oats was the wrong gamble!"

"So what's your story?" Dan growled. "What you packin'?"

"We's got a whole gawddamned wagon o' punkins!" Calvin said with pride. "We turned every acre into punkins! There's gonna be a big grab for our tradin' stuff, sure!"

"Gawdamighty!" Dan yelped and began to laugh. "Punkins! Punkins?"

"Punkins!" Calvin said, mocking him. "You damn betcha, punkins. Bet you wish you would o' thought 'bout that one, huh?"

"Won't bring a good swift kick to your haid!" Dan laughed out of control. "There ain't one jackass in the whole county 'cept me which ain't got punkins!"

"You ain't got punkins?" Pearlie asked with concern.

"No, I ain't, Miss Pearlie," Dan smiled. "I used every inch o' ground for this here oat load, 'cause I'm needin' bad, same as you. An' my gamble is gonna pay off, sure."

"Then you's gonna be layin' out a sack or two for some punkins!" Calvin grinned. "You's our first taker!"

"Maybe so," Dan frowned. "But I'll be the only one."

Later, back on their own wagon, Calvin began to laugh.

"We're up an' drivin' a deal, sure!" he smiled. "Punkins is same as goal."

"We got our oats for the stock, but these is gonna have to fetch up salt an' the rest, sure," Pearlie said, showing her worry. "We should o' not poked in so much wheat."

"We had to!" Calvin yelped. "What if these punkins don't trade? We had to have wheat for flour, sure."

They worried every mile, with every step taken by the mules. They held their breath as they came around the last bend. The wagons of the other farmers would already be there, most of them anyway, and what they carried would be easily seen.

"Hogs," Pearlie said, her voice showing her tension as they came within view.

"An' wheat, an' thar's some oats, an'—" Calvin strained his voice.

"An' hens, an'—" Pearlie's voice wavered.

"An' taters, an' corn. Lordy, Pearlie, you s'pose?" Calvin's voice squeaked.

"An', more hogs. Hens, wheat. There ain't no gawddamned punkins!" Pearlie yelled, throwing her hat. "We's rich! By gawd, we's rich!"

"We is rich!" Calvin yelled and laughed.

AND THEN Dancing Tree cried, remembering. The tears poured down his cheeks.

"Oh, Pearlie."

Dancing Tree sobbed, alone in the night.

The next morning everyone sat by the fire, waiting for Rainbow's story.

"Right after Little Wolf left our camp we held a council," Rainbow said without lifting her bowed head. "It was decided that we, too, would be more safe if we journeyed into the mountains." Her voice broke. "We . . ." She began to cry again.

"Is there anyone who still lives?" Crazy Dog asked, putting his hand on her shoulder. "That is all we need to know right now."

"No," she cried. "There is no one."

"By the Holy Power!" Little Wolf muttered under his breath.

The same evening, while Rainbow slept, Crazy Dog called for a council.

"There is a canyon near here that is safe," Crazy Dog said in a dull voice. "I believe it would be better if we spent the winter in there."

"But wood is scarce within these canyons," Little Wolf broke in. "It will be difficult later on to warm our lodges."

"I know," Crazy Dog said. "But I think it would be best. We could begin collecting wood as soon as we put up our new camp."

"Could we collect enough?" Dancing Tree asked, turning to Little Wolf.

"Possibly," Little Wolf answered. "But I think we should take some time to think before we do something like that."

"It will be hard," Dreamer added. "We do not yet have enough food, and we need to tan more robes. Can we do everything all at once?"

"Crazy Dog has more eyes than any of us," Little Wolf said. "I think we should do it. And I think we can do it with much hard work."

"Then Dreamer, Rainbow, and I will move the camp while you two hunt," Crazy Dog said, finishing the decision. "We will be jumping at every sound if we stay here within this valley for the winter."

Soon after the first snow, Dancing Tree began work upon the coil of thin braided rope he would need for his winter traps.

"It looks as if we are going to eat well." Crazy Dog smiled as he sat down to help.

"Little Wolf thinks we will have enough wood," Dancing Tree replied. He did not look up from his work.

"Rainbow has finally told us what happened," Crazy Dog offered.

"I do not wish to know," Dancing Tree growled. "Not one stinking word."

"But you must," Little Wolf said as he joined them. "Because not talking about it will only hollow out your insides. Believe me, I know."

"Why should I listen!" Dancing Tree exploded. "I know the whole ugly story. Whitemen rode into the camp, laughing as they shot down women and children. They—"

"Stop it!" Little Wolf bellowed. "You are acting like a child. You do not have to be so defensive about the whitemen. Do you think we are fools? We have had murderers who were of the People too. You know that! It is all the same. There are those people who kill and there are those who seek peace."

"Those are the exact words of the peacemakers I met at the pony-fort lodge," Dancing Tree said, looking up at the face of Little Wolf. "Exactly the same. Word for word."

"Of course," Crazy Dog broke in. "And Rainbow's story will bear the truth of it. She said that when her camp was attacked some of the People rode with the whitemen."

"And they shot down the People without feeling," Little Wolf explained. "Because they were blind to themselves and to their hearts. You cannot murder unless you first smother your heart. These men who kill are all asleep. They walk within a nightmare and believe it to be reality."

"But is it not real that Pearlie and Thunder Chief are dead?" Dancing Tree asked, feeling sick.

"Yes," Crazy Dog answered. "But remember, my son, the killers create their reality as they walk around dead to the world. They kill principally in order to steal things. They kill to possess, yet what does it do for them?"

"It does nothing but continue their circle of murder," Little Wolf answered. "They kill to possess while they walk endlessly to their own deaths. They never awaken."

"Enough!" Dancing Tree said, holding his head in his hands. "I have heard enough!"

The snow flower is as light as a baby's breath, as real as a memory, more true than pure joy, and as delicate as the child's dream. This is the song taught to every mother who understands. Winter is the time when the streams of water become a path and the northern lights reach down to earth where creation dances among the sleeping. Our mother is preparing for spring!

"OUR WINTER will be much longer than that which visits the low places," Crazy Dog said as he set down an armload of wood. "In the traditional way, winter is called the Ancient Creator. The other name within this tradition is Stone Person."

"Why so many names?" Dancing Tree asked.

"There are more," Crazy Dog chuckled as he made himself comfortable by the fire. "There are seven names. Ring Breaker is another of the names, but the most important to learn first is the name which means Dance Hammer. Dance Hammer is translated from all the names and it means respect."

"This sounds very much like a riddle," Dancing Tree grinned.

"It is no riddle," Crazy Dog answered. "Allow me to place a song within your mind. The song will speak to you for many years. You may forget the song. That is to say, you may not be able to recall it, but it will always be with you. It will not remain as the original song, because it will grow, just like a tree or a flower. It will change as you change. Will you allow me to plant that seed within your mind and heart?"

"Will it do something to me?" Dancing Tree asked, feeling a little apprehensive.

"It is a way of our touching," Crazy Dog smiled. "It will be a name given to you, a name you will never hear. Will you trust me?"

"Forgive me, Crazy Dog," Dancing Tree said. "But somehow I feel there is more to what you are saying than I am able to understand. It makes me feel uneasy. Is this seed you speak of good in its spirit? What I mean is, is it all good?"

"Your feelings speak clearly to you," Crazy Dog smiled. "Very clearly. And my answer is this. All things are equally as good as they are bad. This song is neither all good nor all bad. Throw the seed upon earth that is without water and the seed will wither. Throw it upon good soil and it will grow. Within some people the seed will grow only into a twisted image. Others may grow the plant without ever recognizing what it is. Still others will grow the plant and even speak of it, only to have its power stolen from them. These people are familiar with the plant but are contemptuous of it. Others use the plant to heal or kill, depending upon the person. Some make a powerful bow from its body and others eat of its fruit. The song is simple. All seeds appear to be very small."

"Has that plant killed some of the people who grew it?" Dancing Tree asked.

"Dead," Crazy Dog answered. "Yes, dead. Some have used that plant against themselves. They saw the plant as something that could destroy them, and they warred with it. But to fight these things is to fight against a mirror. This seed will grow into a mirror and much more. Those who despise themselves are killed by what they grow. Those who learn of themselves and respect themselves receive the mirror power, a great gift. Some people have seen the holy tree or flower, and believe that they can capture that power. These people become entrapped in the power, and their own spirit is absorbed. These people become hollow shells."

"Is there no cure for those who are hollow?" Dancing Tree asked, showing his worry.

"Yes!" Crazy Dog laughed. "The cure is within their own decision! The holy flower or tree will nourish them if they will only seek to understand the power for themselves! No man or woman can represent the Power of the Universe. Can you imagine people who believed they could represent the power of Sweet Medicine? Represent the Creator? It is madness! No human can represent the Eternal!"

"I think I understand," Dancing Tree said.

"Would you do me a favor?" Crazy Dog asked, deliberately narrowing his eyes to draw suspicion.

"Of course," Dancing Tree answered warily.

"What did you understand?" Crazy Dog asked, frowning.

"I understood what you meant," Dancing Tree laughed. "Surely you believe that?"

"I also mentioned the Dance Hammer," Crazy Dog said. "How was that part of my explanation?"

"You were trying to convince me to not worry about receiving the song. Is that not right?" Dancing Tree asked, a little annoyed. "Come, admit it."

"Suppose that I was and suppose that I was not," Crazy Dog replied.

"We could ask riddles in this manner for days," Dancing Tree smiled. "Come, tell me what it is you are trying to show me."

"It is easy for you to suppose that I was trying to show you something," Crazy Dog said quietly. "But just suppose I was not. Wrestle with the question, not with your ready answer."

"All right, I will," Dancing Tree smiled. "But if you were not trying to convince me, then what were you doing?"

"That is not wrestling with your answer," Crazy Dog laughed. "It is confronting mine. But enough of that. Let us begin still another way. It is said by the chiefs that the wolf can observe how many other wolves are in its pack, but only the human can number them. Take away four from the family of the wolf, and the wolf will still perceive the pack as complete, a whole. But take away four from the human's family, and they will tell you that their family is not whole. Is this not so?"

"So the human can add and subtract," Dancing Tree laughed. "Is this your example, that the human has a mind that can understand abstractions, and that the animal does not?"

"What abstraction?" Crazy Dog asked. "Is the wolf abstracting or the human? Is it not true that the human's family is just as much whole as that of the wolf?"

"Of course not!" Dancing Tree whooped in laughter. "Some of your explanations are really amusing. The human knows if four are missing from his family. The wolf obviously does not."

"Is that so?" Crazy Dog asked soberly. "The wolf knows of trails that the human can only guess at. The wolf has no need to climb up a tree to see ahead of itself. Can a wolf become lost? Why is it the human can become lost?"

"Wolf pups can become lost from their mothers," Dancing Tree argued.

"Yes!" Crazy Dog said, brightening up. "But not adult wolves. In what way is the adult human different from the adult wolf?"

"The adult human can become lost from its own camp, obviously," Dancing Tree frowned. "But the human ranges over a greater distance than the wolf."

"You joke," Crazy Dog chuckled. "The human circle is much smaller than that of the wolf."

"The wolf is much more familiar with its surroundings," Dancing Tree continued to argue. "Its surroundings are all that it knows."

Crazy Dog folded his hands, not answering.

"You disagree," Dancing Tree sighed. "Right?"

"I can or cannot disagree," Crazy Dog answered. "We have taken the talk to the place where the trails crisscross into infinity. We will begin from still another way."

"I would very much like to run down another trail with you," Dancing Tree said. "But I have one question. I have been thinking about it ever since we first began our discussion."

"Ask your question," Crazy Dog answered. "However, before you do, let me remind you that I do not want you running down my trail. Seek out your own."

"Stop right there," Dancing Tree said, slapping his forehead. "Explain to me what you mean, and don't run in any more circles! My question can wait."

"Very well," Crazy Dog said. "It is like this. Person went to Great Hunter and asked Hunter to teach him to hunt bear," Crazy Dog explained. "Person was young."

" 'My first teaching,' Hunter told Person, 'is this. Respect yourself and respect the bear.'

" 'How can I respect the bear?' Person asked, puzzled. 'The bear is a brute. The bear is dirty and can be cruel.'

" 'Then begin by respecting the bear's strength,' Hunter explained. 'Is the bear not stronger than you? Can the bear not kill you?'

" 'I do fear the bear,' Person answered. 'I will respect the bear's strength.'

" 'There are many hundreds of paths that lead to the valley,' Hunter told Person. 'Go to the valley and find the bear, but stay downwind or the bear will see you. Do you want to fight the bear?'

" 'No!' Person answered.

" 'Stay hidden from the bear. Do not let the bear see you. When the wind changes and carries your scent to the bear, run! Run until you are hidden from the bear again. I want you to watch everything the bear does for seven days.'

" 'With no weapons?' Person asked in surprise and fear.

" 'You do not know how to use weapons,' Hunter said. 'They would only make you clumsy. Do you want to fight the bear?'

" 'No!' Person answered, afraid.

" 'Well?' Hunter asked.

" 'I will trust you,' Person said to Hunter. 'I will go!'

" 'You have seen the first path,' Hunter told Person. 'It is decision. Trusting in yourself was the second path. Go to the valley.'

"Person went to the valley and found the bear. Person watched every move the bear made. Soon Person began to know many habits of the bear. When the wind changed, Person ran! Person ran and hid again and watched the bear. Soon Person began to recognize the bear. Seven days later, Person chose a path back to Hunter.

" 'Here is your knife,' Hunter told Person. 'Make yourself a bow and forty-four arrows and two lances and one shield.'

" 'Where can I get the materials for the arrows?' Person asked Hunter.

" 'The hollow reeds in that lake over there can be made into arrows,' Hunter answered.

" 'Will you show me how to make one arrow?' Person asked.

" 'I will demonstrate how to make four arrows,' Hunter answered.

" 'How can I make the lance?' Person asked Hunter.

" 'I will show you the trees,' Hunter answered. 'Choose your own tree and carve your lance shaft. I will demonstrate how to balance one lance shaft. I will chip four arrow points and one lance point. Watch me.'

" 'How shall I find the right feathers for the arrows?' Person asked.

" 'There are many birds,' Hunter answered. 'Hunt them and experiment until you find the correct feathers. Never waste the meat from the birds.'

" 'How can I hunt the birds?' Person asked Hunter. 'I have no bow and no arrows.'

" 'Borrow my bow and arrows,' Hunter answered.

" 'But I do not know how to use a bow,' Person said.

" 'Shoot seven hundred arrows into that one knot on that tree,' Hunter answered.

" 'But I cannot pull your bow!' Person said in alarm.

" 'Pull my bow until you can shoot seven hundred arrows into the knot on that tree,' Hunter answered.

" 'And the shield?' Person asked. 'How can I make and paint my shield?'

" 'Wait until you have hunted the bear,' Hunter answered. 'Then make your shield and paint it.'

"Person worked for forty-four days. Then Hunter came to Person.

" 'Go into the forest for me,' Hunter told Person. 'Be my eyes and ears. Find seven bears for me, and come back and tell me where they are.'

"And Person did. Person found seven bears and came back and told Hunter.

"Four days later Hunter came again.

" 'Find seven elk for me,' Hunter told Person. 'Then come back and tell me where they are.'

"Every four days, Hunter would come again asking for Person to find seven different animals. Each time Person had to tell Hunter where to find them. This was done forty-four times.

" 'I have no time to work upon my weapons,' Person told Hunter.

" 'Go back into the valley and find the bear,' Hunter told Person. 'Watch the bear for four days and return to me.'

"Person ran to the valley, but the bear was not there.

" 'The bear is gone from the valley,' Person told Hunter when Person had returned.

" 'Go out and find the bear,' Hunter told Person. 'Come back here and tell me where the bear is.'

"Person did as instructed and sought out the bear. Four days later Person found the bear and came back and told Hunter.

" 'The bear is in the canyon,' Person told Hunter.

" 'Work upon your bow, arrows, and lances for four days. Then watch the bear for four days,' Hunter told Person.

"And Person did. After that time, Person had made a bow, forty-four arrows, and two lances.

" 'Go to the canyon,' Hunter told Person. 'Carry my bow and your bow. Carry all of my arrows and all of yours. Carry my lances and all of yours. Watch the bear for four days and return here to me.'

"But Person could not carry all the things Hunter had told Person, and Person returned sad.

" 'Do not be sad,' Hunter told Person. 'Take your own bow, your own arrows, and your own lances. Go and kill the bear.'

"Person returned again, this time even more sad.

" 'I do not know how to kill the bear,' Person told Hunter. 'How do you kill the bear?'

" 'Hunt with me for twelve moons,' Hunter told Person.

"And Person went with Hunter, but Hunter never once hunted bear. Twelve moons later Hunter spoke to Person.

" 'We have hunted forty-four different beings together,' Hunter told Person. 'Now go and hunt the bear.'

"Person returned to Hunter, but Person still had not killed the bear.

" 'At one time I was terrified of the bear,' Person told Hunter. 'The bear was my greatest enemy. Now the bear is like a baby. The bear has no chance with me. The bear has taught me too much for me to kill it. Why should I kill that bear? When I visit the bear now, I do not have to fear the changing wind. The bear knows that I will not harm it. I can now sit within seven steps of the bear. The bear has become so used to me, the bear thinks that I am a tree, leaf, stone, or bird. The bear has met a human being, and I am no different to the bear than the grass, the bees, the skunk, or the fox. How can I strike down the bear?'

" 'Paint your first sign upon your shield,' Hunter told Person.

" 'I am a hunter,' Person told Hunter.

" 'You do not know what you are,' Hunter told Person. 'You are a child who has learned to walk. What is a hunter? Leave me for forty-four years, then return here to me.'

" 'Why return if I know?' Person asked Hunter.

" 'So you can see and know who I am,' Hunter told Person.

" 'But I can see who you are,' Person told Hunter.

" 'What do you see?' Hunter asked Person.

" 'I see my teacher,' Person answered.

"Hunter began to undress.

" 'You are a woman!' Person said in surprise.

" 'I am the earth,' Hunter answered. 'But what is the earth? Go, my child, go into the world and learn who I am.'

" 'I am afraid,' Person told Hunter. 'Can I remain here with you?'

" 'If you stay here, you will never be anything but a child,' Hunter said.

" 'I want to discover who I am,' Person said.

" 'Decision is your trail from here to the valley where you will find yourself,' Hunter told Person. 'Go there upon your Vision Quest. It is from that place you will see many paths that lead into your world.'

"And then she disappeared in front of Person's eyes."

Dancing Tree sat silently, thinking hard.

"Now," said Crazy Dog to Dancing Tree, "what is your question?"

"My question?" Dancing Tree laughed. "My question divided into a thousand different paths!"

Crazy Dog's talk now turned to preparing Dancing Tree for the sweat lodge.

"Many people, many hundreds of thousands of people, even millions of people, have been brought together because they believed that some single person represented the Eternal," Crazy Dog said as he stirred the fire. "They come together! That is true, but this also is all. They are brought together and then organized. It always happens that way. The organizing briefly brings about good things, but then it brings terror. Always it fails, for two important reasons.

"The first reason is that no man or woman upon this earth can represent the Living Spirit of the Eternal. The second is that all of these kinds of organized myth-beliefs mirror only the founder, and then later the people who are its chiefs, its priests. It prevents individuals from ever seeing themselves. It crushes their true spirit. These things have occurred with people everywhere for thousands of years. But it is not the way of the People. When the People come together in a common good they always realize a healing. The coming together has nothing whatsoever to do with powers or represented powers. It is the coming together that is the healer. Religious beliefs are often used as foundations for horror, terror and war. They are not the same as the foundations the Sacred Mountains rest upon."

"That was my question," Dancing Tree laughed.

"Now for the other path," Crazy Dog smiled.

"What path do you mean?" Dancing Tree asked.

"The teaching of winter," Crazy Dog answered. "The teaching of the Dance Hammer."

"I have never seen anyone in my life who hangs on like you do," Dancing Tree said. "Once you take a bite, you won't let go."

"People hang onto ignorance with far more resolution than they do to anything else in life," Crazy Dog chuckled.

"All you are doing is irritating me," Dancing Tree said, almost to the point of anger. "Is this a way to teach?"

"How else can I keep you awake?" Crazy Dog asked. "You insist upon remaining aloof. You play with knowledge as if it were your genitals."

"Is not my patience enough?" Dancing Tree asked sarcastically.

"Your patience?" Crazy Dog laughed. "What kind of trail is that? Why should you be so patient? Am I a slave? Is it my duty to entertain you? Why do you sit with me? You can go out into the snow and entertain yourself, you know. Am I supposed to entertain you? Why should it be me who is entertaining? Why not you? Why are you not teaching me? I greatly desire to learn more. Come teach me! I promise I will sit patiently until you have tired of forcing your knowledge upon me."

"I am sorry," Dancing Tree said in earnest. "Truly I am. Please sit with me."

"You can teach me, you know," Crazy Dog said seriously. "You can reach down into your wonderful medicine bundle and teach me."

"I am not ready to teach," Dancing Tree answered. "I want to listen."

"Teach and you can listen," Crazy Dog smiled.

"Not now," Dancing Tree said.

"Tomorrow we will talk again," Crazy Dog said, getting to his feet. "Come, let us roast a nice juicy rabbit."

The following day Dancing Tree took his first winter sweat bath.

He loved the steam and the singing, but when it came time to jump into the icy stream he balked.

"Jump into the stream?" Dancing Tree exclaimed in surprise. "We're going to jump into that icy water? It will kill me!"

"It will not," Rainbow laughed. "It will feel wonderful. Come, take my hand and jump with me."

"Are you certain?" Dancing Tree said nervously. "Are you certain it won't make me sick?"

"Just the opposite," Little Wolf laughed. "It will make you well."

"Everything seems to be backwards!" Dancing Tree laughed. "Everything! Are you sure?"

"Jump in or we will throw you in," Crazy Dog spoke from the darkness.

"Then let's go!" Dancing Tree whooped and threw back the flap of the sweat lodge.

Later, after Dancing Tree and Rainbow had dried themselves and were back in the lodge, Dancing Tree began to sing.

"That swim has certainly purified Dancing Tree," Little Wolf said as he entered the lodge. "And changed him too. Now he is a bird, or at least he sings like one."

Dancing Tree stopped singing and cocked his head to one side. "Is there a magpie in here?" he asked Rainbow. "Something is chattering like one."

"Didn't that bath help you?" Little Wolf laughed. "I thought it would." He sniffed around Dancing Tree. "No, it did not." He sighed. "Your odor is still that of an old buffalo!"

"Such an insult calls for war!" Dancing Tree yelled, running out into the snow. He grabbed up a handful and threw it into the lodge at Little Wolf.

"Warrrr!" Little Wolf yelled, running from the lodge and scooping up handfuls of snow.

"Wait!" Crazy Dog suddenly yelled. "Something is wrong."

Everyone stood still and listened. Then they heard it, a faint sound carried to them on the wind.

"A thunder iron speaks," Crazy Dog said. "Down the valley. Be quick!"

The women quickly began to gather together enough supplies to keep them alive if they should need to escape. Little Wolf and Dancing Tree threw on warm robes, slipped their feet into snow shoes and snatched up their rifles.

"I will ready the horses and leave them for the women to guard," Crazy Dog yelled as he ducked through the lodge door. He stopped just outside the door and turned back to hold both Little Wolf's and Dancing Tree's hands. "I will wait at the fallen tree," he said, "just as we planned. If you should become entangled in a war, I will signal the women and join you. Peace be with you."

"And to you," Dancing Tree said as he ran from the lodge.

The snow was deep, and the country studded with boulders, but none of it was unfamiliar to Little Wolf and Dancing Tree. They quickly reached the mouth of the valley.

"Can you see anything?" Little Wolf gasped as he sat down, breathless.

"Nothing," Dancing Tree puffed from where he lay. "I can see a thousand steps into the valley, and there is no one. Nothing."

"It is certain that the thunder iron sound came from this direction," Little Wolf said, leaning his back against a rock. "We must catch our breath before we go any further."

"Wait," Dancing Tree hissed between lungfulls of air. "I see something."

"Where?" Little Wolf asked, crawling up beside Dancing Tree.

"There, see those specks at the far end of that small draw," Dancing Tree said, pointing.

"I see them," Little Wolf answered. "I will go along the left side of this ravine." He pointed. "And you take the right. We can support each other in this way. If it is an enemy, we will have him between us."

The two men moved cautiously along until they could see that the dark spots in the snow were the bodies of a woman and three children. They appeared to be dead.

"I will go first. You cover me," Little Wolf said.

Little Wolf dashed behind his cover and ran in a zigzag pattern until he was halfway to the bodies. Then he skidded upon his stomach in the snow and waited awhile before jumping to his feet again and running to the nearest boulder, flattening his back against it.

Slowly, carefully, Little Wolf moved to see beyond the boulder. Then he walked abruptly out into the open and waved Dancing Tree forward.

"Over here," Little Wolf said. He crouched by a man who was sitting with his back to another rock.

"He is alive," Dancing Tree exclaimed.

"Yes, but gut shot," Little Wolf said, examining the man's wound.

The man opened his eyes and looked at them.

"Can you speak?" Little Wolf asked.

"Like me, you are of the People," the man groaned. "But you are too late."

"There is no help for you," Little Wolf said softly. "I am sorry. How did this happen?"

"I killed my family," the man said and coughed. "We were starving to death little by little. They were dying. There was no other way. I am very tired. I broke my leg this morning, bad fall."

"Does it pain you much to speak?" Dancing Tree asked, feeling sick.

"Much," the man answered. "But soon I will no longer suffer."

"We would have helped you if we had known you were here," Little Wolf said and looked down.

"It is ironic," the man grimaced. "Bitterly so. You were camped so close by. Please, my brother, will you use your ax on my head?"

"My ax?" Dancing Tree blurted in horror.

Little Wolf stood up quickly and grabbed his own ax from his side.

"Close your eyes, my brother," Little Wolf said. Tears streamed down his cheeks.

"No!" Dancing Tree screamed as Little Wolf struck.

"It had to be done," Little Wolf said, shaking. "He was in pain!"

"Savage!" Dancing Tree yelled and retched.

Back at the camp Dancing Tree would not speak. He sat apart from the others and brooded.

Crazy Dog walked to Dancing Tree and sat on his haunches across from him.

"I do not want to speak of it," Dancing Tree said angrily.

"The words burn in my mouth," Crazy Dog said evenly. "Words that I want to scream at you, you who call us savage! You had a thunder iron in your hands, a thunder iron that would have blown off a man's head, a weapon no different from Little Wolf's ax."

"It is different!" Dancing Tree scowled. "There is a right way and a wrong way to kill!"

Crazy Dog was crying.

"You would readily shoot down an enemy who was trying to kill you. But when you must kill a friend in mercy, you say that this is wrong?" Crazy Dog asked.

"He was alive!" Dancing Tree spat out the words. "Alive! There is always a chance!"

"Would you think that if a healthy man were running toward you, trying to kill you?" Crazy Dog asked. "Think! Do not be a child! There was no chance for that man. He was in agony so severe it almost makes me bleed even to think of it! Do you think that Little Wolf took pleasure in striking with his ax? Do you believe that Little Wolf could be so cruel? He was merciful! You must stop believing such dreams. Your whole being is sickened by these dreams! If I were begging you to end my misery and I had no chance to live, would you let me suffer needlessly to the bitter end? Why? Do you have some strange belief that people should be punished, that they should suffer?"

"Little Wolf will burn in fire when he dies!" Dancing Tree said, blowing up. "The Creator will punish him for that horrible act. He does not have the right to take human life!"

"Have you gone mad?" Crazy Dog asked, perplexed. "You would have shot that man dead if he had fired upon you, yet you say that Little Wolf will burn in fire when he dies? What fire? Whose fire? How can you burn in fire after you have died? The spirit cannot be burned! Who told you such a thing? Where did you receive such a horrible teaching?"

"My good mother gave me that teaching," Dancing Tree answered in his most sarcastic voice. "My mother. Will you now say to me that my mother was a liar?"

"No, I will not," Crazy Dog said, standing up. "What did your mother tell you?"

"She said . . ." he started slowly, then stopped as Crazy Dog interrupted him.

"What?" Crazy Dog asked in a curt voice.

"Nothing!" Dancing Tree said, jumping to his feet. "Nothing at all! Please take your body and move it from me!"

"Fire?" Crazy Dog said, sitting back down again. "Strange. Why would anyone teach such a thing?"

"I can still hear you!" Dancing Tree said from where he stood.

"Of course you can," Crazy Dog said, scratching his head. "If I were a mother, why would I teach such a thing? I would love my son. Why would I say such a thing?"

"Listen to me. I do not wish to hear this." Dancing Tree fumed. "Take your game someplace else!"

"Burn in fire after death?" Crazy Dog asked, wrinkling his brow. "Amazing!"

"You believe you are wise, don't you?" Dancing Tree finally said, sitting back down. "Well, smart owl, there is a great deal you have not learned."

Crazy Dog waited.

"Did you know that the Evil One and all people who have done wrong will be punished by the Holy Power?" Dancing Tree asked in a mocking tone. "That there is a place prepared by the Holy One for all those people who do not keep his laws? And that those bad people will burn forever and ever? Did you know that?"

"No," Crazy Dog answered. "No, I did not. Why will this be?"

"How should I know why?" Dancing Tree yelled. "Am I the Holy Power?"

"But how do you know?" Crazy Dog asked with interest.

"From the *book!*" Dancing Tree laughed mockingly. "You are surprised, are you not? You did not know that there were such things as *books*, did you?"

"What does the word mean?" Crazy Dog asked. *"Book,"* he frowned. "It is a strange sounding word."

"A book is made from trees," Dancing Tree explained, curling his lip. "Leaves are made from the trees, and they are scratched upon in symbols that mean words. You can read those symbols into words. The words of this book tell that everyone is going to burn in fire after they die!"

"Everyone?" Crazy Dog said in surprise. "I thought—"

"You thought!" Dancing Tree growled. "You thought. Not everybody, just the bad ones!"

"When did the Holy Power make that book?" Crazy Dog asked.

"The Holy Power did not make the book!" Dancing Tree said angrily. "People made the book. The Holy Power told them what to scratch in symbol words, and they did!"

"Who are they, and how did the Power tell them?" Crazy Dog asked.

"You amaze me!" Dancing Tree said. "The people who did the sign scratching were told by the Power in a vision!"

"Was the Power mad that day?" Crazy Dog asked.

"The Power wasn't mad," Dancing Tree laughed, shaking his head. "Crazy Dog, you are but a child."

"I am indeed!" Crazy Dog smiled. "Now tell me when this happened."

"Hundreds and hundreds of winters ago," Dancing Tree said, now very calmly. "It is very ancient, and it is true."

"Has that Power made one of those books lately?" Crazy Dog asked.

"Lately!" Dancing Tree bellowed with laughter.

"Why is that so funny?" Crazy Dog asked. "If the Power could do it once, why couldn't that Power do it again? Is that Power dead?"

"Of course not!" Dancing Tree roared with laughter.

"I think that Power is dead," Crazy Dog said sternly. "Hundreds of winters dead. That Power died when its vision seekers died."

"No. That is not true," Dancing Tree said, angry again. "The book is a history of what the Power had to say. How do you answer this?"

"I say that many hundreds, perhaps thousands of visionaries have died saying pretty much the same things. But it was always humans who said those things, Dancing Tree, not the Holy Power. The Holy Power would never be so simple with creation. The Holy Eternal Power could never do what they said. Could you burn Rainbow or me to death because we broke a law?"

"You are being just a bit silly," Dancing Tree replied with a grin. "Are you not? I would walk very lightly when I say what you are saying."

"I could not burn Rainbow because I would have compassion. The Holy Power of the Universe is all compassion! The Power of the Universe is a hundred times more compassionate than you or I, we who were created by it."

Dancing Tree fumed and searched for more words.

Crazy Dog continued before he could speak. "Anger, hatred, cruelty, fear—these are all powers created by humans. They are not Powers of the Universe. The Power of the Universe is above such petty things. As I told you before," Crazy Dog said with kindness, "there have been many of these human powers created, thousands upon thousands. They are always equally good and bad, foolish and wise. They teach of love and terror, hatred and mercy, and everything else in between. They teach all these things because all these things are human.

"The Eternal Power of the Universe is none of those things. Is the Power of the Universe so backward? Does it depend upon a book that is hundreds of winters old, when that same Power brings each new spring? Come, Dancing Tree, wake yourself! You need no book to know the Power of the Universe! You have a mind, a heart, a body, and a spirit. These are the beginnings from which to learn of your Creator. Now, concerning your brother, Little Wolf. Think: were his actions humane or cruel?"

"His act was humane," Dancing Tree answered slowly. "It took strength for him to do what he did."

"Little Wolf is sick with a broken heart," Crazy Dog said. "He needs your love and understanding."

"Thank you, Crazy Dog," Dancing Tree said. "It is I who have been uncivilized."

"Do not judge yourself," Crazy Dog said. "You hardly know yourself."

Later that same evening Dancing Tree and Little Wolf went together to the tiny stream to find their uncle.

"What have you been doing?" Dancing Tree asked when they found Crazy Dog.

"Fishing," Crazy Dog smiled. "Look, I have caught twelve of the rainbow fish!"

"Beautiful," Little Wolf grinned as he picked up one of the fish. "Tomorrow I will show my brother how to cure them with smoke. Then we can eat them bones and all," he chuckled.

"I brought you your pipe," Dancing Tree said. He sat down on a buffalo robe he had carried with him.

"I want to hear the song too," Little Wolf said, spreading down an elk robe to sit upon.

"So, Dancing Tree has told you of the song," Crazy Dog laughed. "Are you sure you want to hear it? You have to be very certain."

"I am sure, very sure," Little Wolf said.

"I too want to have the song," Dancing Tree smiled.

"Then put your left hands upon your forehead and your right hands upon your heart," Crazy Dog commanded.

Both Dancing Tree and Little Wolf complied.

"The song is a tiny seed," Crazy Dog said. "Take it carefully from me."

"I am ready," Dancing Tree said.

"And I," Little Wolf said.

"How many more of you are there?" Crazy Dog asked.

Both men sat there waiting.

"And?" Little Wolf asked.

"That is the tiny seed," Crazy Dog smiled.

"That is all?" Little Wolf asked. "Why did you have us touch our forehead and heart?"

"As a gesture of trust for me, and friendships towards yourself," Crazy Dog answered.

"I will think about this," Dancing Tree said. "But, like my brother Little Wolf, I expected more."

"Seeds are never large," Crazy Dog grinned as he filled his pipe.

"Have you ever heard a song of the willow?" Little Wolf asked Dancing Tree.

"No, I have not. What does that mean?" Dancing Tree asked.

"They are songs that are sung in the winter," Crazy Dog explained. "Winter is the time of preparation for the Renewal of the Arrows."

"But the Sun Dance does not begin until the sun visits the north!" Dancing Tree said. "Is that not the time for the Renewal?"

"The Arrows have four robes," Crazy Dog explained. "Autumn is the first robe. When this robe is removed the song is heard. The second is the winter robe. This is the teaching time. The third is the bringing-about-the-changing-hoop in the spring. It is at that time we sing the community song. The fourth robe is the golden robe of the sun. The summer is the time of dying and conceiving. The autumn is the time of going to sleep to waken, and the winter is the maturing in the womb of the dream. Within the spring all things are reborn."

"And the willow?" Dancing Tree asked.

"Little girls, with the help of little boys, make willow reed baskets." Crazy Dog smiled. "But what of these baskets? If I suddenly pour water into one of these painted baskets, the water will only pour through. The willow reeds are dry. But if the baskets are soaked in water, the willow reeds become pregnant with the water, swelling together. The baskets can now hold the water.

"The grandmothers and grandfathers go to the places where the willow reeds live, and they make medicine and sing. The women and men who are neither old nor young gather the reeds. After the children make the baskets, they paint them. The paint is given by everyone, and the children are taught how to seek their own personal designs. Here is a basket song.

" 'I am a stone beneath the wheel of stars. No matter where I stand, I am looking up. I am a feather upon the wind that sings the song of the voiceless. I am the breath that calls forth the thunder and lightning. I run along the ground like shadows playing with the tumbleweeds, scattering the seeds. I flutter magically, like the eyes of children watching a flower. Who am I?' "

"Am I supposed to answer?" Dancing Tree asked.

"You are to say what you will," Crazy Dog answered. "Now I will sing another song inside the song."

"The little child lived by an ancient lake and was both happy and afraid. 'What bow shall I choose?' the child asked. 'What bow?' "

"The black bow!" Little Wolf laughed. "I pick the black bow!"

"The black bow is the bow that is the most powerful when the sun is in the middle of the sky," Crazy Dog said.

"I will shoot my arrow first at the joyful things I have learned; then my second arrow toward the sorrowful things!" Little Wolf smiled.

"The child shot the arrow at happy first," Crazy Dog said. "And the arrow changed his reflection in the mirror lake. The child shot his second arrow and saw a bear and an eagle."

"I will choose the next bow," Rainbow laughed as she sat down beside Dancing Tree.

"What bow was already picked?" Dreamer asked as she sat down beside Little Wolf.

"The black bow," Little Wolf answered, hugging her.

"The child saw an eagle and a bear," Crazy Dog said to Rainbow.

"An eagle and a bear," she repeated, frowning as she thought. "Then I choose the bright sun bow!" she laughed.

"Can you answer?" Crazy Dog asked Little Wolf.

"The sun bow cannot be pulled by the child," Little Wolf explained. "So I will make it into a moon bow. The night helps the child pull the bow. The child shoots her first arrow at the eagle."

"The eagle becomes a reflection of fire in the mirror," Dreamer joined in.

"I am Winter Man," Crazy Dog said in his deepest voice. "I will bring my powers against you because now I can see you. You cannot hide! Fire eagle will light up your eyes, and no matter where you run in the night I will find you!"

"My!" Rainbow exclaimed. "That is a problem, let me see." She wrinkled her nose, thinking. "I will not shoot my second arrow! I will give the arrow to the bear."

"And the bear shouted in a great breath for the wind to come," Crazy Dog said, "and the wind moved the water. Now the child's eyes were reflected a million times over in the great mirror, and Winter Man could not find the child. Winter Man begged for mercy. 'Please do not harm me,' Winter Man called to the child. 'Now I can see you clearly,' the child said to Winter Man. 'You are only a child just like me.' And winter became a child and began to play in learning."

"I next choose the red bow," Dancing Tree chuckled, joining in.

"The red bow!" everybody exclaimed all together, putting their hands over their eyes.

"What's the matter?" Dancing Tree asked nervously. "Am I not supposed to pick the red bow? Have I said the wrong thing?"

"Earthquakes and flames roared from the depths of the earth!" Crazy Dog bellowed and roared. "The ground trembled and great

stones fell from the mountains! The stars blazed and the moon shone crimson! Explosions shook the lodges. The mirror broke into foam and surged against its place, and great luminous clouds churned in the sky!"

"Quick, shoot an arrow!" Rainbow cried.

"Ah! Ah!" Dancing Tree stammered. "Ah, I will shoot my first arrow, ah, where?" he exclaimed.

"Where?" Crazy Dog bellowed and roared at Dancing Tree.

"At the earth?" Dancing Tree said meekly.

"And a flower grew," Crazy Dog said in his most musical voice. "And the sun came out, and the birds began to sing. It was very beautiful! 'Where is the child?' a gentle woman asked. Her hair was as green as the grass."

"In a hailstone that had fallen from the sky," Little Wolf answered.

"What if the sun should melt me?" Crazy Dog asked in his highest voice, sounding like a child.

"Quick, Dancing Tree," Rainbow laughed. "Offer the second arrow to the beautiful young woman."

"Here is my second arrow." Dancing Tree smiled as he playfully handed Rainbow an imaginary arrow.

"And now the child stood in the place of ice and snow," Crazy Dog said, sounding like the cold wind. "In the child's hand was the great white bow."

"It is painful," Dreamer shivered. "But I choose to take both arrows to the woman of the north as a gift to her."

"And the child did," Crazy Dog said, pretending he was walking against a severe winter wind. "And suddenly the child saw the great lodge of ice crystals! Two twins stood at the door of the lodge, roaring 'Kill! Live!'

" 'I have come to see the woman of the north!' the child said to the twins.

" 'Starvation! Gluttony!' the twins growled.

" 'Sing! Cry!' the child answered.

" 'Fight! Love!' the twins roared even louder.

" 'Cold! Warm!' the child answered.

" 'Enter! Stay out!' the twins thundered.

" 'Power! Weakness!' the child answered.

"And suddenly the child stood in front of the People. He carried a design upon one of his willow baskets."

"Is it always the same?" Dancing Tree asked.

"What do you mean?" Little Wolf asked, puzzled.

Dancing Tree grinned. "You know, are the answers and questions always the same?"

"Are the trees not different from the mountains?" Crazy Dog asked. "And yet is it not true that the mountains and the trees are one? And are the stones not different from each other? But yet the same? And how many faces does the lake have? Are there any two clouds exactly the same in their shape? No, they are always different, and yet they are always the same."

"You ask strange questions," Little Wolf said to Dancing Tree. "Why did you ask that?"

"His questions are not strange," Crazy Dog explained gently to Little Wolf. "Our brother has come here upon great wings from another place. He has much to give, and he has great strength. Children in our own camps ask the same questions. Dancing Tree is no different. It is hard for him because he has two circles to fit together, one from where he flew from his nest and the one that now spins around him. When he speaks we all learn. Then when we speak together we all learn again. Is this not a good way to prepare ourselves for the Arrow Renewal?"

"It is!" Dreamer laughed. "Can we hear the second song inside the song, Crazy Dog?"

"The wind is beginning to blow and drift the snow," Crazy Dog said, getting to his feet. "Because I am older, I feel the cold more than you. I will continue when we are inside a warm lodge. A bite to eat would also be welcome."

Crazy Dog continued the story painting after they had eaten.

"What if the child had flown into the valley but had found no food?" he asked.

"Are there trees?" Little Wolf asked.

"There are many trees," Crazy Dog answered.

"Then I would become a porcupine," Dreamer said.

"But then I would be hunted for food myself," Rainbow smiled, looking at Dancing Tree.

"Ah," Dancing Tree said, trying to think. He hesitated. "But the wood I eat is also, ah, you know, is it not the same with what I hunt to eat?"

"The story has become a skeleton which needs its flesh to become complete," Crazy Dog said, smiling at Dancing Tree.

"Let me observe this teaching," Dancing Tree said to Crazy Dog. "I have no idea what is happening."

"We continue the story of how the porcupine learns," Rainbow explained to Dancing Tree. "We always begin these stories with a baby.

In this case, a baby porcupine. Crazy Dog is our story mirror. We must try to understand what he is saying at the same time that we try to learn along with the porcupine. Do you understand?"

"Just let me watch and listen," Dancing Tree smiled. "It is too much for me. I am dizzy with it."

"It is a training of mind," Little Wolf explained. "Crazy Dog is supposed to trick us, thwart us, tease us, and much more. But he can only do these things within the discipline of symbols. We, on the other hand, can do as we please as long as the story does not become a game. It is very difficult to keep the story from becoming a game. We create a world, and then we take that world to its most intelligent end."

"Not tonight," Dancing Tree said, getting up and stretching. "I think I will go watch the moon rise."

"What is the matter with you?" Little Wolf asked with disappointment. "It is no contest! It can be a joy! Come, do not leave us."

"I think it is a silly game," Dancing Tree growled. "I do not wish to play."

Dancing Tree grabbed his robe and left the lodge.

"Do not be disappointed," Crazy Dog said to Little Wolf. "Put yourself in his place. You might have walked out even before now. He is not trying to destroy anything; his actions are very understandable. He is frustrated. To sit here longer would only be to punish himself. He has spoken out with honesty, whether he realizes it or not. Go watch the moon with him. He stands in a very lonely place, a place I have stood in many times."

Little Wolf found Dancing Tree lounging upon a buffalo robe Rainbow had taken to him while Crazy Dog had been explaining. Little Wolf sat down with him, back to back.

"You are difficult, but you make a wonderful back rest." Little Wolf laughed good-humoredly.

"When Rainbow brought out my robe she said that the Dance Of The Four Bows is a teaching for children," Dancing Tree sighed.

"I know," Little Wolf answered. "It is strange though." He paused. "It is a teaching for children, and I enjoyed hearing it again. But you know, Dancing Tree"—he turned around so that he could see his brother—"all of us first heard it many years ago. I think everybody was remembering." He looked down at his hands.

"Remembering how much fun it was?" Dancing Tree grinned. "I know what you mean. I had those same wonderful times when I was a child."

"Some of those winters were wonderful!" Little Wolf smiled. Then he frowned. "But you know, I never knew until right now, tonight, just how powerful those teachings are. I see now that they were not children's games at all!"

Little Wolf began to fill his pipe.

Dancing Tree waited, not answering.

"My head was reeling with the meanings of the teaching," Little Wolf said as he puffed. He handed Dancing Tree the pipe.

"I never understood that, not when I first heard those stories," Little Wolf went on. "I shrieked and laughed with the other children, saying almost anything that came into my mind. Those Medicine Men and Women must have been very patient," he laughed. "My head was as thick as a stone. It is a wonder I learned anything!"

"Did all the adults teach in that way?" Dancing Tree asked.

"Some mothers and fathers did," Little Wolf answered. "But mostly it was the Medicine People. Everybody participated though, and everybody enjoyed it. The contraries used to act out the teachings, and those funny, happy people used to bring everybody into their act."

"What do you mean?" Dancing Tree smiled. "Tell me of it."

"They used to dress up and paint themselves," Little Wolf laughed. "They were unbelievably funny! Sometimes they pretended to be the twelve dwarves." He laughed, remembering. "Here comes Crazy Dog, ask him of those contraries. He can tell you much more about them than I can. He is one of them."

"You were a clown?" Dancing Tree teased as Crazy Dog joined them.

"I *am* a clown," Crazy Dog smiled as he sat down.

"I can remember when you were one of the twelve dwarves!" Little Wolf laughed. "Remember how my mother yelled and kicked when you and the other contraries carried her off?"

"What was it all about?" Dancing Tree smiled. "It sounds as if it were great fun!"

"It is. It is a means of teaching the People. Many of the People are not able to learn any other way than seeing the teachings acted out. It enriches everybody! The story you have just heard about the bow is one that was acted out."

"But what are the twelve dwarves?" Dancing Tree asked.

"They mean many things," Crazy Dog answered. "They represent first the full cycle of the seasons. Three are representative of each of the four seasons," he chuckled. "But that is only the beginning. They are also earth, fire, air, and water. There are three elements to each of these forces. These twelve forces are mirrored to the right, just as the rainbow separates the light from the sun into its many colors. There are also twelve dwarf women. They are equal in all ways to the twelve male dwarves, but they mirror the light to the left. The ancient Medicine People who brought us our teachings said that all things in time and space are mirrored this way. Your left hand is exactly like your right, is it not?"

"It is," Dancing Tree said.

"Lay them on top of each other," Crazy Dog instructed.

"A thumb on each side," Crazy Dog said after Dancing Tree had put his hands together. "They appear to be the same and they are the same, but they are different," Crazy Dog chuckled. "Good, bad, up, down, in, out, right, left, power, weakness, full, empty, male, female, light, dark. One could go on forever!"

"Please do not lose your patience with me," Dancing Tree said. "But what good does it do to know of those things?"

"Do you know of the embryo?" Crazy Dog asked.

"Much," Dancing Tree smiled. "Little Wolf has taught me well. Over the years I have observed."

"You have hunted a great many animals," Crazy Dog explained. "And you have seen the embryo in its many stages. At first the embryo is only a speck, but within that speck are the twelve mirrors. These mirrors of building determine what that animal will be. The speck grows and changes until finally it can be recognized. With the recognition there is birth!"

"I see," Dancing Tree frowned.

"You have been taught many things," Crazy Dog went on. "Little Wolf has brought much to your attention. You have seen all of the organs of the animal, and you have learned of their functions. This I know Little Wolf has taught you, because it is the way of the hunter."

"It is true," Dancing Tree smiled. "But these things I can understand. The way of the other teaching is difficult for me."

"It is not," Crazy Dog said sternly. "You must learn to expand the examples you have learned into other forms. The Medicine Wheel is no mystery. You have seen what the animals eat, and you have seen how the food is changed and absorbed by the animals. Do you think it would be different with the food of knowledge?"

"I have not argued that," Dancing Tree said.

"You *have* argued that," Crazy Dog smiled. "Are all flowers the same? The animal eats the flower when it is only a tiny shoot, but the animal also eats the matured flower and its seeds. It is one flower but is it not different? Too many times you learn of the flower, but refuse to recognize what that flower can be within its many forms. Is this not true?"

"I suppose so," Dancing Tree said. "But why do I do that?"

"That is the point." Crazy Dog laughed. "That is what you must consider. Why do you do that? I am asking you."

Dancing Tree frowned. "I have no idea. Am I perhaps slower than you?"

"There is no race, as I have told you many times," Crazy Dog laughed. "But you insist upon a race. Now think of it, why do you? Why is it so important to you that it always be a race?"

"I do not know," Dancing Tree frowned again. "I really do not know."

"You were taught that it is a race," Crazy Dog smiled. "You were taught! Think of it! Think about that! You were taught!"

"Not everything we do is taught," Dancing Tree balked.

"It is all taught," Crazy Dog said. "The twelve mirrors teach the embryo to grow. Those mirrors do not disappear when the animal is born! They change. I, Crazy Dog, tell you that you are taught everything!"

"I cannot believe that!" Dancing Tree insisted.

"What have I taught you of the mice?" Little Wolf smiled. "Do you remember?"

"I remember," Dancing Tree said. "It was the time I did not know if the mixture of roots and berries were poisonous."

"What did you do with the mice?" Crazy Dog asked.

"The mice tasted it for me," Dancing Tree answered.

"And what did I tell you?" Little Wolf asked.

"You said that the mice are that kind of introducer," Dancing Tree answered.

"Did the mouse not teach you?" Crazy Dog asked.

"I see," Dancing Tree frowned, thinking.

"Did your first people tell you when you were a child that you would be taught by many teachers, including the mouse?" Crazy Dog asked.

"Mice were never mentioned as teachers," Dancing Tree laughed. "Unless it was in a patronizing way. The mouse would never be considered an equal teacher to a human."

"But the mouse is indeed a teacher in its own way, as is the flower, the bee, the embryo. Everything!" Crazy Dog said. "It is presumptuous for humans to believe that they are not equal with the mouse! The mouse is a great teacher! Everything has its own language and its own message, my son. Everything! The twelve dwarves are teachers that are invisible. They are also called the introducers!"

"Where did the twelve dwarves come from?" Dancing Tree asked.

"Asking that question is like trying to hunt before you learn to walk," Crazy Dog said.

Dancing Tree began to fidget.

"Please do not curl up in a ball," Little Wolf smiled as he slapped Dancing Tree gently upon the back. "You become embarrassed at the strangest things!"

"It is not a strange action," Crazy Dog said, looking into Dancing Tree's eyes. "Our little brother has been taught that it is embarrassing not to know." He roared with laughter. "Contraries believe themselves to be clowns. Some of your teachers have been unbelievable clowns if they have taught you such a thing!" Suddenly he became very stern. "Do not think that you are the same, my son. Those teachers were fools if they taught such a thing. Come! Speak what you will! Not to know is only to say that you are learning! The ancient teachers tell us that the twelve are like this sign." He drew a triangle in the snow. "But they are like the left hand and the right hand." He drew another triangle interlocking into a star. "The same but different."

"I never knew that," Little Wolf said with a frown, looking at the two triangles. "Are these the same sign as the hoop of the snake?"

"It is the same sign," Crazy Dog answered. "There is the power to create, and the power to destroy. For every possible action there is a counteraction. Whatever is done can also be undone. For every positive action there is a negative. To move ahead is to push back. Every energy force must depend for its existence upon altering another force. We kill the buffalo in order that we might live. It is all the same."

"This sign tells us that we change the buffalo. We alter the form of the buffalo when we eat it in order that we might have energy," Little Wolf said.

"When we learn, we alter ourselves," Crazy Dog added. "We use the energy force of ourselves in order that we may grow."

"Amazing," Little Wolf frowned. "When the dwarves carried off my mother they were demonstrating through their act how I was to be weaned from my mother."

"Yes," Crazy Dog smiled. "But we also made a circle around you and then took you to where your mother was hiding."

"The Mother Earth," Little Wolf mused out loud.

"And do you remember what it was your mother had changed into?" Crazy Dog asked.

"The twelve little girls danced around my mother," Little Wolf answered.

"We hunt," Crazy Dog said, turning to Dancing Tree. "But what is there to hunt that has not already been invented by the Eternal? All things are created by the Power of the Universe. All things exist because the universe exists. We only discover them. If we should ever discover all there is to discover, we then would alter what was and become what it was we altered. We are what we eat. We are what we do. What we change with our hands we must live with. If we tear the earth, we must live with that tear, unless we alter it once again."

"The whiteman is destroying the earth," Dancing Tree grimaced.

"Then our children must forage in the ruins," Crazy Dog answered. "It is the children who suffer because of these things. Do we love our children if we throw them into our ruins? No, we do not!"

"But we are tearing everything to pieces," Dancing Tree cried.

"The tearing will cease when the people awaken," Crazy Dog said. "They are a passing thing, these destroyers of the earth. They believe their day will be forever, but they are only one tiny breath within the shouting voice of those who wish to live."

"Words," Dancing Tree said with anger. "Words, many words. We must do something to stop the destroyers."

"The destruction will stop when the People themselves want it to stop," Crazy Dog said. "The People have what they make. If their camps are foul, then that is their choice. If their children are strangled, then it is they who strangle them. The People must awaken and realize that this is their world, and that what they build here they must live with."

"Will we live through this terrible winter?" Dancing Tree asked.

"Winter?" Crazy Dog smiled. "How do we know it is not spring? We as an entire People must listen to our Mother the Earth. We must honor her all together, and then we can honor ourselves. Maybe we are just about to be born?"

"What do you think about the whiteman People?" Dancing Tree asked.

"I must respect them," Crazy Dog answered. "But I cannot honor them. How can I? They have a weapon in their hands, and they are about to cause my death. This is not to say that I do not believe them to be children, but they are too uncivilized for me to approach. So I stand back and weep as they kill each other, especially their children. Why are they so greedy and violent? I have asked myself this many times. There can be only one answer. Someone has stolen their love.

They are not themselves. They follow a way that teaches them violence. Is this not so? What symbols are painted upon their moccasins? I have asked this, and I believe their moccasins are painted with violence. Who are their teachers? What kind of teachers would have their children despoil their own home? This, our Mother the Earth, is their home. Why do they hate her so? Do they like to live in filth and horror? I can only wonder, Dancing Tree. I can only wonder."

At the change of the moon, Crazy Dog gathered together the small camp.

"There are seven feathers in my medicine bundle," Crazy Dog said, opening his pouch. "Seven ragged, tattered feathers that were given to me by Two Worlds Bird. They are the only possessions I have. Many things have come to rest within my hand, once even a very powerful glittering stone. But I kept none of these. Somebody always wanted or needed these other gifts. But no one ever wanted these seven ragged feathers.

"Two Worlds Bird was a man who was neither tall nor short, fat nor lean, fast nor slow, good hunter nor poor. He sat with great teachers and seemed not to learn. He never was a hero nor ever really alone. He was always present in the camp, but he was also very invisible. When he died even his dogs never really knew he was gone. He was forgotten because nobody really remembered him even when he had been sitting right at their elbows.

"I had been thrown by a bull. I was healing in the camp of Rapid Hawk. I was there for five moons, and I never once saw the man called Two Worlds Bird. He was invisible to me too.

"The camp of Rapid Hawk was strange in a way that surprises me yet. Everyone was beautiful to look at. There was never any sickness, no tears, no deformity. There did not seem to be even a mole on anyone's cheek. The people were all perfectly healthy and beautiful. No one was poor. They were all perfect mothers, perfect hunters, perfect children, and of course they lived in perfectly built and painted lodges. It was amazing! Truly amazing how smoothly everything went in that camp. Everyone was friendly, well mannered, well dressed, full of good stories, intelligent, warm, generous. There was not one among them who did not have a beautiful mouth, bright shining eyes, luxurious well-groomed hair, strong, wonderfully formed limbs, bright faces, and perfect teeth.

"Nothing in that camp was out of order. Nothing! Everything was kept tidy, clean and new. Those people were the luckiest hunters I have ever seen! They hardly had to go beyond their first hunting circle to bring back enough food to feed a camp ten times the size of theirs. Even the location of their camp was perfect. There was no mud when it rained, no mosquitoes, and I only saw one or two flies. In all those five moons there was always a wonderful sky, and a rainbow after each little shower of rain. It was amazing!

"I was well cared for and the center of attention. They could not hear enough. I told story after story and, of course, they were perfect listeners and asked just the right questions! The young women paid me compliments, and every man was my friend. I was given every opportunity to visit and made completely at home. Everybody there had had wonderful experiences and had received unbelievably wonderful visions. It was truly amazing!

"Then one day we had a visitor. The visitor was a powerful woman, and she was a good teacher. She was also entertaining and knew many wonderful ways of making you laugh. And then suddenly I noticed that everything had changed! You must believe me when I tell you that I have never been so horribly shocked! Now, because those people had someone new to entertain them, I had become worthless. Worthless! Worse than nothing! I was more alone than if I had been thrown on the top of a mountain. I was completely ignored. And when I decided to leave, absolutely no one cared. I doubt if they even saw me leave.

"While I was packing up my possessions I noticed that every gift that had been given to me was perfect, without flaw. Suddenly it sickened me. I felt cheapened. I decided to leave them all behind and was just about to go when this man of whom I have spoken walked up to me.

" 'My name is Two Worlds Bird,' the man said, shaking my hand. 'Thank you for coming to our camp. You are a very powerful man.'

" 'You live here in this camp?' I asked in surprise. 'I have never seen you.' Then I suddenly remembered that I had. He had always been there, right in front of me. In fact on many occasions he had tried to be friends, but I had ignored him for the beauty that had been all around me. I felt crushed.

" 'I want to be your friend,' he said with gentleness.

"I have never felt such shame. I could hardly speak.

" 'I have a gift for you,' he said, and he put these seven pitiful feathers in my hand.

" 'How did you get these feathers?' I asked, sitting down with him.

" 'I got them when I went on my Vision Quest,' he answered.

" 'Tell me of that Quest,' I asked.

" 'No,' he said, lowering his eyes. 'I cannot.'

"After much persuasion I finally got him to tell me his story.

"He had left upon his Vision Quest by himself. He had been completely alone. He had asked, of course, for help. Each time those perfect people had promised to go with him, but when it came time to go, they had always managed to forget.

"He actually apologized to me for their actions because he loved them. I do not think that he ever at any time realized just how horrible those people were to him."

Crazy Dog stopped and looked at his hands. He cleared his throat and began his story again.

"He walked out onto the prairie alone, utterly alone. No matter how many times he looked back, no one appeared to help him. He never told me, but I know that he must have cried.

"Then is when he decided that he would climb the highest mountain he could see. From that lofty place he would seek his Vision. By the time he reached the foot of the mountain his feet were already raw from walking. He only had one pair of moccasins that he had made himself.

"He reached the foot of the mountain limping. His feet were bleeding, and he was almost exhausted. He wanted his family to have the greatest gift ever imagined. I know that that man did not do what he dreamed to do to win acclaim. It was to be a gift of love.

"It took him thirty days to climb what he believed to be the mountain. Thirty grueling, painful days. But when he finally reached his goal he realized that he had only crossed a hill. It was a pitiful hill compared to the mountain that now reared up high above his head. The great hill he now stood upon had only hidden the powerful mountain that stood before him.

"He wept. He wept because he knew that what he had dreamed was impossible for him. He would need help, he would need preparation, and he had neither. He had nothing.

"He tried to pray, but his swollen feet pained him so much that he could not bring even a plea to his lips.

"He struggled back down the great hill, and when he came to the prairie he lay down to rest. He awoke the next morning and began to crawl. He struggled to his feet and began to walk.

"He needed help! He stopped and fell upon his knees and cried out, but nothing happened. Then suddenly he saw seven feathers fall from the tail of a powerful eagle that circled over his head. They fell right at his feet.

"He picked them up and a wonderful calm came over him. Then a miracle happened. His feet and torn hands began to heal. He was refreshed!

"Shouting and laughing, he ran into his village to tell of his wonderful gift. But the camp had a visitor, a man whom Rapid Hawk had sent for. The visitor had come from a very great distance and was the center of attention. He could do wonderful tricks. He could roll and flip in the air while holding a firebrand in each of his hands, and he could sing very beautifully.

"This had happened ten years before I had been forced to take refuge in that same camp, and now at last he was telling his story to someone who listened. He was telling that story for the first time.

" 'Will you keep the feathers?' he asked when he had finished his story.

" 'I will try to keep them,' I said, shaking his hand. 'And I will try to tell your story every winter when the woman of the north dances.'

" 'You will?' he asked with excitement. Then, 'You really will, won't you?'

"He was crying.

" 'Yes,' I said, laughing. 'I will, Two Worlds Bird. I will!' "

"Did that camp actually exist?" Dancing Tree asked.

"Do you see these feathers?" Crazy Dog asked, holding them up. "These feathers exist. If I were to answer *yes* to your question, I would cheat you. To answer *no* to your question would be to cheat these powerful feathers. To say nothing would be to shame me and to dishonor Two Worlds Bird. I have spoken."

"That teaching was one of the Dance Hammer, wasn't it?" Dancing Tree asked and smiled.

"Yes, it was," Crazy Dog whooped and threw his buffalo hat to the ground.

"Then it is a yes-no story," Little Wolf said.

"It is equally true as it is false," Crazy Dog answered.

"My grandmother once told us a story like that," Dreamer said. "And she said that the four-leggeds see each day as a whole thing but the humans count each day. What did she mean, Crazy Dog?"

"Both beings, the four-leggeds and the humans, possess mind, body, spirit, and inward teaching," Crazy Dog answered. "It is a question of how these differ from one another. When you consider these things, dance around them before you give yourself ready answers. Consider with me the dogs. Humans have always lived with the dog. The dog is useful to the humans. Consider also the horse. The horse is also important to the humans. Why have these two beings come to be part of the human camp? Many creatures have been made into slaves.

But what does that mean, and why have other creatures refused to be part of the human camp?"

"Is it because the humans have not found a way to control many of the other creatures?" Little Wolf asked.

"Control is an important consideration," Crazy Dog agreed. "But we must consider beyond these thoughts. If the creatures of our world are here for our benefit, then how is it we also benefit them? And more, consider the trees, flowers, rivers, and all else. We obviously can control these also. Are these here for our benefit? Yes! They are! But how do we benefit them?"

"By caring for them," Rainbow answered. "My mother told me that all things are our children. She said that the world is our magical lodge, and we must care for that lodge. We are to learn how to care for our home. Our world teaches us everything, she said. Every thing imagined or known is taught by our Mother the Earth. She said that everything is here for our growing. There is corruption, pain, healing, love, hate, everything! Each thing is within change and all things are within a counterchange. So also are the People."

"Many people dream of a perfect place," Crazy Dog said. "But what of that perfect place?"

"Obviously, being entertained is not an answer," Dreamer smiled.

"Many people demand that they should be entertained," Crazy Dog answered. "They demand a perfect place but do not try to create one. They are willing to live in one but do not wish to make one."

"That place in the story was not a perfect place," Dancing Tree said. "Because of Two Worlds Bird."

"True and untrue," Crazy Dog grinned. "As with everything else in that story. But consider this: is that place not a perfect place for a martyr?"

"I never thought about that!" Rainbow laughed. "Of course it is!"

"The story is a mirror, as all stories are," Crazy Dog said. "But consider how many people try to act out a story in their own lives."

"What do you mean?" Little Wolf asked.

"Many stories try to instruct how to do some particular thing," Crazy Dog answered. "Subtly, many fathers and mothers, teachers and societies, including religions, tell stories of instruction. They are usually stories that force people upon a singular path, or way. Children are vulnerable to these stories. They may not be able to recall them, but nevertheless they remain inside them dictating their life way. This is a crippling thing, a very dangerous thing. And these crippling stories are as common as flies."

"Then these stories are bad?" Dancing Tree asked.

"Bad, good, and indifferent," Crazy Dog laughed. "They are a human folly. They are also among the most terrible of monsters, because they destroy the individual path. They are also meaningless, my children, because every human upon the face of this earth has a decision to become a whole being, even the child. But let us move to another question. Why did the great eagle in the story not enlighten the camp? Why only the seeker?"

"Was it because the others only sought entertainment?" Dancing Tree asked.

"Yes, no, because the martyr also sought entertainment, did he not?" Crazy Dog answered. "They all were seekers in their own way, were they not?"

"I think so," Little Wolf answered.

"No, yes, again," Crazy Dog said. "Did they seek individually as Two Worlds Bird? Or were they a pack?"

"They were a pack," Dancing Tree answered.

"Being a pack crippled them," Crazy Dog said. "But did it not also strengthen them?"

"One could go on forever!" Little Wolf sighed.

"Especially if the story were to be overlaid upon other questions and beliefs," Crazy Dog laughed. "Old, ragged feathers like these which I hold are everywhere! They are falling out of the sky all the time!"

"I have never seen magical feathers like that," Little Wolf said.

"No?" Crazy Dog asked in surprise. "They fall by the hundreds from the trees every year," he laughed. "Have you not heard seven very tattered and ragged stories?"

"Most of the ragged ones I've heard were really ragged," Little Wolf smiled. "Covered with eagle droppings instead of big medicine."

"Eagle droppings are big medicine," Crazy Dog grinned. "So is stupidity, magnificence, boredom, love, and sharing. It is what you make of it. It is what we make of everything within our world! Two Worlds Bird's feet and hands were healed, but what of it? How did he use his hands? How did he use his feet? How did he use the miracle? Is it enough just to experience a miracle? What is a miracle of life? Isn't everything? And if this is not so for you, then why is it not? And if you find out why, then is that not a miracle?"

"Amazing!" Little Wolf frowned. "Just amazing!"

Crazy Dog smiled. "It is not amazing. It is only knowledge. Why not argue with me? Are you afraid? How do you know that I am not telling you another story of instruction?"

"Are you?" Dancing Tree asked, showing disappointment.

"Am I?" Crazy Dog laughed. "Come, awaken! What are you learning?"

"Just how tricky you can be," Little Wolf laughed.

"That is one ragged feather for you!" Crazy Dog said. "It fell right at your feet. Can you recognize six more? What if Two Worlds Bird had never recognized the feathers as a sign?"

"What if he hadn't?" Dancing Tree asked.

"Are you asking me?" Crazy Dog replied, sobering.

"Why not?" Dancing Tree smiled. "That is my argument."

"You tricked me!" Crazy Dog whooped with joy. "All right, I will answer. I will tell you a story that will reflect my way of self-perception.

"Within my mind, Powerful Person walked with indifference into the place where Four Magical Drums speaks. Four Magical Drums represents the voices in our mind that allow thought to develop. Four Magical Drums will never be mentioned again because her voice was stilled by Powerful Person's indifference. Powerful Person's body was that of a lion and his head was that of a man. His hands were claws and could not hold his bow.

"The bow was a brilliant, sparkling clean stream of wondrous dreams made from the shadows of lightning flowers.

"Powerful Person saw all of this when I closed my eyes. So Powerful Person watched as I, Crazy Dog, searched among the flowers.

" 'I think I will call him Heyoehkah,' Powerful Person thought.

"And Crazy Dog was born.

"He looked around and found he was upon a desert where nothing grew. Now I knew that I must ask to borrow a star, and so I borrowed it from the Powerful Person.

"I heard crying. I turned around and saw a beautiful woman wearing a blue robe.

"I touched her because I knew she was crying for Powerful Person.

"And her tears became a rain, and everything grew.

"Powerful Person shouted with joy, and Crazy Dog saw the sun. But wouldn't you know, Crazy Dog was the night, and because it was morning I went to sleep, right beneath your feet as your shadow."

"Horns!" Little Wolf yelled. "That is your answer?"

"No and yes," Crazy Dog said. "It was yours and mine, ours and nobody's. It was just a ragged feather."

"Another feather!" Little Wolf shrieked with laughter. "Now I have two of them, and I still have no idea what to do!"

"Now you have three," Crazy Dog said soberly, then smiled.

"Then we must use what we have," Dreamer said.

"Are you asking me?" Crazy Dog asked.

"I think we had better ask ourselves!" Rainbow laughed.

"Another feather!" Crazy Dog grinned. "It is raining feathers in this lodge!"

"Will you tell us another story?" Rainbow asked Crazy Dog.

"I will tell the story of Fox and Crow and how they stole a prairie dog hole," Crazy Dog said.

" 'Why have we stolen this hole?' Fox asked.

" 'It was your idea,' Crow answered.

" 'Whose idea?' Fox frowned.

" 'Our idea,' Crow admitted.

" 'But what are we going to do with it?' Fox asked, curious.

" 'It is valuable!' Crow answered. 'You know that! We can trade it for something!'

" 'But what?' Fox asked.

" 'What?' Crow frowned.

" 'I see,' Fox admitted.

"So Fox and Crow took that prairie dog hole back to their camp. They were very careful not to let anyone there know about it. They put the prairie dog hole into a bundle made from the robe of a coyote.

" 'What have you got in there?' Bear asked.

" 'Something,' Fox answered.

" 'Something?' Bear frowned.

" 'Nothing,' Fox lied.

" 'Why would you have nothing?' Bear asked puzzled. 'What can you do with nothing?'

" 'Trade it for something,' Crow explained.

" 'Trade something, I mean nothing, for something?' Bear asked, still puzzled.

" 'You just do not understand these things,' Fox said. He frowned with impatience.

" 'I see,' Bear said. 'But who will want it?

" 'That is our problem,' Crow said angrily. 'Can't you see that?'

" 'Yes! Yes!' Bear said with sympathy. 'I can see that.'

" 'There is nothing in that bag,' a voice said behind Fox, Crow, and Bear.

"They all turned around. It was Magpie.

" 'You didn't let it out!' Crow exclaimed.

" 'Let what out?' Magpie asked.

" 'Our prairie dog hole, the one we stole!' Fox cried.

" 'No wonder!' Magpie laughed. 'You can't steal a prairie dog hole!' She almost flew off the ground, she was laughing so hard.

" 'Why not?' Crow asked with suspicion.

" 'All you can do is steal a prairie dog hole shadow,' Magpie explained.

" 'That's something!' Bear smiled.

" 'I tell you, it's nothing!' Crow insisted. 'And don't get any ideas!'

" 'Like what?' Bear asked, puzzled.

" 'Like stealing it yourself!' Fox immediately said.

" 'But,' Bear stammered, 'if nothing is something, I mean, if nothing can be traded for something, it has to be something! And besides that, it's a shadow, and shadows are something even if they are nothing!'

" 'I agree completely,' Magpie said.

" 'All right,' Crow said. 'I will admit it, it is something!'

" 'You have to share that shadow,' Magpie said with insistence.

" 'Among four of us?' Fox asked in disgust. 'There won't be anything left when we trade.'

" 'How's that?' Bear asked, puzzled.

" 'Before there were only two, right?' Fox explained. 'And now there are four, right?'

" 'Right,' Bear answered.

" 'And now we are going to trade that shadow, right?' Fox asked.

" 'Right,' Bear agreed.

" 'And after we split that shadow between four of us, how much do you suppose we will have to eat, I mean, with four of us eating?'

" 'Eating?' Crow asked, puzzled. 'Eating what?'

" 'What we're going to trade that shadow for,' Fox explained.

" 'Who are we going to trade that shadow to?' Bear asked.

" 'A prairie dog, of course!' Fox exclaimed.

" 'I see,' they all three said.

" 'Now all we have to do is find us a prairie dog that wants a shadow!' Magpie yelled for joy. 'And then we eat!'

" 'Wait!' Fox yelled as loud as he could. 'Wait! Now just how much do you think we will all get if we split the food four ways? Answer me that!'

" 'Not much,' Bear answered. 'Not with the bites I take.'

" 'Exactly,' Fox fumed. He was very mad.

" 'I am a crow!' Crow exclaimed. 'My bites are small!'

" 'And mine are even smaller!' Magpie cried.

" 'What bites?' Badger said, sitting down.

" 'Now there are five!' Magpie squawked.

" 'It is too late!' Crow cried. 'Tell him!'

"So Bear explained the whole story in detail to Badger.

" 'What story was that?' Weasel asked, sitting down.

" 'Impossible!' Crow yelled and fell upon his back as though he were dead.

" 'Is he dead?' Bear asked Fox.

" 'I am not dead!' Crow said from where he lay. 'What a mess,' he grumbled.

" 'What mess?' Porcupine asked, sitting down.

"Bear carefully explained everything in each detail.

" 'Why are you all sitting here?' Otter asked as he sat down.

" 'Is this a meeting?' Eagle asked, flying down.

" 'Is there something wrong?' Owl asked as he, too, sat down.

" 'What is going on here?' Wolf asked, taking his place.

"Bear explained the whole story to everybody.

"And one by one they came from every direction until there were thousands of them.

" 'Enough of this!' Crow cawed. He was at the end of his patience.

" 'We are going to trade that shadow right now, before the whole world is here.'

" 'We can't,' Bear said.

" 'Can't!' Fox asked. 'Why?'

" 'Because while we were all talking, a prairie dog came and stole the shadow.'

" 'Now what are we going to eat?' Crow yelled. 'Now what are we going to eat?'

"Everybody looked at everybody else. Then suddenly there was an explosion of dust, fur, feathers, and sounds greater than anyone had ever seen or heard, and everyone disappeared!

" 'Where did they all go?' Crow asked Magpie.

" 'They ate each other up!' Magpie exclaimed in surprise.

" 'But there is no one here!' Crow said, puzzled. 'Just you and I.'

" 'Because we had the last bite,' Magpie explained.

" 'I'm still starved,' Crow grumbled. 'It was like taking a bite of that shadow.' "

Crazy Dog reached for his pipe.

After their laughter had subsided into chuckles, Little Wolf spoke.

"That is enough for me today," Little Wolf giggled. "Tomorrow Dancing Tree and I must hunt."

The following day Dancing Tree and Little Wolf were successful. A white bighorn gave-away to them, and there was a feast.

After the feast everyone had a question for Crazy Dog concerning the story he had told the day before.

"I will say this," Crazy Dog smiled as he lit his pipe. "It is a teaching for you. I have spoken."

"But I have a question for you now," Dancing Tree said playfully. "What is the cure for violence?"

"Violence has many forms and faces," Crazy Dog answered. "There is the violence of birth, as an example, but how is this different from the thunderbolt?"

"I cannot truly answer that," Dancing Tree said.

"Then tell me the difference between the violence of a charging bull and a person who insists upon recognizing only one interpretation," Crazy Dog asked.

"The bull has only one recourse," Dancing Tree answered. "And the person has many."

"Now let us go beyond these answers," Crazy Dog smiled gently. "How does the violence of a child differ from that of an adult?"

"A child must be cunning, I think," Rainbow answered. "Because it is the child's only recourse."

"I agree," Crazy Dog smiled. "But now let us separate these things again. Can you, Rainbow, defend yourself from the violent actions of Little Wolf?"

"Only with my mind, my intelligence," Rainbow answered. "It is impossible for me to physically defeat Little Wolf."

"Would your answer be the same if you were a child?" Crazy Dog asked.

"Yes. A child would use its instinctive mind," Dreamer replied.

"Exactly," Crazy Dog smiled. "But we must go even further, rather than just speaking of what we can readily see. What would you say concerning the adventure, the drama that is derived from violence? Or what of the fantasy of violence?"

"You are referring to fantasies of murder or perhaps rape?" Dancing Tree asked.

"Yes," Crazy Dog said. "In what manner, would you say, is violence taught?"

"Is it the acting out of the stories?" Dreamer asked. "Would you say that the stories that teach violence are stories of instruction?"

"I would," Crazy Dog answered. "I would say that, but why would violence be so easily taught and not, let's say—"

"Love?" Rainbow interjected.

"The human being craves power," Crazy Dog said as he took a puff from his pipe. "The human being's greatest fantasy concerns power. We were placed here upon our Mother the Earth within limitation. We humans substitute power for many things. If something does not fit, we hit out and try to force our will upon it. This gives us a release from frustration. Sometimes the forcing of things satisfies us, but very rarely. Violence is the lowest of all actions. It is always a substitution for what is real. Violence replaces thinking. Thought is the deterrent of violence, and yet thought also is the aggravator of violence. Mind is the greatest of forces and the most beautiful of actions, but only when the mind is within balance.

"Now we come to the teaching of the Medicine Wheel. If we truly look within ourselves, we understand our feelings and know of our hearts, our passions. Then we must think deeply, so we can fly into the place of illumination. When we do these things and are illuminated, we can see that violence is only a shadow of the mind. But be very thoughtful, my children, because of your ignorance."

"You mean even beyond the teaching of the Medicine Wheel there is still more to be understood?" Dancing Tree frowned.

"More!" Crazy Dog laughed. "Much more! What if we have a problem concerning a person, and we decide that the best thing for that person to do is learn of our way. But a person who learns of our way will then fit into our camp circle."

"What is wrong with that?" Dancing Tree asked.

"What if our camp circle is lacking?" Crazy Dog smiled. "Or what if we are not taking into consideration everything that is causing that person not to fit? Now we must begin all over again upon the Medicine Wheel. As a People we must learn introspection. Above all, we must counsel together. Not to decide, but to talk. We must ask what is wrong with our camp circle that one among us might not fit? Why is our camp so intolerant? Is it that we have no place in our camp for that person? But then why not? Why would a circle of human beings not have a place within it for another human being?" Crazy Dog laughed.

"Is what you are saying that the camp might become violent if it did not accept that person, and learn of whatever that person had to offer?" Little Wolf asked.

"I am," Crazy Dog answered. "Doesn't this also occur within each of us as individuals? Are we always so tolerant of each new thing that suddenly enters our mind lodge?"

"Amazing!" Little Wolf whooped.

"It is not amazing," Crazy Dog smiled. "It is a learning. When we become violent with those new ideas that enter our mind lodge, we suffer."

"And we suffer as a People when we do not accept the person who does not fit," Dreamer said.

"It all centers within ourselves," Crazy Dog smiled. "Any action of a camp is only the extension of what exists within the individuals making up the circle. As a camp mind are we acting out a story fantasy? Are we charging like the bull? Are we feminine? Are we acting like a child? That, Dancing Tree, is one of the problems I see concerning the 'book' you mentioned. Those teachings are ancient and bring only partial understanding to what is happening now. They are now just a study in brilliance and stupidity, nothing else. To try to walk such an ancient road would be insane. That road no longer exists. Every People has its prophets and lawmakers. Learn from these things, but never try to live them. The Eternal Power did not give the ancients of any People a perfect answer." He laughed. "Many times the answers of the ancients can be quite humorous. These histories are trails, my children, simple trails. A trail that can be intelligently understood. Look at each history as one hunter, one hunter who is walking down a trail. That trail is no different than any other trail. What is he doing? What does he seek? How does he seek that for which he is hungry? How does that hunter go about his activities? But ask yourself, does this hunter know all that we know? No! We can look back upon his path, the path he has not even covered yet. Think of that! He has not even covered the ground we can look back upon. Are we going to be so foolish as to try to walk his path?" He roared with laughter.

THE YELLOW LODGE

THE MIRROR has great power," Estchimah said, looking up into Twin Chiefs' eyes.

"Yes, it has, my child," Twin Chiefs smiled.

One morning soon after, she noticed that the old man was breaking camp. She ate some dry meat and drank the soup he had prepared. Then she began to help him pack.

"Where are we going?" she asked as she helped him harness the dogs.

"To the mountain place where my sister lives. Her name is Four Sleeping Lions," Twin Chiefs answered.

That night they arrived at the camp of Four Sleeping Lions. But it was not what Estchimah had expected. Instead of a comfortable camp like the one Twin Chiefs and she were used to, there was rubble everywhere. The home of Four Sleeping Lions was within the ruins. The biggest surprise was Four Sleeping Lions herself. She was leaning against the door, drunk, and she looked like a scrawny, scraggy owl.

"Well! Well! Welcome!" Four Sleeping Lions burped. "Come on and make yourself at home."

"Are we going to sleep in this mess?" Estchimah whispered to Twin Chiefs.

Twin Chiefs seemed to ignore her as he sat down upon a large broken stone with Four Sleeping Lions. They seemed to talk about nothing. Estchimah looked around the small room, wondering were they could sleep in all that disarray.

"Well, my child," Four Sleeping Lions said, turning to Estchimah. "Twin Chiefs tells me that you would like to visit the power place."

"Power place?" she thought as she looked into the old woman's wrinkled face. "Yes, yes," she quickly lied, looking toward Twin Chiefs, wondering.

"Good!" the old woman said with a grin. "Tomorrow I will show you."

Estchimah watched fascinated as the old woman dragged herself shakily up from the floor and staggered to her cooking fire. She poured the steaming water from a blackened kettle into three battered cups. She tottered, swayed, staggered, and bumped as she stirred the tea. But what astonished Estchimah most was Four Sleeping Lions' speech. There was absolutely no doubt the old woman was totally drunk, but her speech was as clear as a sunrise.

Estchimah wanted to stay awake and listen, but she couldn't keep her eyes open. She grabbed an old buffalo robe, rolled up into it, and was soon within her dreams.

The course of a new river is never determined for it. The young stream must seek out its own way. Old river beds are chosen by flash floods and spring run-off. These old harmonies remember many of the great villages, because it was here the first medicines were made.

Kindness is a soft melody that is heard by the gentle pines. To speak loudly to these is only to deafen them. Whisper your

message and these pines will speak of it with all of their brothers and sisters.

The blue sky is the Mother's robe, covering all. The stars write tomorrow and yesterday within the Mother's introspection. The Mother paints the sun, moon, sunsets, and sunrises for all of her children.

The wind is caught within memory of the people. Its song is of the earth's movement. Those who have lived braid the hair of the wind and dance within the simple harmonies of each whirlwind. This brings the dry times and the rains. The wind walks in the mountains, touches the snow, moves the grasses, and speaks to all who will listen.

THE NEXT MORNING Estchimah woke up alone. She looked around the dingy room to see if anyone was still asleep, but everyone had gone. She walked out into the beautiful day, happy to breathe the sweet fresh air.

Four Sleeping Lions was staggering about her campfire, cooking the morning's meal, when Estchimah started for the stream to wash. She noticed that the old woman was still drunk, and it made her feel uncomfortable. Twin Chiefs was coming up from the stream with a catch of fish.

"I'm sorry, grandfather," Estchimah said, stopping Twin Chiefs, "but the old woman's drunkenness bothers me. When are we going to leave?"

A mixture of surprise and pity showed in Twin Chief's face. "My child," he said gently, "Four Sleeping Lions is not drunk! She is afflicted."

Estchimah's shame made her angry, and she cursed the old woman's home and its condition. "Why did you bring me to such a filthy place?" she howled, trying to hide her shame.

"This is all-important to you," Twin Chiefs said, touching her shoulder. "I

have walked in many places with you, and you have always been brave. Have courage now. This is a different way, but it is a teaching."

"A teaching?" she asked. "It's hard for me to believe—"

"It's hard for you to believe that you are bigoted," Twin Chiefs broke in, "and it has shamed you. This is not the home of Four Sleeping Lions. It is the visiting room. Four Sleeping Lions is the keeper of this place. No one lives here. No one can."

"I must apologize," Estchimah choked.

"There is no need to apologize to your grandmother, my child," Twin Chiefs smiled. "The old woman understands. Come! Let us cook these fish and begin our journey within the walls."

After breakfast they followed the old woman back to the entrance of the visiting room.

"It is through here," Four Sleeping Lions said.

Estchimah followed, wondering but hopeful. She imagined a wondrous place of hidden gold and sparkling gems, but as they walked it seemed as though they would never get beyond the old rooms. In some of the rooms were overturned statues and broken altars. In others were remnants of pottery and crumbling tablets. In all of the rooms was turmoil, misuse, and decay. Finally they came to a courtyard that was formed from natural stone. In the middle of that small open area was a very tiny spring-fed pool of clear, dancing water. Estchimah turned to look back from where they had come and saw only ruins built upon ruins.

"Stop here," Four Sleeping Lions said as she sat down.

Twin Chiefs and Estchimah sat down, facing the old woman, and waited.

"you will brush away this dust," Four Sleeping Lions said, as she ed her hand in a circle around herself, "you will see a symbol of the

"It is beautiful," Estchimah exclaimed, as the motion of her hand revealed the painting. "What is it made of?"

"It is made of those things that are very rare to human beings," Four Sleeping Lions answered. "The shamaness who first brought me here called it the Black Shield. The Black Shield is brought into existence only when we perceive the inward signs."

"I wish to learn of this teaching," Twin Chiefs said to the old woman. "But I am curious about this symbol. Did the builders of these ruins create it?"

"They walked over it, but they did not create it," Four Sleeping Lions answered. "They dreamed and understood that the dream was important, but they ignored the Black Shield."

"How did they ignore the Black Shield?" Twin Chiefs asked.

"They had visions concerning the inward signs, and they believed those signs to be gods," the old woman answered. "But this is not the way of the Black Shield.

"When we dream of going into the earth, we are entering into the world of the Black Shield. Within the world of the Black Shield there is every law and no law. The Black Shield is the Fountain of the Children's Maze.

"The People knew of this great shield and taught concerning the double circle of authority. But before I speak of this double circle, I wish to talk to you about the lodges of learning given to the People by the Buffalo Teachers.

"There are two lodges. One is the lodge of the man, and the other is the lodge of the woman.

"Let us consider the lodge of the woman first. These women had a first law which permitted no men to come into their lodge. These same women had a second law that all men must approach their lodge and ask permission to enter. If they did not, then they were forbidden to speak to any woman or girl."

"Those two laws seem to present a paradox," Twin Chiefs said, smiling and glancing at Estchimah.

"The woman's lodge as a Sacred Lodge," Four Sleeping Lions went on. "There was no authority above the authority of the woman in that lodge. In that lodge was the world of the woman. Only things of the woman were permitted in their lodge, and all things of the woman were holy in that lodge. So when the men entered that lodge, they entered it as women. They spoke of women's things and learned what it was to be a woman, and they learned of the laws of the woman."

"I have a question within my mind," Estchimah said, frowning, "but I cannot put it into words."

The two chiefs waited.

"It's the circle," she laughed. "I understand it and yet I do not."

"All things occur first in the mind—every action and every circle," Four Sleeping Lions said. "This way is called the Foundation Circle. It is also called the Contrary Circle, and it is called the Eastern Lodge Door. There are two persons—twins—who are the keepers of these doors. One twin puts the world around them into order in a way that pleases them; the other twin dances through everything that already exists. These twins must always balance one another. If either of them should ever rule the other, then war results. This war is always a battle between our Mother the Earth and ourselves. This can be very destructive!"

"I want no war!" Estchimah exclaimed.

"Then be mindful of the twins," Four Sleeping Lions said gently. "The female understands how to become pregnant; it is, of course, basic to her. However, in order that she might learn of the balance of the twins, she must also learn to impregnate."

"How is that possible?" Estchimah laughed.

"These things are more of the mind than you would at first believe," Four Sleeping Lions answered. "When a woman brings herself into marriage

with a man, she dances with the circles of powers within and around her. This is the Foundation Circle. However, if that woman does not also learn how to impregnate, she will be seized and used by everything around her. She will place herself within a circle that will victimize her. She will expect creativity to be placed within her, instead of marrying with the world around her and placing the seed of her own creativity in the outer world.

"The man expects to impregnate. It is a driving force within him. However, the male must also learn how to become pregnant. Otherwise, he will be in direct war with his inward half and with the world around him.

"The woman opens herself to everything that exists around her and is receptive to everything that has intercourse with her. She is receptive to every thought, every action. She believes she is a vessel to be filled. The woman waits for creation to occur within her. It is a very subtle realization, my daughter, but a woman of this mind believes that once she has been impregnated, the natural laws of her physical body will complete the circle of creativity, totally without any effort of her mind.

"The man's approach to this circle is to conquer, to bring submission to his demands. If the man's mind knows only the first circle, he will become a rapist and he will breed only slavery.

"The woman can only impregnate through the mind; the man can only become pregnant through the mind. Not *in* the mind, but through it, as you will soon discover."

Four Sleeping Lions touched the Black Shield that surrounded her patting it gently as she did her grandchildren. "To the North in this mirror," she smiled, pointing to the northern half of the Black Shield, "is the male, the aggressive. And to the South is the female, the receptive.

"When we study closely the woman's mind, we will see that she has been given the mind of the North, because she must be completely

within reality concerning childbirth. However, remember the paradox: the Foundation Circle is found within the South for the woman.

"The man is far less wise about childbirth and its realities. He was given the mind of the South to consider these things. The man never assumes the burden of the pregnancy. The woman must. Consequently, we can see how these things of the mind have influenced the People."

"I am afraid that I have become lost upon these paths," Estchimah said with a shake of her head.

"When we enter into a new land, a new place, a new thought, a new circle, we always experience these questions," Four Sleeping Lions laughed.

"I have seen it knot many men's braids to hear these things," Twin Chiefs chuckled. "The man immediately tries to be aggressive with the teaching. He wants it to submit to his demands. His first reaction is to spread the legs of some young lady in order to fill her up with his own image. It is a fantasy of the South for the man, a fantasy with which he wishes to have intercourse. However, women react differently to these teachings. To them, the teaching holds great wisdom. They experience this wisdom within themselves and become pregnant with it."

"These questions are themselves part of the Foundation Circle," Four Sleeping Lions went on. "Let us consider these things within the realities of how men and women behave within the circle. If a man does not learn how to become pregnant with the dance of the Mother Earth, he will bring himself into direct war with her. He will not be satisifed until he has tamed the world he lives in. He will manipulate. He will try to order the world around him in his simplicity, placing in that world only what he wants to be there. He places his own image into the world around him, and demands that his efforts be multiplied. He demands multiple births. If a man approaches all things within this path of mind, he will become more and more aggressive. Soon he will be enslaving everything in the world around him. It is at this time he will become dangerous.

"Within these men there is a fear that their children are not their own, but another man's. These men will love their children and hate them at the same time. Remember, we are speaking of the men who have begun to divide their world. These men who are out of balance with themselves will become violent. This happens because they believe it becomes easier and easier for them to conquer the women around them. However, they then believe that if it is so easy to conquer the women, it must surely be even easier for other men. The war is begun, because these men then fear that either none of the children are theirs or all the children of the camp are theirs. Numbers and the power of those numbers become all important. The power these men hold over those numbers is their only concern, their only satisfaction.

"Now let us look at the women. What of them? Can they also divide their circle? If the woman's only way of perceiving is that of a receptive vessel, waiting to be filled, then she also will bring herself into direct war with herself and the Mother Earth. This happens much more subtly with a woman than it does with a man, because the woman perceives within a passive mind. Instead of reaching out into the world and seeking to bring herself into completeness with it, this unbalanced woman will draw herself into an ever-smaller circle of mind because her only consideration will be to become pregnant. She will feel compelled to make herself available to the men around her. This can become a force too powerful for her to resist, and it is at this time that she will begin to divide her circle. Every woman quickly learns that she must be beautiful in order to attract the male. However, there is no woman alive, or who has ever lived, who believes herself to be beautiful enough. Because of this, she quickly learns how to manipulate, how to order the people and events around her to satisfy her needs. Those needs are always simple and direct. They concern themselves only with attracting men and becoming pregnant. Two very powerful forces enter into the world of this woman. She becomes dependent upon the male, and she begins to war with the female. And, Estchimah, because she herself is a woman, she comes into direct war with herself. The war that ensues between these females

gives the males a tremendous advantage of mind and opportunity. Now, instead of the males pursuing the females, the order is reversed and there is a flood of females pursuing the males. Because of the war between competing women, each woman becomes alone, completely separated from the world. I say completely separated because she cannot enter the world of men and she has cut away the circle of women.

"This way of mind not only removes her from her family, but it also alienates her from everything else. Everything either has intercourse with her or ignores her. The world around her is out of her control, she believes, and she must tolerate it.

"This brings us to the matter of the children. A child born to a woman of this mind is both loved and hated. The woman's entire world of mind, her myth, reality, dreams, and need for creativity is literally embodied within the birth of the child. But, Estchimah, let old Four Sleeping Lions say this: there is not a woman alive, or who has ever lived, who can have her entire life, her every need fulfilled, through having children. A woman in this mind is cheated—trapped by the birth of children.

"The older this woman becomes, the more terrified she becomes. She waits in desperate fear for the day when she no longer will be youthful. This happens because all of her mind, all of her efforts, have been placed upon her body.

"The woman with this approach of mind curls herself up into a very tiny circle. She begins to hate the world around her. She sees everything as a threat to her fragile circle. She will begin to manipulate her husband, her children, anything to maintain the walls that she believes protect her tiny world. This is when that woman becomes very dangerous: dangerous to herself, to her children, and to everything around her.

"The woman is a circle of power. When this circle is combined with the power of other women, that greater circle is the most powerful force upon all of the earth. That combined force literally dictates how the

world will appear. Strange as it may seem, men only extend the world of the woman. Only the outward world is the child of the man. It is what he gives birth to, because here it is the women who impregnate the men."

The old woman stopped. She reached into her medicine pouch and brought out a necklace made of tiny crescent moons of silver and gold.

"You will wear this upon your Vision Hill," she said, smiling as she handed Estchimah the necklace. "It is a gift from the Maze."

Estchimah took the gift and placed it in her medicine bundle.

"Thank you," Estchimah said as she touched the old woman's hand.

"The men had their lodge also," Four Sleeping Lions went on. She was looking directly into the eyes of Estchimah. "And when the women entered that lodge they entered it as men. This is another of the ways of the Black Shield.

"This third lodge is called the Lodge of the Thunderbird. This was the lodge of death and birth.

"The People learned within the teaching of the Black Shield that it was important for them to wean their children from themselves and from their camp circle. If they did not do this, their children would live, but their spirits would die.

"When each girl or boy returned from their Vision Quest they entered the Lodge of the Thunderbird. When they entered, the People of the camp mourned and wept. They lamented because the seeker they had known had died. But when the seeker came out from the Lodge of the Thunderbird there was rejoicing and singing, because a new person had been born among them! A shield was painted, and the newcomer was given a name. This new person was celebrated.

"When this newcomer was ready to enter the fourth lodge, the Lodge of the Sacred Arrows, the mood of the entire camp was changed. Now they would watch the newcomer hold the four sacred powers of authority.

"Two of these powers were of the man, and two were of the woman. There were the sacred bow and the lance, and the sacred herbal sweet grass and the fire.

"Sometimes new people would enter the Arrow Lodge within the same twelve moons in which they came to the camp. Sometimes it would be years before they would enter, but they always entered.

"When new people came from the Lodge of the Sacred Arrows they came out with the bow, lance, fire, and the herbal sweet grass of authority. These are the words they would say:

> *I have come from this lodge with singing!*
> *I am within this world!*
> *I hold the bow and the lance of authority!*
> *I hold the fire and the herbal sweet grass of authority!*
> *I hold my own authority!*
> *I have been given the power of the human being!*
> *I have the power given to me by Sweet Medicine!*
> *I have chosen the power of the human being!*
> *Approach me!*
> *I am standing among you!*
> *I have my authority!*

"Each person did this. Girl children, boy children, women and men all did this, and they had authority. It was upon their authority that they married. Within their own authority, they chose the people they would live among. Their authority determined how they lived, dressed, ate, taught, learned, and moved among the people. It is still a good way, this way of the Black Shield.

"This double circle of authority of the Black Shield is only one illumination among many that may be found within this teaching.

"All these teachings are known as the Medicine Wheel. The Wheel is all things. It is the Great Hoop among the People. This Wheel is the Sweet Medicine. What is within it is also without it.

"When we see the powers within us, it is our choice which of these powers we choose to show to ourselves and to the world. If we deny our powers, we will be only half a person because we will have chosen to smother our gifts.

"We can hide many things within the Black Shield, but the Black Shield loves us and will dream with us. The Black Shield sees all things, remembers all things, and sings to us from the center of the earth. Within us is the Power of the Universe. The Black Shield is a teaching sign, but its wonder is the symbol of the sun.

"Here is an ancient song," Four Sleeping Lions continued.

"We are gathered together within an illusion. We dance into the sunlight and touch the moon within our memory.

"The twin sign of the Black Shield is the White Shield. There is a teaching reflected upon this shield of the twin circles. It is the shield of the hunter and the planter, the builder and the destroyer.

"The double circle upon this White Shield is black because it reflects its sister shield of the West, the Black Shield. The feathers upon this shield are also black, and the feathers and the twin circles upon the Black Shield are white.

"Within our world circle we see those things of the Black Shield that we have brought into the world of the White Shield.

"Reflected opposite the great White Shield is the Red Shield of the South. This is the way of the human being. The feathers upon this shield are gold, and the double circle upon its face is bright gold.

"The shield of the East is gold and the circles painted upon it are red, as are its feathers. This is the shield of all powers, symbols, and signs. It is Sweet Medicine."

"What is the history of the shields?" Estchimah asked. "And could you explain more to me concerning this Way?"

"I will," Four Sleeping Lions answered as she lit her pipe. "This Way grew among a powerful People of the South who lived in a great city. The people whom these Star Dance People lived among hated the Way of the Shields and what it taught concerning the dream, the earth, the stars, and the medicines.

"Here is a memorized portion of the history of these People:

"They walk among us with shields of gold, and their sand armor protects them. They come to destroy us because they have no understanding. We will go among the wild people, and we will live.

"Four Mirrors, Sweet Medicine, Erect Horns, and Medicine Coyote, all these and more were the names of the man and woman who led their People into the world of the wild people.

"These People were of a race that had built cities and temples twenty thousand years ago.

"These People who came into the land of the wild people were astronomers, builders, teachers. They were the learned.

"Here is another portion:

"The pyramid of power, the hierarchy, is dangerous because it is an artificial law. It is not real, and it imprisons the human mind as powerfully as it imprisons each stone within itself. All the stones in the pyramid support every other stone, and those who live within such a false reality are imprisoned within it.

"As an example, children within such a community do not know how to touch the earth, nor do they understand the reality of the earth around them. They believe they are ready for life. They believe they have control of their world; some even believe they have created the world that exists around them. But the world which they believe supports them is a false world. If they should ever be removed from the pyramid they

would falter and die. Only the very strong can stand up against such a crushing realization. This is not to say that their world is not a real world. It is real to them and to those around them, but only within the illusion their society has created."

"I am surprised to hear you speak in this manner," Twin Chiefs interrupted. "You have taught me to picture a teaching in its bright and happy form, but now you choose not to do so yourself. Is this part of your teaching?"

"It is," Four Sleeping Lions answered. "It is best always to take the bright and happy path to any teaching, as I have said. People are like trees and store their learning within the roots of their minds. If a teaching comes to a person in a dark and fearful way, that is how the roots of the mind will perceive it and feed upon it."

Twin Chiefs laughed good-humoredly. "I had thought that this teaching was only for Estchimah," he chuckled. "But now I see that I too am upon the journey."

"The peace chiefs of your People must never forget this!" Four Sleeping Lions quickly answered. "We are all upon the journey, and even though we have been shown the shields and the painting of the teachings, this does not mean we must fall asleep!"

"Please continue," Twin Chiefs said as he looked at Estchimah.

"I have flown up from the center of my painting," Four Sleeping Lions went on. "It is my way to teach in this manner, but there is a problem that exists among us. It is a very old problem, which many Peoples have had to face and overcome. This problem is language. The language of the People who rule our world is a language trapped inside the pyramid of authority which the language itself has created. People of power always assume that there is a higher law than the people of the community. Our chiefs have learned this. The People of power who now live around us follow the law of the pyramid. The Buffalo Teachers knew that such a way was dangerous."

"Then our chiefs left their cities because they feared the pyramidal rule?" Twin Chiefs asked in surprise.

"They did," Four Sleeping Lions answered. "The rule of the pyramid is not the rule of law. This rule is primitive. It can be used and twisted in such a way that it is above the laws of the People. The law must always come *from* the People and be understood by them. No law can be above any person within the community. Each person must be the equal of the law. I will speak more of this at another time.

"Here is another portion:

"We saw the pyramid begin to become law for the People, and we were alarmed. We witnessed the enclosing of the thunderbird nest. We saw the children and ourselves being entombed within the pyramid.

"The mother's circle is the most important circle in the world. This is the introduction to the world for everyone.

"Every mother holds absolute power over her child. The circle the mother lives within describes reality to her, and she in her turn describes reality to her child. She does this by her every breath and action. Even her heartbeat is a model to the child.

"As children grow, they quickly learn all the invisible trails of the world they live within. They learn the language of the People they are born into. They learn both the spoken language and the unspoken language.

"Everything within this first tiny circle is a force that teaches the child.

"All human beings are individuals, powers unto themselves, and each human determines a part of his world reality. But this reality we possess is only one tiny flower among the many that are our Medicine Wheel.

"The peace chiefs never sat in places of judgment to decide what was real. Never! It was their way to allow the People to seek this illumination themselves."

Four Sleeping Lions paused to light her pipe, then spoke again.

"Here is another portion," she said, continuing the story.

"The medicine woman whose name was Carving Dogs On The Temples began to teach our young concerning the Black Shield. She told us that our children were learning the language of the pyramids, and that these children were being cut away from the principal person in the mirror of the Black Shield. The language of the pyramids is entombing them, she explained. Their language is becoming the language of the pyramids. These children are being separated from the natural law.

"The People of the law and the astronomers had always been concerned with the gentle weaning of the children from their first circle. This was acted out in the naming ceremonies, where the children were transformed into their new selves. Thus the message Carving Dogs On The Temples brought to the People's councils moved them to take positive action.

"I will describe this action, but before I do, I wish to speak about the first circle.

"Children are provided for. The father, the physically stronger of the two most important people in the child's world, is a provider, equal to the provider-mother. Each child sees this in a unique way and structures it into its own world. As the child grows, its circle grows with it until it encompasses its entire camp. That child in its own unique way introduces into its own world what it is able to perceive of the larger camp circle.

"When they have begun to understand how to dance with this larger circle, the children then begin to mimic this larger circle of the People. This is a time of change for them. The child has emerged from its second womb and been born into the world of the People. This important time is to be celebrated with ceremony.

"The ceremony is simple. The child is placed before the entire camp and a circle is drawn around it.

" 'We have noticed you are aware that we exist,' the Medicine Woman or

Man tells the child. She or he does this in a loud voice, so that everyone can hear.

" 'We are honored to have you among us,' the Medicine Person continues. 'Play among our lodges and know that you are welcome here. But remember this. I, your aunt-uncle, tell you this: you are yourself. That is why we have held this ceremony for you.'

"The children are very young when this ceremony takes place. They quickly structure it into their world as a matter of fact.

"From this age onward the child is given every opportunity to touch the things of the People.

"The child holds the hunter's bow, sews moccasins with the moccasin maker, participates in sacred rituals. It does this not as a game, but as an equal with the shaman. It is in this way that the child sees a baby born; sees the buffalo hunted and sees it butchered; sees the making of the bow, arrows, and lances; sees how the sick are cured, sees the wounded and bleeding mended; sees the dead, sees the flowering and the withering. Nothing is hidden from the child, absolutely nothing! The child touches reality!

"The child does not, of course, carry scalding water or try to drive a lance into a charging buffalo. To assume this would be foolish. The child participates in the only way a child can, which is as a child.

"But this is true only in a balanced camp, a circle camp. It is not the same with the pyramid People. The child who lives within the immovable blocks of the pyramidal camp can never do this. The peace chiefs saw this."

"Why did they not take action?" Estchimah asked.

"I will answer you briefly, Estchimah," Four Sleeping Lions replied. "But I will not criticize the People of the Pyramid because I do not recognize them nor their powers. It is for those who want such a way to argue with it," Four Sleeping Lions chuckled. "When you are caught in a trap, that

is when you hear great arguments about what it is, or who was to blame for it. But to me this is foolish. Everyone in a pyramidal camp is in a fixed position. They can never really move. To move in such a hierarchy is only an illusion supported by the very myths which support the structure. People within such a structure can only perceive the supporting stones around them, above or below. The realities they are taught have no relationship to anything natural. They learn only that which is relative to where they are within the pyramid.

"Anything or anyone outside the pyramid is an enemy and is either ignored, destroyed, or forced to fit. This law is very primitive, of course, and it invites destruction."

Four Sleeping Lions paused for a moment and then continued.

"Here is another portion:

"We fought this way and war was brought upon us and many fell to the sword axes and arrows of our own People. In the year of the Moving Snake In The Stars we gathered together and began to move north to the land of the wild people.

"One thousand canoes, each with twelve people in them, set out from the great cities and moved north to find the Grandfather River.

"The year of the Moving Snake In The Stars was three thousand years ago," Four Sleeping Lions said. "The land of the Sweet Medicine is the land where you and I now live. The Grandfather River is the river also known as the Mother of Waters," Four Sleeping Lions continued.

"Such terrible things visited us. We were torn and killed. There was much misery and weeping, and many wished to return. Three hundred canoes were all that were left of our world. Sixty of our canoes turned back to beg the forgiveness of the priests.

"Forty of the canoes of the People reached their destination. The entire journey lasted eighteen years. After these People left The World Under The Ground, the world of the pyramids, they called themselves the Lodge Builders, the Mandans. The People who were called the In The

Pyramid Priests became known as the Hopi, the artisans. A part of the In The Pyramid Priests People moved further north and became the People known as the Haida. All these Peoples were to marry with the wild Peoples, and all of them were altered forever by the customs of their new families.

"Here is another portion:

"Four Mirrors and his wife, Carving Dogs On The Temples, brought us overland, and we fought desperately for our lives. We met great forces of warriors who wanted us for slaves. Hundreds fell in battle. We left a trail of blood. Falling Into The Sky was stricken. His legs would not move. Four Mirrors wept and tore his breast. Four Mirrors would not speak for one moon. We all were crying.

"Four Mirrors and his People struggled north until they reached the land of the Silver People. It was in that place they first settled.

"Four Mirrors called a council.

" 'We are within the land of the Sweet Medicine!' Four Mirrors said to the People. 'It is here we will Sun Dance and teach our children.' "

"The land of Sweet Medicine," Estchimah smiled.

"Yes," Four Sleeping Lions said, touching Estchimah's hand. "Now you, my daughter, are going upon your Vision Quest. You must be mindful of what you gather within that wonderful dance with our Mother the Earth. Each person's Quest is always the same, just as it is also different," she smiled, looking into Estchimah's eyes. "You have been born into a world in which everything has been divided into blocks within a pyramid, but your own inward world is the circle. You must learn how to reflect that inward world into everything that is around you."

"How can I do that?" Estchimah asked with emotion. "I truly wish to do that, grandmother."

"You must be awake," the old woman answered. "The circle of change begins with you."

Estchimah began to cry.

"What is wrong?" Twin Chiefs asked with concern.

"I understand the pity you have for yourself," Four Sleeping Lions said gently. "But you are dancing yourself into a closed circle. Awaken, my daughter, and speak of what is in your heart."

"What is in my heart is awful!" Estchimah said, brushing away a tear. "You have shared beautiful dreams with me, but what have I given you in return?"

"There is something else you wish to say," Four Sleeping Lions said, leaning closer. "Tell me what it is."

"The world I live in is beautiful," she answered, hesitating. "Yet it is awful!"

"Speak of it!" the old woman commanded her. "Do not fall asleep!"

"It embarrasses me," Estchimah said, as the tears rolled down her face.

"Tell us," the old woman insisted. Her voice was kind.

"Promise you will not get angry," Estchimah asked, looking at the old woman from beneath her eyelashes.

"I promise," Four Sleeping Lions said gently. "Tell us."

"All right," she said, sitting up and brushing away another tear. "I, I have . . ." she hesitated. "I have heard . . ." She then raised her voice. "All my life I have heard many false and unreal things. These things were paths that twisted and turned and led nowhere. They were no better than buffalo dung." She looked at Four Sleeping Lions. "I must understand, grandmother."

"If what we have been sharing with you is the same?" She laughed heartily. "Of course it is! It all is!"

"It is?" Estchimah asked, frowning in surprise.

"Everything is dung," Four Sleeping Lions laughed. "If you try to eat that dung it will sicken you. Does the buffalo eat dung? No, my daughter, it

does not! However, Estchimah, the dung from the buffalo is food for the grass. It is a circle." She smiled. "Our words are also grass, grass for the buffalo. The buffalo eats the grass, and the power of its body transforms the grass into food. There are many people who try to keep the grass just as they find it. These people never eat the grass. There are others who discover the grass and want it to remain in its perfect form. When these eat the grass they refuse to let it change." She laughed heartily. "Place everything we have shared with you in the wonderful garden that is within yourself. Let each symbol be a seed of your own learning. Learn to say what is in your heart and mind, and it will become food for you. But keep it secret and it will become foul."

"I thought myself dishonest for holding doubts in my mind," Estchimah said, still frowning. "I have been afraid to go upon my Vision Quest," she said, brightening up. "I have been afraid that I would learn nothing!" She sought for words. "I have been afraid that nothing would happen, and yet at the same time I have been afraid that something horrible would happen."

"Are you still afraid?" the old woman asked.

"Of course!" Estchimah answered and smiled. "But now I will place whatever happens in the wonderful garden within me."

"The Vision Quest is a marriage with ourselves," the old woman said gently. "And it is a marriage with the Earth. Let me tell you of the four walls."

"The four walls?" Estchimah frowned. "I feel trapped just hearing the words."

"It is common for all People to build the four walls," the old woman smiled. "The Buffalo Teachers call it the Place Where All The Mirrors Are Hidden."

"How is it possible to hide the Great Mirrors?" Estchimah asked.

"Not the Great Mirrors," the old woman laughed good-humoredly, "but

the little ones. To the South, in the place of trust and innocence, is the wall of your childhood. The powers that make up that wall are all the children you grew up with. The wall grew as you grew, a living wall with your beginning years. You, my daughter, are afraid to walk through that wall.

"To the North is another wall. That wall is made up of every teacher you ever had. Even Twin Chiefs and I are there, and so are you. There is every kind of teacher there, living or dead. Everything that ever taught you is there within that wall. You, my daughter, are also frightened to walk through that wall.

"To the East is another wall. That wall is made up of everything dead. All religions are there. You, my daughter, are frightened to walk through that wall.

"To the West is the fourth wall. That wall is the wall of dreams. A portion of that wall is reflected into the wall of the East, just as the North and the South walls are reflected into one another. Those things of the dead that are mirrored into the West wall are the many dreams that you have let die. You, my daughter, are afraid to walk through that wall."

"Is there no way out?" Estchimah asked emotionally.

"There is," the old woman smiled. "But first we will speak of the many tiny mirrors from which the floor of that place is built. Can you guess as to the nature of some of those mirrors?"

"I have no guesses," Estchimah frowned.

"Many of those tiny mirrors are from the world into which you were born. Some of them are from the world of your mother," the old woman explained. "There are old images in that world, the world of remembrance. Each one of those tiny old mirrors blinds you to the path that can free you from that world."

"What is the path?" Estchimah asked with fear.

"If you truly begin to question each of the mirrors you have placed in

that world," the old woman answered, "or question who it was that placed those mirrors into your world, then you will see the path through the West wall."

"But you said that I was frightened to walk through that wall," Estchimah said with emotion.

"You will walk through that wall on your Vision Quest," the old woman smiled. "There have been many who have walked through the West wall. They have walked through that wall in as many ways as there are People. The West wall is the wall of dreams. Many fear that there is nothing beyond the wall and that they will be alone," she chuckled, "but these, of course, have never questioned and have never walked through the wall. Beyond the wall is reality. Within the enclosure of the walls is unreality. Beyond the wall is the great world of your own mind. It is a world as beautiful and varied as this one we call the earth."

"Would you give me an example?" Estchimah asked.

"I will," the old woman said. "But you must understand that it is only a tiny reflection of what awaits those who walk through the West wall. If I were to try to explain reason to a child of seven winters, that child would understand only that portion of the circle she could see. Do you remember the little girl that you once were?"

"When I was seven winters?" Estchimah asked.

"When you were seven winters," the old woman replied.

"Not very well," Estchimah answered.

"But who can remember that child more completely than yourself?" the old woman said. "Not even your mother knew that little girl as completely as you did. However, that knowledge is now in the past. What would you teach that little girl if you could meet her right now—if you could meet your seven-year-old self? Where would you begin? What would you say? How would you introduce yourself to the knowledge you would need?"

"It makes my head spin," Estchimah laughed.

"There are many who experienced much pain as children," the old woman said evenly. "It is not amusing. The child's world is very small. It is always just big enough for the child to comprehend. The chiefs who live in The Place Of The Maze saw this phenomenon, and they marveled at it. They saw the children building the four walls around themselves, and they saw how the People added to those walls. It frightened them, Estchimah, because they saw that the walls could destroy the mind, the heart, the body, and the emotions of the human being. They saw many fight against those walls only to become frightened, lonely people. They saw others shrink into one corner of their worlds and go insane. We begin to see, as those chiefs began to see, when we teach the children within us concerning ourselves and the world around us. It was these chiefs who discovered the way called the Vision Quest."

"Is my necklace magic?" Estchimah asked.

"Why did you ask me that?" the old woman smiled.

"I . . ." she said, wrinkling her brow. "Because I was wondering about it."

"The necklace is somehow mirrored into your world," the old woman said, emphasizing her words. "It has some direct connection to something that existed in your past. The connection you made in your mind was a simple response. You wanted to speak of what I had just told you, but you could not find the words. You sought for a symbol, something to say, and the necklace formed itself within your mind. What you did, Estchimah, was to substitute the necklace for thinking."

"I do not know what to say," Estchimah said, gesturing. "What you are saying is true!"

"There is no substitute for thinking," the old woman said. "You are fortunate in that you were born into two circles, two camps. You have two approaches of mind. One is the square, the pyramid. The other is the circle, the sphere. You have learned from both."

"I feel what you are telling me, but I still cannot put it into words," Estchimah said.

"You think!" the old woman said with emphasis. "Feeling is only the shadow of thought. It follows thought. Estchimah, look at me. What do you see?"

"I see my grandmother, a woman with white hair," Estchimah answered. "I see a wise woman, a gentle person and gentle teacher."

"Is there anything strange about me?" the old woman asked.

"Strange?" Estchimah asked, scrutinizing the woman who sat before her. "No, I see nothing strange."

"What am I wearing?" Four Sleeping Lions asked.

"The dress of a shamaness," Estchimah answered. "Upon your dress are painted four plumed serpents. You have four mirrors tied into your braids with the sign of balance painted upon them. Your moccasins have beautiful tiny moons made of silver and gold sewn upon them. I think that you are wise and—"

"That is enough," the old woman smiled. "Now, what do you see that is different?"

"From what?" Estchimah asked, perplexed.

"That was what I was hoping you would say," the old woman laughed. "I appear quite ordinary to you because we are both of the same People, the same circle." She laughed again. "But to someone from the world of the pyramid, I would be considered different. The ordinary, or what we think is ordinary, is almost invisible. The invisible is what I have been trying to help you see. This is of utmost importance when we consider the many symbols of the mind. You were searching for recognizable signs, for symbols within your mind. You wished to respond to what I had told you. The new symbols within your mind were waiting for you to give them meaning within your own perceiving. You chose to not speak

within the power of the new signs because you did not see a recognizable path. Consequently you chose the necklace path."

"There is magic in the necklace then," Estchimah smiled. "Because now I have learned."

"You learned because I walked down that path with you," Four Sleeping Lions said evenly. "You could have walked the same path alone and learned from your own Chiefs, the ones who are the Law Circle within you."

"I will be mindful of my Circle of Law, of my Chiefs," Estchimah said. She clapped her hands together in the sign of celebration.

"There are no teachers as great as the powers that live within you," the old woman smiled. "It is these principal people who dream with you. Protect them, love them, give them information. All this is food to help them grow. But above all, you must council with them."

"This is your third gift," Four Sleeping Lions said as she folded a bright Sun Dance robe about Estchimah.

"And this is your fourth gift," Twin Chiefs smiled as he handed her a white buffalo robe. "Sit upon this robe, my daughter, it will comfort you. I will be waiting below your Vision Hill."

He turned, picked up his pipe, and slowly walked away.

"Below your memory is power," Four Sleeping Lions sang. Then a beautiful rainbow began to dance around her. It shimmered and sparkled like the northern lights. The circle of light began to move faster and faster until it became a surge of lightning mixed with thunder. Slowly, gracefully, within the circle of moving power and light, Four Sleeping Lions began her transformation. First she was old; then she changed into a beautiful young woman; she changed again and became a laughing girl; then within her fourth transformation she became a little girl of seven winters.

"Below your memory is power," the little girl sang.

The Black Shield began to reflect the star-filled sky, becoming a Medicine Pool.

"The Pool of Memory," the little girl sang.

The light spun, dazzling in its brightness, and the little girl became the beautiful Plumed Serpent Of The Stars.

"Below your memory," the Plumed Serpent whispered as she disappeared gracefully beneath the mirror of the pool.

The light rippled the surface of the water, and the pool became smaller and smaller. As the pool changed, its color changed, first to brilliant red, then into a fountain of sparks. Then quietly, in one blink of Estchimah's eyes, it suddenly became the flames of her campfire on the Vision Hill.

"Below my memory," Estchimah whispered to herself as she looked into the coals of her fire.

A WEEK LATER Little Wolf told Dancing Tree that Crazy Dog wanted to speak with him.

"Why did he not ask me himself?" Dancing Tree asked in surprise.

"I do not know," Little Wolf answered. "He left before the light this morning. He went to Medicine Hat Butte. He asked that you meet him there."

It was noon before Dancing Tree came into view of the butte. He searched for signs of Crazy Dog's horse. It wasn't long before he found a clear trail, and he set off to follow it. It pointed straight toward the butte. The tracks were so clear he spent little time studying them, until suddenly he noticed that they stopped abruptly at the very face of the butte.

"His tracks lead right into solid rock!" he thought out loud. "But that is impossible."

He searched a little more. There was something strange about the tracks. When he dismounted to study them he heard Crazy Dog's voice above him.

"It is an old trick," Crazy Dog laughed. "I did it just to give you a good laugh while I waited. The trick is to ride your horse up to the.

rock and then away, then brush out the returning tracks with pine boughs. It looks strange, doesn't it?" He laughed.

"These prints are not deep enough for a horse to have made them," Dancing Tree said, examining them.

"Right again," Crazy Dog laughed. "That was my second trick. I made the tracks with the hooves of a dead horse."

"What does it mean?" Dancing Tree asked, smiling. "Crazy Dog, you are a master trickster. You must have suckled from mother coyote herself."

Crazy Dog laughed and disappeared behind a large boulder.

Dancing Tree led his horse a short distance away and picketed it in good grass. Then he found himself some shade.

"He isn't going to have me chasing my own shadow today," he said, leaning his back against what appeared to be a tree.

"Are you not already doing so?" Crazy Dog laughed. "I am not just any old tree you can lean upon, you know."

"That is the most wonderful trick you have ever done," Dancing Tree laughed. "You did not make a sound as you came up behind me."

"Last winter you asked if I would give you some power medicine," Crazy Dog said as he sat down. He opened up a small pouch. "And I, in my turn, asked you to tell me of the circle of foxes."

"I guess I forgot about it," Dancing Tree laughed. "It made no sense to me then, and it still does not."

"There are many people," Crazy Dog said as he drew a circle upon the ground, "very many, who walk all of their lives within the fox circle. The fox circle is a spherical world that has no up, down, in, or out."

Dancing Tree laughed.

"Here," Crazy Dog grinned. He handed Dancing Tree a bowl of roots he had gathered. "You have never tasted these before. Try them."

"They are good!" Dancing Tree said, taking a bite. Then he shook his head. "But they are a bit sour."

"If I were to tell you to find some of these roots, what would be your approach?" Crazy Dog asked.

"I would first ask you where you found them and then how to identify the growing herb. I would also ask you at what time of the season they should be gathered," he answered with a tone of certainty.

"What if I told you that you needed to learn of the fox circle first, before you could identify the herb?"

"Then I would naturally ask you about the fox circle." He laughed. He was expecting to be tricked, and he enjoyed the game of it.

"Consider with me," Crazy Dog said, looking into Dancing Tree's eyes. "Consider your mind as you speak with me. Also consider the two circles that I have drawn for you here upon the ground." He pointed. "One circle is the fox circle, and the other is the learning of the lightning root. If I described the herb physically to you, where it grows, and the season to gather it, you could find it, could you not?"

"Easily," Dancing Tree answered.

"Now, consider this," Crazy Dog said, pointing at the other circle. "Suppose with me, that if you were to walk within this circle of foxes, you could no longer recognize the herb."

"That is ridiculous!" Dancing Tree laughed. "Funny, too!" He laughed again. He was feeling flippant, playful. "It seems to be one more Crazy Dog circle to me! Little Wolf's circles are much easier for me to walk."

"To the South, in the circle of foxes," Crazy Dog went on patiently, "you will discover the people who lived within your immediate family, the persons who shared their world with you. To the North, reflecting what you can discover in the South, is the camp circle, the circle you grew within. To the West, in that circle of foxes, you can discover power, authority, dreams, and laws. Reflected into the West are the children, the Eastern side of the circle of foxes. These are all the children that grew up with you.

"You have already learned the language of that circle of foxes. Also its songs, its laws, and its dreams. These are four powers: language, song, law, and dreams. These dreams are not of the West, even though they were taken from that place. Instead, they are of the circle of foxes. The songs are not of the North, even though they were borrowed from the North. Instead they are the ways of that circle of foxes. Those ways, the paths within the songs you learned within that circle where you grew, are the songs of your People. The language of that circle of foxes was taken from the South, but it is not reflective of the South. Instead, it also was the language of the circle of foxes. These laws of the East are also borrowed; they are of the circle of foxes."

"I agree," Dancing Tree said. He laughed and slapped his leg. "That would get a hundred wolves lost on one trail." He laughed even harder at the image that formed itself in his mind. "Even though they were all four steps apart!"

"I see," Crazy Dog said, as he moved to make himself more comfortable. "What if I told you that those roots you have just eaten are poison?"

"You do not poison me," Dancing Tree smiled. "You nourish me." He meant to flatter Crazy Dog. "All the food you give me is good for me. It strengthens me!"

"You are too ignorant to assume so much," Crazy Dog answered. His face was hard as stone. "You trample the flowers I point out to you, no differently than if you were a stumbling blind bull."

"Why do you insult me?" Dancing Tree asked, sobering. "You embarrass me!" He moved uncomfortably. "Why do you try to cause me anger?"

"You should not be embarrassed," Crazy Dog answered, his face still not showing one movement. "Do you even know when you are insulted? The circle of foxes you grew within assaulted your mind, insulted your presence of being, poisoned you with violent symbols of language, and destroyed your integrity within the laws they taught you. Those laws stripped you naked, left you with no authority of your own, and imprisoned you within an unnatural world. You move through the circle of time and the country changes around you, changing you and changing itself, but your mind does not change. It remains exactly the same! Your dreams must be unbelievably boring!"

"I must tell you something," Dancing Tree said, leaning forward and placing his elbows on his knees. He looked directly into Crazy Dog's eyes. "You are the strangest man I have ever met! I do not have the vaguest idea of what you are talking about!"

"I know," Crazy Dog said, letting out his breath. He reached for one of the lightning roots and slowly began to chew it, thinking.

Still looking at Crazy Dog, Dancing Tree shook his head and smiled. He also reached for another of the foods within the painted bowl.

"Zaaugh!" Crazy Dog smiled as he ate. "Eating these lightning roots reminds me of the time I visited the camps of the Wood Carvers. I made the journey with my wife, Two Dawns. We walked north, walking because there were no horses in those times, until we came to the place known as Two Medicine Hats Dancing. We lived among a tiny camp of People who called themselves Black Moccasins. We lived with them until the spring, and then they had a big give-away for us. We were given clothes, bows, arrows, robes, traveling food, and a beautiful canoe.

"On the way we stayed with the Snake Water People and the Crow People. Then we traveled by canoe until we came to the Great Water. At the Great Water we danced with the Wood Carver People.

"We had taken four pipes with us when we first set out. These four pipes were to be given to four Medicine Women."

"What do you mean?" Dancing Tree interrupted. "Were those real pipes, or stories from your family?"

"Both," Crazy Dog answered with a smile. "We had left one of the pipes with the Black Moccasin People, one with the Snake Water People, one with the Crow People, and the last one we gave to the Wood Carver People."

"Had this been done before? Was it a custom?" Dancing Tree asked, intrigued with the story.

"It had been done before," Crazy Dog answered. "It was called Taking, Giving, Holding, Loosening Medicine Arrow Journeys, at least by the circle of foxes within which I grew. Other Peoples call them other things, but it does not matter what they are called. It is still the same journey.

"Two Dawns and I had pledged to make this journey at the Sun Dance the year before. We knew that at other Sun Dances within the land of the Sweet Medicine there were other people who had made the same pledge. It is a very ancient custom! Four Mirrors, thousands of years ago, taught the Sun Dance People of these ways."

"Did only the young make these journeys?" Dancing Tree asked with curiosity.

"No," Crazy Dog answered. "It was not just the young that made these long journeys. Sometimes it was the old. Age had nothing to do with it. It could be a very dangerous journey, and many times the people who went upon these journeys never returned. But each person who made the journey wore a spirit shirt. This was the sign for all the people they might meet, saying they were walking the path of peace and carrying the journey pipes."

"But there were times these people were killed or captured?" Dancing Tree asked.

"Many times," Crazy Dog answered. "But there were also those who did not suffer hardship. One man and woman came among our People and lived twenty-four changes of the moon south of us. Then finally they returned to their People. When they left they told us that they would return as they had come and that they would exchange songs with each camp they met along the way.

" 'We will exchange songs with the people we walk among,' they told our camp. 'It is a great sign for you, this Sun Dance way. When we reach our own People and our own lodges we will send this camp a necklace of green turtle shells. We will send seven of them. Count them, and know that each one is a touching, a coup. It will be a sign for you that we had a safe journey, and that we are telling your stories at our fires.' "

"Did you receive the necklaces?" Dancing Tree asked.

"Only one," Crazy Dog answered. "Six disappeared somewhere upon the journey trail." He smiled. "But we recognized the sign of those two visitors. Their signs were upon the shells of the necklace. We knew that they were back among their People, and that they were telling our stories. It was a good feeling! Guess with me. How many winters do you think passed before my camp received that necklace?"

"Two. Three, perhaps," Dancing Tree answered.

"I was sixteen winters old when the visitors left our camp," Crazy Dog smiled, "and twenty-one when the necklace was brought to our council fire! The power of that sign danced with me and sang to me in my mind and in my dreams. Two Dawns was also very much moved by the power of that sign. The following year at the Sun Dance, we spoke to the People and decided to make one of the journeys ourselves."

"How long was your journey?" asked Dancing Tree.

"Eight years," Crazy Dog answered. "We were five years getting there and then three years returning."

"Eight years!" Dancing Tree exclaimed, blowing out his cheeks. "That is a long journey!"

"There are much longer journeys which can be taken within one very tiny circle," Crazy Dog smiled. "Everybody journeys, I learned that. When Two Dawns and I returned we were both pleasantly surprised and horrified."

"Why? What had happened while you were away?" Dancing Tree asked, frowning. "Did something terrible happen while you were gone?"

"We were very happy to be back among our People," Crazy Dog answered, "but surprised that we had never truly known any of them. We were also horrified at the ignorance we found among our People."

"Then what happened?" Dancing Tree asked.

"We began to sing of the People we had met," Crazy Dog answered. "We told of their ways, their medicines, their laws, and their dances. We gave our People the last of the four beautiful dance masks that had been given to us by the Wood Carvers. But when Two Dawns told our camp of the balance we had found between the women and the men in the camps we had visited, we experienced the wrath of the camp. The People I lived among would not hear this teaching. Our Medicine People instructed us to tell the others we had lied.

"I knew that we were in tremendous danger, more terrible danger than we had faced in the eight years of our journey! I cautioned my wife of this danger, but she insisted upon confronting the Medicine People." Crazy Dog looked down at his hands. "I did not have the courage to confront my family, the camp, myself, or the Medicine People." His voice lowered, became saddened. "I was very much prepared to lie." He shook his head. "It was a horrible time for me, and yet it became the most powerful in my life." He made the sign with his hands that a circle had been completed. "I did the worst thing I could possibly have done. I became neutral. Two Dawns fought by herself." He began to rub his knees with the remembrance. Pain showed itself upon his face. "The argument grew, and the camp became divided. Still I persisted in my fear! I tried to find the courage to fight with Two Dawns, but I could not. Then one day, just as the hunting summer ended, we were both summoned to the center of our camp. Two Dawns and I knew we might be banished, or worse." He rubbed his arms, partially hugging himself. His eyes showed pain. "I wanted to run, but Two Dawns would not hear of it." He stopped.

"What happened?" Dancing Tree asked, leaning forward.

"I was just remembering," Crazy Dog said, straightening up. "Our People had received their first horses two years before our return." Again he paused briefly. "A warrior, a reckless young man, came charging over the hill straight towards us. I knew that he meant to kill us. Behind him rode another, another, and still another!

" 'What should we do?' Two Dawns cried. 'We cannot fight! We cannot kill our own family!'

" 'Run!' I said as I hit her horse with my quirt.

"We raced away from the camp. The war arrows of our brothers were hissing past us! I turned to look back just as one of the arrows caught my horse low in the leg. He jumped. It threw him off stride, and we both rolled into the dirt.

Two Dawns jumped down beside me and helped me from the ground. We strung our bows, waiting. The warriors had jumped to the ground to fight us hand-to-hand. There was a fierce fight! It sickens me to even retell it! We fought a defensive fight because we did not wish to kill!" A small quiver appeared in Crazy Dog's voice. "But I felt their hatred. I have never felt so much hatred in my life!

"Then suddenly everything became quiet! I had been hit by a war ax, and it had driven me into a sleep near death.

"When I awoke I immediately tried to jump to my feet! It seemed that I had been stunned only for the briefest of time, but no," he said as he touched his forehead. His voice was filled with pain. "I had been asleep for nearly one full day! I awoke within the lodge of my uncle, Diving Hawk. He grabbed me when I jumped to my feet and helped me to lie back down. The pain in my head was almost unbearable!

" 'The war is over!' he said to me as he comforted me. 'Two Dawns no longer lives!' He was a man who always was direct. He believed that knowing the truth saved people pain.

"Instead of crying," Crazy Dog's voice raised, "I laughed! Yes, my son, I laughed." His voice began to take on new strength. "I never would have believed it, but I laughed. Then I began to cry. I do not know how long I wept. When I awoke the second time, I was changed! I had become very bitter. My heart had hardened.

"I left my camp and I began to wander.

"Nine moons later I met the Medicine Man called Littlest Creek. It was that man who cared for me, taught me, and at last caused my heart to heal. Two years after I had left my camp of People, I heard the story of the circle of foxes for the first time. Would you care to hear that story?"

"I would," Dancing Tree answered, almost in a whisper. He was not looking at the man who sat in front of him.

"Sit up," Crazy Dog said in a commanding voice. "Look at me and hear this story."

Dancing Tree slowly raised his head and looked into Crazy Dog's eyes. "I am ready," he said.

"This story," Crazy Dog began, "was brought into the land of the Sweet Medicine by the two Medicine People called Wears Gold South People.

"The person who told me the story was a young and powerful man whose name was Bird In Ground. His home, where I then visited, was in the great stone ruins in the south.

" 'Well,' Bird In Ground smiled as he began telling me his story, 'it seems that all of us here have one thing in common.' He clapped his hands together. 'All of us have experienced a tragedy! We are within the circle of tragedy together, brothers and sisters. We are learning the song that the Wears Gold South People brought to this camp we now sit in,' he said, 'in fact, to this very lodge!'

"We all sat in silence.

" 'This is the story of the man called Circle of Foxes,' Bird In Ground said with a powerful voice. 'This is how he freed himself from slavery!'

"Bird In Ground spoke my language, but he also signed because many were there who did not know his tongue. He signed to these people as he spoke.

"A tall man named Sword Axe Person slowly stood up. Possibly he had been wounded in battle because he favored one leg, leaning slightly. He appeared to be even taller in the firelight. He was a kind man, very powerful. We shared a sleeping room together, a room within the great stone ruins.

"'Bird In Ground,' Sword Ax Person signed, 'we have no names here!' He stopped and looked at the people who sat around him, especially at me. His eyes held me for a very long time. Everyone waited. It was the custom to wait, to be patient. 'You have asked us not to speak while we are in the rooms of the ruins.' He stopped again. He seemed to be thinking. 'But you also explained to us that we could speak while we sat with you here in this kiva.' He stopped again. He seemed to be warring with his decision to speak. 'I speak now because in my sleeping room I have been placed with a brother who is a gentle man, yet he is also a man of war.' He turned and looked at me. 'I feel that his heart is caught within a violent dance. It disturbs me greatly.' He stopped again. It was easy to see the pain robed behind his eyes. 'I have grown to love that man.' He straightened. 'I have never sung a song of comfort to any man.' He hesitated. His signs hung in the air as an eagle would hover on the wind. 'Never to any child or woman. To no one!' He was keeping himself in perfect control. 'It is now my wish that we all sing the quiet song together.' He looked around and slowly sat back down upon the painted robe that had been provided for him.

"A long silence followed. I sat feeling tense, nervous, and angry! It embarrassed me that a man would request a comforting song for me, a child's song! The silence seemed to grow.

"'Are they also embarrassed?' I thought to myself. 'Or is it that they believe that I am embarrassed?' I tried to find a word, an image in my mind that spoke of how I saw myself. I was becoming even more angry. The silence grew. Everything waited. The whole world seemed to be waiting.

"'Are they laughing?' I asked in my mind. A cold panic, then a fierce determination danced up within me, as water boils up from the earth. The silence remained. Now it seemed to be watching me, peering into every detail of my existence! A good looking woman of strong presence suddenly let a string of beads she had been holding fall from her hands to her lap. The sound of them made me jump! I felt in my whole being that she had purposely dropped them because of her contempt for me.

"The silence continued. Then suddenly Bird In Ground lifted his arms. His swift movement startled me as if I had seen lightning! My entire being shrank. The muscles in my body jerked, causing me to tremble. I was determined to leave the kiva and never look back! I despised everyone there, especially the man who had embarrassed me!

" 'We have sung the quiet song, each one to ourselves, because that is the custom,' Bird In Ground said and smiled. 'It is a good custom!' He clapped his hands.

"I tried to move, testing my muscles to see if they would answer to my commands. I planned to stand and walk away. It was important to me that I not show panic. I did not wish to wobble, to appear in any way affected!

"Suddenly the woman began to cry. I bit my lip. My head was bowed, I could not look anyone in the face! I watched the woman and the others from beneath my eyebrows. I was angry and determined.

"Then the woman spoke. 'I have never sung the quiet song, the comforting song,' she said in a halting voice. Her head was bowed just like mine. 'It embarrassed me, at first . . .' She stopped and wrung her hands. 'At first I was angry, I felt it was an imposition!' Suddenly she raised her tear-streaked face and looked around the room. 'To sing a child's love song to a man.' Her voice trembled slightly. 'Especially to that man.' She pointed at me. 'It tore at my heart like a badger tears at the ground with its digging claws! I felt humiliated that I should be asked to participate in such a thing!' Her eyes dropped. 'The man for whom we have all sung appears to be overly confident; he almost swaggers with strength.' She spaced her words, searching among them. 'I despised him for that! But then I saw that his flippancy, his arrogance, his entire being was only a robe. His robe hides a very ordinary person. I saw that our song embarrassed him, even frightened him!' Her voice became warm. 'I saw into him and through him. He was angry, frightened, and no doubt determined to leave us forever! But somehow, he found the strength to stay.'

"The silence that followed her talk was even more oppressive than the first. I struggled in my mind, trying to find something to say, some action to perform. I thought I would laugh, tell them something funny, but the words that came from my mouth surprised me.

" 'I stayed because I was unable to move,' I confessed in a shaky voice. I would have said more, but I could not. My breath seemed to leave me, to dwindle in my throat! I was stung with shame! I knew that I was too weak to stand, otherwise I would have run!

" 'It was the same for me,' an older man said very quietly. His voice shook slightly with emotion. 'I also could not move.'

" 'Nor I,' another man signed. 'I thought that the beautiful robed woman who just spoke,' his signs wavered nervously in the air, 'I thought that she was laughing at me.'

" 'When she dropped her beads,' a round-faced man from the far north signed, 'the sound of those beads was like the breaking of ice on a lake ten thousand steps wide.'

" 'I knew that it shamed him,' a tall young woman said. 'At first, it delighted me to know he suffered. Then I pitied him.' She looked directly into each of our faces. 'Then I saw that Sword Ax Person had deliberately chosen to speak of one among us, the only person among us who would not immediately react in physical violence.'

" 'He did so choose,' Bird In Ground smiled. 'That is the teaching.' He clapped his hands. 'As is everything else that happened within each of you! Sword Ax Person has danced a mirror dance with you. All of you in this kiva, this ruined world, are violent. You perceive the world in violence. Each one of you came here because you walk the trail of death. Each one of you has experienced tragedy. Each one of you is captured within the circle of determination and revenge.

" 'All of you have been harshly cut away from the world you once lived within. All of you wander aimlessly upon the paths of the great earth.' He raised his voice, becoming very hard in his face. 'You expected that we would entertain you with a medicine story, but let me tell all of you this.' He leaned forward. 'You are already within the story! We have driven you into the first circle!' He leaned back against the western wall of the kiva and lowered his voice. 'Each one of you knew the custom. Each one of you had the way of this kiva carefully explained to you before you came here. Outside the circle of these ruins,' he pointed, making a circle above his head, 'are warriors. They are dog soldiers, dedicated people. It is their duty to bring themselves into combat with any person who tries to leave this circle.

" 'There are those of you who have thought of killing themselves.' His voice again rose and became very clear. 'It is easy to die. Step across the line of this circle and you will be dead. No one may leave this circle until the dance has been completed. Each of you has a story. Every evening, we will meet at the council fire and tell our stories, the stories of our personal tragedies. We will do this for forty-four nights.

" 'Over and over again, you will tell your stories. You will tell them until you have wrung every tiny part, every detail, from your experience! Those who do not tell their stories will not be punished. Not to dance is punishment enough! There may even be those among you who will derive pleasure from that kind of punishment. Indulge in it! We will make sure that your dance lasts longer than the rest. You will indulge until there is not one tiny twinge of feeling left.

" 'You are all within the story. You are dancing within the fox circle. You are within a war, a war of the mind. All twelve of us who dance here are your combatants! We will engage each of you in conflict with us, and in this way you will encounter each other!

" 'You are dogs, dirt under our feet! You are sniveling cowards, stupid children. You are petty, whining fools! Not one of you has mind enough to help yourselves! Become violent! Become violent!' He raised his voice until it filled the cavern of the room. 'We will drive you ever deeper within your violence! If you find pleasure in this, if you find release from pain through violence, we will oblige you.' He lowered his voice, causing it to become threatening. 'Become violent and we will starve you. When you become hungry your thinking will change. You will approach violence differently than if you are well fed. You cannot escape this story! There is no other way out of this circle of foxes except through the dance of the mind.

" 'The questioning dance is the Northern Dance. We are within it!

" 'The answer dance is the Southern Dance. You are within it!

" 'The old mirror dance is known as the Dance of the West. You are within it!

" 'The new mirror dance is the Eastern Dance. You are within it!'

"He stopped, cleared his throat, and looked around at us.

" 'This is the dance lodge called the Earths Of Foxes,' he said. His voice was suddenly kind. 'We have brought you here because of our love for you. Each one of you has come here because a beautiful part of yourself still lives and cares. Each of you has a strong mind, and each of you is a strong person.

" 'The council fire has been lit. Go now from this kiva and bring yourselves into a circle around that fire. We will hear your stories until the dawn and beyond. When we have all become exhausted, we will roll up in our robes and sleep beside the fire. When we awaken we will begin again. You will tell your stories for twelve days. For these twelve days that is all that will be spoken of. After that, we will discuss your stories in every detail until the dance of the forty-four days has been completed.' He quickly rose to his feet and walked out of the lodge. We all followed.

"The stories began. They were all horrible; each one seemed more terrible than the next. By the time the first twelve days had ended, we knew each other's stories in intimate detail.

"We then began the second part of the dance. Again the stories were told, but now we began to talk among ourselves about them. There was only one incident that broke the rhythm of this walk. A young man, a fiery, headstrong young man tested the dog soldiers. He threw himself against them with all of his frustration and pain. They responded in terrible violence, but they never once attacked. Instead they waited for him to attack them. But when he attacked, they answered viciously. He fought on and on until he could no longer move. It was very strange. The dog soldiers never struck first. They only retaliated; they only gave back the blows he gave to them. It was no different than if he had run with all his strength against a stone cliff. He would crash into their ranks and they would repel him. He would actually bounce off them. Over and over again, he ran headlong into the wall of dog soldiers, and over and over again he was bounced back. We all watched in silence. It was forbidden that we should speak.

"We sat in silence for seven days while he healed from the beating he had given himself. He was comforted by the twelve Medicine People. They were six men and six women. We learned of his childhood in all of its detail because that is how those Medicine People spoke with him. To our surprise we learned that the tragedy he had told us about was false! His real tragedy had not been so violent. It was much more subtle but actually more terrible than the wild adventure story he had first told us.

"When he had healed, we all began to tell our stories again. To my surprise many of them were now changed—about half of them! I laughed when I learned this and told everyone that I should have been more inspired. Everyone laughed, especially the young man.

"The stories droned on. Finally they became boring. Over and over, the same trails were walked. We waited, listened for the tiniest change, and we watched each other. Everything was noted, argued about. We cajoled and teased each other about the changes. We accused each other of lying. The stories went on and on and on and on."

Crazy Dog stopped and began to prepare his pipe. He took his time as he filled it, watching Dancing Tree. He lit his pipe from a tiny fire he had built. He started his story again. He began, slowly, patiently, as he always spoke. "Gradually we became more harsh with one another." He lowered his eyes. "I became angered when a man accused me of cowardice, and I hit him across his mouth. The blow slapped him onto his back! Frightened, I jumped to my feet and turned to defend myself from the attack I thought would come from the dog soldiers, but they did not move! They only watched me quietly from where they stood. Not one lance moved. Confused, I turned again to the assembled people, expecting a fight from them. No one had moved! Silence filled the air. Not even a night bird or coyote sang its song. There was no sound of the wind. Not even a cricket chirped.

"I turned again, spinning on my heel to face the dog soldiers. They still had not moved! I became crazed, maddened by the silence. In my insanity I charged at Bird In Ground! He was an expert warrior, a very powerful man, much older and more experienced than I. Skillfully, he caught me by one arm and my long braids, driving me face down into the dirt. I roared like a wounded bull and jumped to my feet. For the briefest flicker of my eye I looked to where the dog soldiers stood. Still they had not moved! I dove blindly for Bird In Ground only to bounce off a shield he now held. I found myself once again upon the ground.

"I should have rested. My mind cried out for me to rest, but there was another part of me that screamed at me to fight! The battle raged within me. Then I heard a voice, yelling. 'Stupid!' the voice yelled. 'You are just a foolish boy!'

"I leapt from the ground, trying to get under Bird In Ground's shield. Again, my hair was grabbed, and I was hit in the face.

"I bellowed in rage, but my voice sounded pitiful, tiny and far away. I yelled again, and then I realized that I was on one knee and staring into the upraised shields of the dog soldiers. Bird In Ground had fallen back into their ranks.

"I heard the voice again and looked to see who it was that was yelling. It was the woman!

"She was standing beside the fire, and in her hand was a burning piece of wood. The firelight contorted her features, causing her to look very fierce.

" 'I want to die!' she screamed. She was crying, the tears flowing down her cheeks. 'She is dead! They have killed my sister! Dead!'

"She rushed past me and hit the wall of shields! One of the dog soldiers easily grabbed the burning piece of wood, no differently than he would have wrested a war ax from the hand of a child, and threw it over his head. It arched behind the wall of shields, where it landed with a thump upon the ground.

"The woman threw herself against the shields and then fell to the ground, sobbing.

"Stupidly, as if I were in a dream, I walked to the side of the fallen woman.

" 'Two Dawns?' I asked. My vision seemed blurred, and I had a difficult time focusing.

"The woman moaned. It was a pitiful sound, and she buried her face in the dirt.

"I looked around myself. Slowly, my mind began to clear.

" 'Lightning root!' my mind yelled. 'You have eaten the roots of the lightning tree!'

" 'We—' I stammered to the people assembled around the fire. 'We—we have been tricked! We have eaten the lightning root!'

" 'Exactly,' Bird in Ground said as he stepped from the line of shields and lifted the woman into his arms. He faced all of us, the woman still cradled in his arms. 'All of you,' he said in a clear voice, 'are still violent! You have not helped one another!' He gently laid the woman upon her sleeping robe beside the fire and walked back to the powerful row of shields.

"The following day the talk began again. Again, we began to walk into the stories. However, now I added even more detail to my story and everyone else did the same. Two more stories changed. There was weeping and sometimes tremendous anger. The days circled on and on, and the stories were drawn out longer and longer.

"On the fortieth day, we were fed an herb that put us to sleep. We awoke together on a high mesa. We were all lying upon our sleeping beds in the middle of a tiny camp. There was a circle of lodges around us. Each of them was painted differently.

"I sat up, rubbed my eyes, and looked around. I looked at the lodges and the people. They were just awakening. Down the slope of the mesa I saw more lodges. These appeared to be those of the twelve Medicine People and the dog soldiers.

"The dog soldiers and the twelve Medicine People were sitting around us, each of them on a buffalo robe and each of them holding a shield. They began to sing, chanting a song together about a rose.

"After everyone was awake the chanting stopped. Then Bird In Ground approached us. He held his shield in front of him.

" 'This Sun Dance is over,' he said with a clear strong voice. 'We have brought ourselves into this dance with you because we wanted to learn of these ways.' He pointed to where four old women were sitting. 'Those are the teachers of these ways. They are named for the four directions: North, South, East, and West. Their dresses are reflected within their names.'

" 'It is truly over?' the round faced man from the far north asked in signs.

" 'It has just begun,' Bird In Ground answered as he reached for his hand to help him to his feet.

"All of us stood. The dog soldiers lay aside their weapons and shields, placing them neatly upon their buffalo robes. Then they came to us and greeted us, telling us their names.

"The following day the dog soldiers and the twelve Medicine People took down their lodges and left for their camps. Many of the people who had danced in the ruins called Earths Of Foxes also left, either by themselves or with the dog soldiers.

"I camped alone beside the river. The only other person who stayed was the tall young woman. Her temporary camp was not very far from mine. A man whom I had not seen before was with her.

" 'My name is Grass,' he said as he approached me in my camp. 'Are you going to stay and learn from the four Medicine Women?'

" 'No,' I said as I shook his hand. 'I am going to visit with the People Of The Stone Hammer.'

" 'My sister, Listening Water, is going to stay and learn from those women.' He smiled. 'They are camped down beside the place where the river has a crossing.'

" 'I see,' I said as I began to ready my horse for my journey.

" 'She wants you to have this,' he said with a bright smile as he handed me a necklace.

"I took the necklace and looked at it. It was made of yellow iron. 'Tell her I think that it is beautiful,' I said to Grass.

" 'Those are all different kinds of birds,' he said, pointing at the pieces of flat yellow iron.

"I smiled and touched his hand. I realized that he was very young.

" 'It is very pretty, is it not?' he asked and smiled.

" 'It is beautiful,' I said with a dramatic voice. 'Here, let me share this with you.'

"He watched me take the necklace apart, watching me with the excitement of a little boy.

" 'Here,' I said, handing him half of the necklace. 'Tell your sister that I wished you to have half of it.'

"He looked at the two newly strung necklaces, and his eyes shone. He turned suddenly and ran down the river, back to his sister's camp."

Crazy Dog leaned his elbows upon his legs, reflecting the way Dancing Tree sat.

"I want you to have the other half of that necklace," Crazy Dog said as he reached into the pouch that had held the lightning root. He took the necklace from the pouch, looked at it for a moment, and handed it to Dancing Tree.

"That yellow iron is pure!" Dancing Tree exclaimed as he examined the necklace. "I wonder where it came from?"

The following morning before dawn Little Wolf and Dancing Tree rode to the butte called Sleeping Child. From its summit they would

be able to see a great distance. Buffalo were what they sought. They dismounted when they reached the top of the butte and hobbled their horses. They would have to walk the remainder of the distance to look out over its edge.

As they neared the rim, Little Wolf stopped.

"Look," he said, brushing the ground. "There was a winter camp here."

Dancing Tree looked.

"How could anybody live up here in the winter?" Dancing Tree asked as he looked around.

"No one could have survived," Little Wolf answered.

They both began to search.

"Here they are," Dancing Tree pointed.

"They were only boys," Little Wolf said with emotion showing in his eyes. "Some one must have left them here."

"He is over here," Dancing Tree called down to Little Wolf.

Little Wolf came to Dancing Tree's side.

"The hunter broke his leg," Dancing Tree explained. "He crawled from that small valley down there. I am sure of it, because of the way the skeleton is lying."

"It does not make sense," Little Wolf frowned. "No hunter would try to live up here, not in the winter."

"I know," Dancing Tree answered as he looked around. "It is very strange. Let us look to see if there are any more signs. You go to the right and I will go to the left."

Dancing Tree began to search through the huge boulders that covered the top of the butte. Then suddenly he saw a man armed with a rifle.

"Do not move," the man signed.

"Who are you?" Dancing Tree signed.

"My name is Lives In The Meadows, and I do not want to fight with you or your brother. I do not wish for there to be killing. Turn around and walk out and tell your brother that I am not upon the path of war," he signed.

Dancing Tree did as he was told and walked out into the open.

"Little Wolf!" Dancing Tree called. "Come to me in peace. I have met a man who tells me that he is not upon the path of war."

There was no answer. Dancing Tree turned around to face the man.

"You are at a disadvantage," Dancing Tree signed. "Little Wolf will come, but not so that you can see him. Lay down your weapon, and he will see that you mean well."

"I knew that it would be this way," the man signed. "I will now lay down my weapon."

"Who is our visitor?" Little Wolf said as he stepped out from behind the rocks.

"He is called Lives In The Meadows," Dancing Tree answered.

"I am the eyes for the pony soldiers," Lives In The Meadows signed. "The soldiers are looking for some of the people who attacked the whitemen who live in the rolls-along-the-ground-on-hoops. I think that I have found three of them. There were ten others."

"But why did they leave three of their brothers alone to die up here?" Little Wolf signed. "Two of them were only boys; this we can see by their skeletons."

"The two boys were stolen from the people who were attacked," Lives In The Meadows signed. "They were left here to starve to death."

"But what of the man?" Dancing Tree signed.

"If you will examine the dead man's skeleton closely, you will see that he was shot," the man signed. "They shot him as they would a horse, because he had broken his leg."

"Thieves," Dancing Tree signed.

"There are very many," Lives In The Meadows signed. "They take what they want. It is not uncommon. The pony soldiers fight all of the people equally, the thieves and the ones who fight only to protect their camps. It makes no difference to the pony soldiers whether they are warriors or thieves. They are paid to fight. It is their lives."

"Then there are those who have come together to fight the soldiers," Little Wolf signed. "I have been tempted many times myself to kill as many of them as I could. But why are you the eyes for those soldiers? I would be shamed!"

"I am not shamed," the man signed. "My eyes hunt for only the murderers. I refuse to search out the warriors. My father was of the People, and my mother was a whitewoman. They lived in the camps of the Shoshone. I am torn. My heart aches. Tears have filled my eyes many times."

"Then why do you do what you're doing?" Dancing Tree signed.

"Because the pony soldiers do not know the difference between the warriors and the murderers. I do. It was thieves who killed my father and mother. Some of those thieves are still alive. There are many of them, maybe a hundred. They have separated themselves from the People. They are enemies of both the whiteman and the People."

"Then you are upon a revenge path," Little Wolf signed. "Have you protected the warriors as you say you have? Do the pony soldiers know the difference because you tell them so?"

"I do not truly know," Lives In The Meadows signed. "It is no concern to me if they refuse to believe me. I have told them, told them many times. I have seen councils called for peace. I do not know if these councils were called because of my word or not. It matters little to me. Yes, I am upon a revenge path, and I will see it to its end."

"I have walked close in your shadow," Little Wolf signed. "I know what you feel. But now it is different with me. I have spoken with a Medicine Person. Come with us and your heart will be healed. Your path is a straight path. It does not encircle those things that are gentle. The revenge path is a harsh way."

"Thank you, my brother. But I do not wish to be healed," Lives In The Meadows signed. "The murderers will not rest. I will hunt down every one of them. I have spoken."

"Tell us," Dancing Tree signed. "Tell us of the good things. What has come of the peace meetings? Has there been success?"

The man laughed bitterly.

"You are ignorant of your own People if you ask a question like that," he signed. "You are a whiteman. Who are their chiefs? Have we ever seen the chiefs? No! We have seen pony soldiers and those who sit in councils, but where are the chiefs in all this? Do you know the chiefs? Who are they? Where do they live? Why do they want everything?"

"I have never met a whiteman chief either," Dancing Tree signed. "There are many of them, this I know. They live in a place very far from here."

"Why have you never spoken with them?" the man signed. "You are a whiteman. Why have you not gone to their lodges and spoken with them? Are they not killing your relatives?"

"They are," Dancing Tree signed. "The whiteman's chiefs are many. I do not know if they would listen to me."

"Are you afraid of your chiefs?" Lives In The Meadows signed.

"I am not afraid of them," Dancing Tree signed. "I am afraid of no person. You must understand, they are not my chiefs. I am of the camp of Crazy Dog. I have left the whitemen's world far behind."

"You sicken me," Lives In The Meadows signed. "You should speak to your chiefs for peace. You would not be killed if you tried. I have tried, and they only laugh. You are half, they tell me. Then they laugh. You are not half, are you?"

"I am not half," Dancing Tree signed.

"Why are you cruel to your brother?" Little Wolf signed to the man. "Dancing Tree has been kind with you. Would you come into war with my brother? You must apologize. I have spoken."

"I am sorry, my brother," Lives In The Meadows signed. "I hate those chiefs I have never met. They are murderers no different than the men I hunt. The hate I feel towards those men, those chiefs, caused me to speak cruelly to you. I am sorry. If you were to choose, within custom, to slap my face, I would understand."

"I would not slap you," Dancing Tree signed. "I have had enough of this talk. I wish to return to the lodges. There will be no hunting for me. This place jolts my heart, and I am sickened."

"It has been a strange day," Lives In The Meadows signed.

"It has," Little Wolf signed.

Dancing Tree spun on his heel and began to walk to where they had left the horses.

"Wait!" Little Wolf yelled as he ran after Dancing Tree.

"That man has poisoned me," Dancing Tree exclaimed.

"Why let this meeting ruin our hunt?" Little Wolf asked, coming up beside his brother. "There are still buffalo down upon the prairie. Come, hunt with me and your heart will be easier."

SEVEN DAYS LATER Little Wolf and Dancing Tree finished their hunt.

"Enough buffalo have given-away to us that we have plenty of meat for the whole winter," Little Wolf said, reining his horse. "Come, let us go for a good swim."

But Dancing Tree seemed not to hear. He raised his thunder iron to his shoulder and fired, knocking down another young bull.

"Why did you do that?" Little Wolf frowned, showing his annoyance. "That bull will be wasted. We do not have time to care for it."

"That was the last time I will ever use a thunder iron," Dancing

Tree answered. "Do not be angry with me, my brother. This thunder iron is empty forever for me. I will dress this one out and even help in the drying of its meat."

"Then I will help you," Little Wolf smiled, jumping down from his pony.

That evening Dancing Tree took Crazy Dog the horns from the bull he had killed.

"What can I do to find the medicine within these horns?" he asked, sitting down.

"Do you feel there is a power within them?" Crazy Dog asked.

"Yes," he said. "I mean these horns to be a symbol reflecting my decision never to use a weapon of murder again."

Crazy Dog wrinkled up his nose, thinking before he answered.

"You could kill me with the string that holds your leggings up," he finally answered. "Could these horns be a symbol of your never using that string to kill? Strings such as that one have killed, you know."

"You mock me!" Dancing Tree said with anger.

"No, I do not," Crazy Dog said. "Come, tell me what teaching these horns have given you."

"It is just as I have already said," he answered, still angry.

"And you drove a thunder arrow point into the heart of that bull to prove it," Crazy Dog frowned. "We had no need for its meat. Why did you kill it, my son?"

"Because it was the last thunder arrow point I ever desired to see," he replied nervously.

"But why did you not shoot it into the air? Or into the ground?"

"Enough!" Dancing Tree said, getting to his feet. "You choose not to understand."

"Sit down!" Crazy Dog commanded. "We can talk."

Reluctantly, Dancing Tree sat back down.

"Many times all of us feel that a certain gesture or movement will fill a void that exists around us," Crazy Dog offered. "I think maybe that is what happened with you."

Dancing Tree sat quietly, listening.

Crazy Dog went on. "When we touch the hand of an enemy to show them love, we are making a gesture that is full. Or when we tousle the head of a child, that act also is full. But many of these acts are thrown into blindness. Do you understand?"

"What you are saying is that I have thrown away my gesture in blindness," Dancing Tree replied in a dull voice.

"Not completely," Crazy Dog said kindly. "Because you have a good heart. You see," he said, drawing a circle upon the ground, "we all want to touch the hurt we see around us. It is no different than the time you blessed the power place. Do you remember?"

"I do remember," Dancing Tree said, relaxing a little.

"These gestures are of many kinds," Crazy Dog continued. "But one thing certain is that they are all learned. When we are still children we might bring a flower to our mother, and we see her smile. She shows us her love. At another time we may be standing on one foot on a log over a dangerous river, and she will scold us. This scolding also shows us her love. It is all the same. But all too often we forget the flower and remember the time we stood upon one foot."

Dancing Tree laughed. "I guess I am remembering the scolding."

"It is something like that," Crazy Dog smiled. "We are beings of symbol, my son. When we remember the scolding we should connect it to the time we stood out over the river and understand the reason, but we do not. Way down deep within us we remember it, but only in those times when we are again standing upon one foot. It is at these times that we feel strange, and we look around." He laughed. "We are expecting the scolding. But, of course, now we are standing upon one foot because we have a need to, not like before, when we were a child standing on one foot on a log over the river. It was for putting ourselves into danger, not for standing on one foot, that we were scolded. This we must seek to remember."

Dancing Tree shook his head, laughing. "Crazy Dog, you amaze me. You can make such a little thing so complicated." He laughed again.

"It is you who is complicating a simple thing," Crazy Dog said, looking into his eyes. "Did you not try to substitute that bull for something around you that felt empty?"

Dancing Tree jerked visibly.

"You have performed many acts like this before, my son," Crazy Dog said, still looking into his eyes. "I believe your mother must have taught you these ways. Think. Can you remember any act of hers that tried to fill an emptiness?"

"Yes," Dancing Tree said, suddenly remembering. "She would set an extra bowl at our table for my father, who had gone and never returned. She continued to do it even after we all knew he had deserted us."

"These symbols can become very confused within us," Crazy Dog explained. "But it is not for us to chase down each of those trails. That would take a lifetime of running backwards. There is a better way."

"What way is that?" Dancing Tree asked.

"It is the way of understanding," he smiled. "When we become angry for no apparent reason, or suddenly become frightened because we are standing upon one foot, we should stop right then and think."

"Think of what?" Dancing Tree asked with interest.

"First think by asking yourself why you are so frightened, then think to act with reason," Crazy Dog answered. "It is the same with gesturing. When you begin to do these things, you will become less afraid and little by little you will understand yourself more. In this way you will also learn of your brothers and sisters."

"I see," replied Dancing Tree. "But why did you ask me to look upon the circle you drew?" Dancing Tree asked. "You said nothing about it."

"I did," Crazy Dog laughed. "I did, but I said it without pointing at it. These things are all a circle, as you already know."

"You tricked me," Dancing Tree laughed.

"You tricked yourself," Crazy Dog smiled. "So now tell me about these horns."

"These horns mean nothing," he laughed.

"Those horns mean very much," Crazy Dog corrected.

"Why?" Dancing Tree asked, confused all over again.

"Why?" Crazy Dog asked. "You ask *me* why? I did not kill the bull. You did!"

"Forgive me, my father," Dancing Tree complained, "but many times I have an empty head. Nothing will connect to anything."

"You killed that bull because you were unable to act with reason. Your heart and mind were not within a circle of harmony," Crazy Dog said, leaning closer. "You knew that the very thunder iron you held in your hands was made by our relatives, the whitemen. And you felt that the iron was made only to murder. But reflect! You reject the thunder iron with one of your hands and yet you secure food for your family with the other. You remembered only the three dead men, and your sorrow."

"And I remembered Thunder Chief and my sister Pearlie, and much more," Dancing Tree added.

"Then what do these horns represent?" Crazy Dog asked again.

"Death and ignorance," Dancing Tree frowned. "My own."

"They do not," Crazy Dog corrected him again. "They are a gift to you. They have brought you into a wondrous new circle. That buffalo bull was very important to you because it gave you a new understanding."

"It is painful to me that I do not see things as fully as you do, my father," Dancing Tree complained. "Am I so slow-witted?"

"You are not stupid," Crazy Dog laughed. "It is simply that you have been taught to see things within a circle that divides itself and wars against itself. That is all. But this is not the way of the universe. We all must learn to perceive, to look clearly at our gifts."

"Forgive me, Crazy Dog," Dancing Tree explained, "but I cannot help it. I must say that I see much pain within our world."

"There is indeed much pain, my son," Crazy Dog answered. "The pain of winter awakens us to our need for shelter. The pain of our stomachs opens our eyes to our need for food. The pain of our brothers and sisters has opened our eyes to their needs. And our own personal pain of heart has opened our eyes to our need to touch the circle. There is pain, my son, but much of it we cause ourselves. We create our own pain when we refuse to open our eyes to the needs of our brothers and sisters, and to the world that exists around us."

"But then how can I learn to perceive clearly?" Dancing Tree cried. "I am tired of being so blind."

"You are not blind, my son," Crazy Dog smiled. "You have eyes. You *wish* to understand. It is the most important step into the circle. But let me tell you of Crazy Dog and his blindness."

Dancing Tree laughed. "It is hard for me to believe that there is anything at all you do not see."

"I have been blind to many things," Crazy Dog said. He frowned, then laughed. "So many that they are half of my experience. Let me tell you of my visit with Crying Owl."

Crazy Dog began to fill his pipe.

"You are not going to put me to sleep again, are you?" Dancing Tree asked nervously.

"No, not this time," Crazy Dog laughed. "I am only making myself a smoke."

He took a coal from the fire and lit his pipe.

"I was wandering about in those days," Crazy Dog began. "I was searching for places of power. In one of the villages I came upon I met Crying Owl.

"I feared him immediately because there was something about him that constantly made me feel unbalanced. I asked an old Medicine Woman who lived in the same village about this. She told me that he was absolutely insane.

" 'Insane!' I babbled.

" 'Insane,' she repeated, matter-of-factly.

"For awhile I wandered about the camp, trying to decide if it made any sense that I should be so curious about Crying Owl. I decided that it did not, so I started off to the next village.

"As I was walking to the next village, I met the same old Medicine Woman. She was carrying wood. When she saw me, she put her load down and motioned for me to sit with her. So I did.

" 'Where are you going?' she asked.

" 'To the next village,' I answered.

" 'Why?' she asked, wrinkling up her nose.

" 'Because I am seeking the holy places,' I answered.

" 'Why do you not speak with Crying Owl?' she asked.

" 'Because you told me he was insane,' I answered. 'What can I learn from a crazy man?'

" 'He is not crazy,' the old woman frowned. 'I am. You should not listen to the advice of an insane woman, you know.'

"I just sat there, too surprised to speak.

" 'Were you not sent here upon this path by Beaded Horn?' she then asked.

" 'I was,' I answered with surprise. 'How did you know that?'

"She chuckled and handed me some dry meat instead of answering.

" 'He is crazy too, you know,' she laughed. 'Old Beaded Horn is as crazy as a bug's ear!' She whooped with laughter again.

" 'Come,' she said, taking my hand. 'I will introduce you to Crying Owl.'

" 'But,' I protested, 'I have already met Crying Owl.'

" 'No, you have not,' she insisted, and pulled me along.

"What could I have done? Knock her down? Her, a Medicine Woman? So I went meekly along, wondering.

"I noticed when we entered the camp that everyone was staring at us, which caused me to wonder even more.

"We walked on until we came to the lodge of Crying Owl.

" 'Crying Owl!' she yelled so loudly that the whole camp could hear her. 'Come out! A young man is here who wishes to meet you. He is as crazy as a buffalo that tries to live in a tree!'

" 'Are you crazy, my son?' Crying Owl asked with concern as he came from his lodge.

" 'No!' I quickly replied. 'I am not!'

" 'Then why have you come here?' Crying Owl asked in a very kind voice.

" 'I am searching for places of power,' I began to explain, but was interrupted by a loud snort from the old woman.

" 'He is as crazy as a tick on a snowball,' she snorted again.

" 'I am not! I am totally sane,' I replied in confusion.

" 'How do you know if hunting these places is crazy or not?' he asked in a kind voice.

" 'It is not!' I protested. 'My teacher is Beaded Horn and—'

"She interrupted again with an even louder snort.

" 'Beaded Horn is as crazy as a swimming rabbit!' she explained to Crying Owl.

"Now everybody was staring! Even the little children who did not know any better! I had never been so embarrassed!

" 'I can prove that I am not!' I yelled.

" 'Can you?' Crying Owl asked with concern. 'Come. Let us take a walk into the mountains and see if you are right.'

" 'You'll see!' the old woman said, shaking a finger at me.

"We walked and walked until I thought I would drop with exhaustion. Finally, Crying Owl stopped and pointed to a cave.

" 'Inside that cave are some people who need your help,' he said, turning to me. 'They are a very desperate people who have suffered much. Do you think you can help them?'

" 'How can I know that?' I asked.

" 'Do you want to help them from their suffering?' he asked.

" 'Yes,' I answered.

"He sat down beside me and took his pipe from his medicine bundle.

" 'Here,' he said, handing me a turtle shell. 'Take a coal from my carrying shell and start a fire for me.'

"I did as he instructed and sat down again to see what would happen next.

" 'There are many people,' he began as he smoked, 'who are blind and in need of seeing. Most of these people do not know this. They do not realize that they cannot perceive. Strange, is it not, my son?'

" 'It is,' I answered.

" 'Over there,' he pointed at the cave again, 'is a suffering people. They are trapped within that mountain. Open that door and they will be able to come out into the bright sun of the day.'

" 'Is that all?' I asked.

" 'That is all,' he answered.

"I walked quickly over the cave and discovered that what I thought was the cave opening was in truth a black door. It looked like stone and it appeared to be very heavy. I pushed at the door with both of my hands. To my surprise it opened easily and without a sound.

"Curious, I stuck my head inside and saw the most shocking thing of my entire life. All the people he had said would be there were really there, and they were *eating* each other!

"It was ghastly! They were eating each other alive, and the people they ate upon were screaming in pain!

"Suddenly everybody stopped and looked at me. Then slowly they turned and all together reached out their hands toward me! I screamed and slammed the door just as they were about to grab me! I could hear them crying!

"Sick and frightened, I sat down upon the ground and began to cry myself.

" 'Get up upon your feet!' Crying Owl ordered me. 'You must have a strong heart!'

" 'They are terrible!' I gasped. 'Horrible! I cannot do it! I cannot help them!'

" 'Try it again, and remember your teaching!' he said, his face rock hard.

"I tried again and then again, and each time I could not do it. I became so sick I was retching. I could hardly see because of the tears in my eyes.

" 'Remember your teaching!' Crying Owl seemed to beg. 'Have pity upon them!'

"Crying and shaking like a leaf I approached the door again. It was my fourth time. I could hear their agony and their sobbing from within.

" 'I will give-away to them!' I yelled, shaking so badly I could hardly open the door.

"And there they were again, just as before. They stopped their screaming and reached out to me, but this time I waited to let them touch me. My eyes were wide open. I could not have closed them if I had wanted to.

"Then they touched me!

"And they ran by me into the sun, laughing. I saw that they were little children.

"I fainted.

"When I awoke I was back within the camp in the lodge of Crying Owl. The old Medicine Woman was there too. She was caring for me.

"I washed and then rested until my stomach stopped jumping. Finally I calmed enough to have a meal.

"After I had eaten, Crying Owl began to speak.

" 'It is very difficult to perceive with the eyes of the spirit, my son,' he began. 'With your human eyes you saw the horror of the people within their pain. But your heart saw them as they really were, as children. In their agony, they were reaching out for your help. Your human eyes saw this as a threat. But, my son, you also saw with your spirit eyes, and because of this they were set free from their darkness into the light.'

"I could only sit there, stunned.

" 'And you have a new name!' he said. 'It is Crazy Dog!' "

Dancing Tree sat, unable to move or speak.

"Come!" Crazy Dog said, laughing. "Let us, you and I, throw these horns into the river together! They have been a wonderful gift to you. Let us return that gift to our Mother Earth with thanksgiving!"

"HAVE YOU ever noticed how close the stars appear to be at times?" Rainbow asked, hugging Dancing Tree.

"Yes, I have," he said, turning to look at her.

"My grandmother used to say that we see them because we wish them," she smiled. "They become even more beautiful when you think about the teaching of the twelve magical worlds."

"The twelve magical worlds?" he asked.

"It is a Sun Dance teaching." She laughed a beautiful laugh and lay her head back upon her soft pillow of white ermine.

"Isn't everything?" He laughed with her. "Please tell me."

"Well," she began, "the Medicine Woman said there was a dance of prophecy that began a very long time ago. It began out among the stars, she told us. It was a song that belonged to the great universe. The song grew within its fullness, until finally everything began to sing with it. It was a pure song of the harmony of all that exists, and it painted its brilliance across all time.

"The beings upon the twelve worlds blinked at the light and

wondered concerning the song. And so each of them made medicine. And the medicine flew from one world to the next until it was reflected everywhere. The beings upon the twelve worlds had seen the sign of the thunderbird. And the thunderbird held up an image to each of the worlds, until all twelve could see the next. They were very surprised to learn that they were not alone within the universe.

"But more important than this, my little children, all the beings upon each of the twelve worlds now knew they were not complete. 'We are only partial beings,' they cried, and their sadness moved out into the universe until it was heard.

" 'It is so,' the universe answered their cries. 'You have awakened!'

"The Great Spirit of all the universe walked upon each of their worlds and everyone became refreshed. Now they felt the joy of birth.

" 'Where should we go to meet ourselves so that we can become whole?' the beings from all twelve worlds asked.

" 'Walk upon my robe,' the Mother Earth answered. 'Walk here, my children, and you can know of each other.'

" 'The Mother is made up of all things,' the universe sang. 'She is part of all twelve. She is part of all the beings upon all the twelve worlds.'

"And the Mother made medicine. The medicine was love and the universe knew that it was the song of the light.

" 'Come,' the Mother sang. 'Come and be born. You will leave your memories behind. Come and be children together. Come and be sisters and brothers, mothers, fathers, and relatives. I will provide everything. Come and dance together.'

"And the beings, many of them, wanted to dance. They wanted to become. And so they were born.

"Little by little, more and more of the beings wanted to become. And the Mother sang her wondrous song. Each of them was given a body-lodge made from the Mother Earth. And the spirit of these things grew among the people of the earth.

"Each being from each of the twelve worlds brought a special gift with them. This gift was their way of perceiving. It was their spirit. And each of these beings had a special power.

"The Mother sang to them of these things, saying, 'You will become complete people when you have danced with the powers that each of you has brought. Learn together. Teach each other. Care for one another and you will learn of your love for each other.' "

"What are those powers you spoke of?" Dancing Tree broke in to ask.

Rainbow laughed. "Do you not remember your teaching concerning the medicine wheel?"

"You mean the reflections?" he ventured.

"Of course!" she smiled. "Are you not different from Crazy Dog or Little Wolf?"

"Yes," he frowned, "but we are the same, too."

Rainbow sat up.

"There are special things given to all of us, but all of us can learn about our gifts within the Sun Dance."

The next morning, while everyone was swimming together in the nearby stream, Crazy Dog decided to prepare their meal. While he cooked, he sang a song he had learned from his wife, Two Dawns. He had loved her very much, and he often sang the song in remembrance of her. But this time his song was suddenly interrupted.

"Move plenty quick your hands up," a voice hissed quietly behind him. "And not make noise or me kill."

Crazy Dog lifted his hands slowly.

"Run!" he screamed at the top of his lungs as he spun on his heel.

The thunder iron in the hands of the man behind him roared, spinning Crazy Dog onto his face. But it had not killed; it had only grazed his ribs.

"Evan!" Crazy Dog gasped in surprise from the ground.

Evan's hands were shaking. "Crazy Dog?" he mumbled. "It you?"

"Yes," Crazy Dog said, getting to his feet. The blood spilled between the fingers of the hand he held over his wound.

"No!" he shouted when he saw Little Wolf pull his bow taut behind Evan. "It is Evan!"

"Evan?" Little Wolf exclaimed, loosening his pull. Then he shouted, "Do not pull your arrow, Dancing Tree! It is Evan, our brother."

"Evan?" Dancing Tree repeated, unable to believe his ears. "What is he doing?"

Little Wolf ran quickly to Crazy Dog's side and examined his wound.

"He very nearly killed you," he exclaimed.

"I sorry," Evan said evenly. "I thought you other man I want kill."

Dancing Tree looked into Evan's eyes. What he saw made him feel suddenly tired, and a fear close to nausea rose within him. He hardly recognized him. Evan looked old, and his eyes were brutal.

"You Calvin," he grinned, showing his yellowed teeth.

"This is Dancing Tree," Little Wolf explained. "Are there more with you?"

"Calvin now all injun." He used the white word instead of People. "He even look injun." He laughed and spat upon the ground.

"Are there more?" Dancing Tree asked coldly.

"There is much great more!" Evan laughed. "Whole big soldier party comes."

"We must hide!" Little Wolf said, turning to Dancing Tree and then to Crazy Dog.

"Run quick!" Evan roared with laughter.

Everyone grabbed what they could and mounted to ride. Evan could still be heard laughing from the nearby thicket.

"You have become insane, Evan," Dancing Tree yelled over his shoulder.

"And you dead injun," Evan yelled and laughed again.

When they topped the rise of the mountain, about three miles away, they stopped to rest their horses.

"Smoke!" Dancing Tree said. "Look! He is burning our lodge."

"And our food, everything," Little Wolf said, showing his grief.

"Many of our things are well hidden," Rainbow said, turning to Dancing Tree. "He would have to dig to find them."

"He will." Little Wolf spit out his words. "He knows us. He is our family." He laughed bitterly. "He knows of our hiding ways, and he will destroy everything."

"The winter will be here soon," Dreamer said, trying to fight back her tears.

"We will not die," Crazy Dog said. "I do not think he has burned everything. I think he burned our lodges to keep away the pony soldiers. He is insane, but he does not hate us."

They stayed hidden within the canyon for one day, until Little Wolf decided that it was time he and Dancing Tree scouted the valley.

"I will circle to the left and you to the right," Little Wolf said to Dancing Tree. "We will meet at the Place Of The Two Standing Trees below the valley."

"You can see the camp from the first ridge," Dancing Tree told Rainbow. "Watch for us from there, but do not go into the camp unless I am wearing my leggings. If my legs are bare, we are a decoy."

"A decoy?" Crazy Dog asked, alarm in his voice. "Why?"

"I do not share your heart, my father," Dancing Tree answered. "I think that our brother, Evan, is capable of murder. I think it has become a game with him. In fact, I do not believe he is a scout for the pony soldiers at all. I believe he roams with a pack of thieves who take what they can. I think he is still searching for the yellow iron, but he takes anything else he might also find along the way."

"Then we are in even more danger than I believed," Crazy Dog said with worry.

"No," Dancing Tree corrected. "There is less danger than you might think, because he will tire of the game quickly. If there were soldiers it would be organized."

"True," Crazy Dog agreed, "But if he is with other men, it is still an organized thing."

"You do not have the knowledge I have concerning the whiteman," Dancing Tree explained. "What you believe is true concerning a party upon the path of war, or the pony soldiers. But it is not true with men who are crazed with the dream of the yellow iron. They are not together for discovery. It is only for protection. They could kill each other without mercy if they were to discover the yellow iron. No. It is different with these men. They will ravage a camp simply out of boredom."

"Then the dream has driven my son mad?" Crazy Dog exclaimed.

"Your son!" Little Wolf said with contempt. "He is not your son!"

"Come," Dancing Tree said, getting to his feet. "Let us begin our search now."

Little Wolf rose to his feet. He stopped, and turned to Crazy Dog.

"Forgive me," Little Wolf said. "I spoke only in anger."

"You spoke with disappointment, too," Crazy Dog answered.

Little Wolf and Dancing Tree made their circle carefully. When they met at the place they had decided upon, they rested.

"I found their tracks," Little Wolf said as he sat down. "They went off to the north. There were five of them together, leading horses."

"Six," Dancing Tree said, rubbing his forehead. "I found one dead. He had been stabbed."

"Then there was an argument," Little Wolf said.

"I think that argument concerned us," Dancing Tree said. "When I found the dead man, I circled back near our camp and I found our stores untouched."

"Then Crazy Dog was right," Little Wolf said.

"Only partially, my brother," Dancing Tree replied sadly. "Evan will be back again, and next time it will be to kill us."

"Why?" Little Wolf frowned. "First he defends us, then next you say he will kill us?"

"They know we have women," Dancing Tree said without feeling, "and they need the stores themselves."

"Then they may be returning right now!" Little Wolf said, standing up.

"We must move quickly, and we must move far," Dancing Tree answered. "We must be certain they cannot find us."

Dancing Tree and Little Wolf moved cautiously, searching as they went, on their return to the ridge. When they reached it they quickly explained to the others what they had found.

"I am afraid that you are right," Crazy Dog said quickly. "I have a plan."

"Tell us," Little Wolf said.

"We will gather our belongings," Crazy Dog explained, "and we will follow their trail north."

"North!" Little Wolf yelled. "That will be right into their jaws."

"No, it will not be," Crazy Dog argued. "Those men know that we have only two paths out of here. They know that we cannot cross the mountains at this place. That leaves only two ways. They will expect us to run from them. They will be waiting for us to ride through the canyon to the prairie. I do not believe they will expect us to follow them north. And we can cross over the mountains if we go to the north, or we can go onto the prairie from there."

"Then it is a game, as I suspected," Dancing Tree said. "Evan knows we have only one obvious escape route." He thought before speaking again. "And I agree with you. I think he would never believe that we would go north."

"I hope you are right," Little Wolf said uneasily.

"I think they went north to the place called Two Broken Rock," Crazy Dog said, "and I believe that is where they would circle back to the canyon to ambush us."

"It is the closest path," Dancing Tree agreed. "I wish we could scout them to be certain."

"But we cannot," Crazy Dog said. "Because too much time would pass, and they would guess our plan."

"If they find us, we would have no chance," Little Wolf said deep in his throat. "Their thunder irons would cut us down from too far away for our arrows to reach."

"Come," Crazy Dog said, getting to his feet. "We will go now!"

They collected everything they had, making sure that it was packed on the animals carefully in case they had to run them, and they set out upon their journey.

Crazy Dog followed directly in the trail Evan's party had made, while Little Wolf and Dancing Tree rode ahead in flanking positions.

As they rode they were nearly sick with fear. Crazy Dog knew that they took a great chance. The weight of it pressed hard upon his heart.

He looked around at Dreamer and Rainbow, who rode behind him, and the skin crawled on his back. Would Evan attack from behind? Would this be how he played his game of death?

It was quiet around them, more quiet than he could remember. The birds would not be of much help to them. They had sensed the group's tenseness and fallen silent. If they had been happy and unworried, the birds would have sung with them, and then if the killers had come the birds would have become silent at their approach. Then they would have had a sign, but now there was nothing. Only silence.

"Around the next bend," he thought. "If we are to be attacked, it will be there."

With his eyes he searched to the left and to the right into the timber, expecting at any moment to hear the roar of a thunder iron.

"Little Wolf and Dancing Tree should be almost around the bend by now," he thought, tensing.

There was still no sound.

Then suddenly Little Wolf rode out into view, waving them forward.

"We were right," he said, sounding out of breath. "We have found their tracks leading back in a circle. We are safe!"

A few moments later they reached Dancing Tree, who had dismounted and was kneeling in the brush to one side of the trail.

"Over here," Dancing Tree signed.

"Hold the pack horses," Little Wolf said to Dreamer and Rainbow. "We will be right back."

He and Crazy Dog rode to where Dancing Tree waited with one knee upon the ground.

"Another one is dead," Crazy Dog said.

"He has been stabbed also," Dancing Tree said as he rolled the man onto his back.

"I have seen enough," Crazy Dog said. "Let us go over the mountain."

A MASSIVE WIND the width of the mountains began to fall from the prairie sky. It surged against the base of the foothills, sighing and gusting through the pines, bending their tops and causing their strong bodies to tremble. Dead branches snapped and plummeted to the ground, clacking wood against wood in a sorrowful voice that made Dancing Tree's spine tingle. He shivered and pulled his robe close about his shoulders, fearful that it suddenly would be torn from his body, leaving him exposed to the awful dread that threatened to break his heart. He glanced about him quickly, searching the faces of his family for the tiniest sign that they had perceived weakness in him. But they all appeared to be calm: expectant, but not nervous.

Crazy Dog walked his horse, not looking back. Dreamer and Rainbow kept the walk of their horses matched; they were listening. Little Wolf tied an eagle feather into his braid as he rode, seemingly unaffected by the ghostly sounds around him.

"Hooooo," Crazy Dog said softly.

Small whirlwinds the height of a man played among the pines, flitting in between the trees like wraiths. Their eerie voices mimicked the hissing of the wind higher in the boughs. Deep pools of darkness shifted on the floor of the forest as the trees bowed and waved their branches in frenzied movements.

A weakened cottonwood that stood alone in a clearing bent nearly double and then suddenly splintered in half, splitting its full length. Dancing Tree jumped as the wood exploded, his heart sickening with the sound and his stomach muscles snapping taut. Then his eyes filled with tears, and he began to cry silently. His thoughts were of Evan. At one time they had been closer to each other than brothers.

Dancing Tree lowered his head against the force of the wind and gritted his teeth. "What miracle could I have done?" he asked in his mind.

The memory of the dead man he had rolled onto his back flashed into his thoughts and his body shook. He realized he had hoped that the face he had turned over would be Evan's. "He has gone mad," he said sorrowfully in his mind.

The wind suddenly ceased its plunge onto the prairie and the remnants of the powerful storm howled forlornly into the deep ravines, moving away forever like the dying breath of an army of ghost soldiers.

Dancing Tree's horse shied from a tumbleweed that bounced in front of it. He jerked the horse up hard. It danced sideways and threw its head. He kicked at it viciously.

Crazy Dog rode up alongside Dancing Tree and touched him on his arm. Dancing Tree's head snapped up, and his eyes glowed with hate.

"You cannot change the dead," Crazy Dog said quietly. "Change is not your concern. It is the concern of the Great Spirit. I know that you sought your brother's face when you turned over that body. I know that right now you think of Evan. You also think of your mother, of the past and its pains. What you do is understandable, but it is a sign of an undisciplined warrior. If you must do battle, then draw your knife and battle me. I am of the living. Do not turn the blade slowly in the past. These things of which you think have gone beyond reaching. Fighting them will bring only pain to your own spirit. Awaken!"

Dancing Tree moaned with sorrow and his vision blurred.

"Such sorrow!" Crazy Dog said with sympathy. "Now you reverse the order of thinking and sorrow for yourself. Much of importance is happening all around you, yet you look only inward at your own emotions. This is pity, and it is dangerous. Be attentive to your illuminations! If you must remember, do so with love, and look with disciplined vision into the twisted mirror that was the past.

"There is much for you to see. From what you have told me of your People they were like spiders caught in their own webs. The boy you knew as Evan has long been dead. The man who now seeks to destroy us is a stranger, a madman who brings his own destruction upon himself."

Dancing Tree narrowed his eyes.

"*Whey-hah!*" Crazy Dog said in his deepest voice. "Perhaps you should spend the remainder of your days upon our Mother Earth making everything right. Make a gift to Evan of as much yellow iron as he wishes, save his sister, call up your mother from the dead and give her all that she ever wished for. Give your father—"

"Stop it," Dancing Tree hissed through his teeth.

"Never," Crazy Dog replied, almost in a whisper. "I will not allow my son to die. You will battle me here and now," he raised his voice, "and you will be a warrior."

"The pass is near," Little Wolf said as he loped his horse alongside. "How shall we cross it? Should we mountain-tie the pack horses?"

"Yes, but the pass is not too dangerous," Crazy Dog said, reining in his horse.

"We are likely to be shot in the back when we enter that canyon," Dancing Tree growled.

"They would have had to run their horses to death to have caught up with us by now," Little Wolf frowned. "Why do you speak this way?"

"Dancing Tree is within a deep chasm of despair, the very same chasm which you yourself once visited," Crazy Dog explained to Little Wolf. "The same troubled spirits haunt him, blinding him to his present realities."

"I do not envy you your future battles," Little Wolf said as he turned his horse. "Be mindful of Crazy Dog's words. They will save you much heartbreak."

"Battles?" Dancing Tree blinked, repeating the word.

Crazy Dog dismounted and began to tie the elaborate loops called mountain-ties into the lead ropes of the pack horses. Little Wolf watched carefully.

Dancing Tree remained mounted, pretending to watch the trail behind them. He needed time to consider what Crazy Dog had said to him. His uneasiness had passed, but his heart was filled with rage and tension.

Rainbow and Dreamer both stole secret glances at their husbands' faces as they prepared their pack animals. Their eyes saw what women's eyes have seen for thousands of centuries: the faces of warriors alert for danger from an enemy they knew they could not overcome. Then the women looked briefly into each other's eyes and recognized another quiet mystery that sparkled from the center of time. They saw the love that grows when women carry the seeds of new life within them. Both women would bear children when the spring came.

THEIR ESCAPE through the labyrinth of mountain passes made it impossible for Evan and his killers to follow. Eight days later Crazy Dog pointed to a valley where they could camp. It was a valley of beauty.

Little Wolf kindled a warm fire, then helped Dancing Tree cut lodge poles. Dreamer began to prepare dinner while Rainbow helped unpack the horses. Crazy Dog sang as he removed the heavy burdens from the horses.

"What is that strange song that Crazy Dog is singing?" Dancing Tree asked.

"It is a thanksgiving song," Little Wolf smiled. "It has something to do with the hot pools here in this valley. He is singing a poem of images." He listened for a moment. "They speak of birth and cleansing, of birth and death." He shrugged his shoulders.

"Why does he keep repeating the words, 'my two little boys'?" Dancing Tree asked.

"He means us," Little Wolf answered, looking up. "We are the two boys he sings about. He says that we are dangerous."

"I do not understand," Dancing Tree frowned, straightening up and looking toward the camp.

"It is simple," Little Wolf said, putting down his ax. "He is thankful that we did not kill. His song says that we wanted to kill." He lowered his head and began to work again. "It is true. I desired to kill."

"Look," Dancing Tree said, calmly pointing at Little Wolf's feet. "Look at what you have uncovered with your snow boot."

"What is it you see?" Little Wolf asked, straightening up.

"This," Dancing Tree said, picking up a large gold nugget. "Yellow iron." He let the nugget drop and began to trim the branches from the tree he had cut.

"So," Little Wolf grinned. "You have given up your desire to be a mole, digging under the ground."

"I am a hunter," Dancing Tree smiled, looking around. "I desire to carry nothing more heavy than my bow."

Little Wolf buried the nugget with the heel of his boot. "Good," he agreed.

The following spring a beautiful baby girl was born to Rainbow. Dancing Tree named her Estchimah.